MILITARY SPENDING IN DEVELOPING COUNTRIES

MILITARY SPENDING IN DEVELOPING COUNTRIES:

HOW MUCH IS TOO MUCH?

Brian S. MacDonald

CARLETON UNIVERSITY PRESS

Copyright © Carleton University Press, 1997

Printed and bound in Canada

Canadian Cataloguing in Publication Data

MacDonald, Brian, 1939-
    Military spending in developing countries: how much is too much?

Includes bibliographical references.
ISBN 0-88629-314-6

    1. Developing countries—Armed Forces—Appropriations and expenditures. 2. Developing countries—Military policy. I. Title.

UA17.M33 1997   355.6'22'091724   C97-900248-6

Cover Design: Your Aunt Nellie
Typeset: Mayhew & Associates Graphic Communications, Richmond, Ontario, in association with Marie Tappin

Carleton University Press gratefully acknowledges the support extended to its publishing program by the Canada Council and the financial assistance of the Ontario Arts Council. The Press would also like to thank the Department of Canadian Heritage, Government of Canada, and the Government of Ontario through the Ministry of Culture, Tourism and Recreation, for their assistance.

CONTENTS

Acknowledgements

List of Acronyms

1	The Conceptual Model: The Purpose of Military Forces	1
2	Modelling Issues	11
3	Northwest Africa	27
	Case Study 1: Morocco	30
4	West Africa	41
	Case Study 2: Burkina Faso	45
	Case Study 3: Mali	54
5	Central Africa	63
	Case Study 4: Cameroon	66
6	Southern Africa	75
	Case Study 5: Zambia	80
	Case Study 6: Zimbabwe	92
7	Eastern Africa	107
	Case Study 7: Tanzania	111
	Case Study 8: Kenya	127
8	The Middle East	143
	Case Study 9: Jordan	149
	Case Study 10: Egypt	161
9	Determining the Extent of Military Overspending	185

Appendix 1 - National Development Tasks:
　　Canadian Defence Structure Review of 1975　　199

Appendix 2 - United Nations Centre for Disarmament:
　　Defence Expenditures Disaggregation Model　　201

Appendix 3 - African Debtors to the Former Soviet Union　　203

Appendix 4 - NATO Distribution of Defence Expenditures
　　by Category: Average 1985-89　　204

Appendix 5 - Distribution of Canadian Military Personnel
　　by Military Occupation Codes (MOCs) 1994　　205

Appendix 6 - Partial Correlation Analysis: Military
　　Imports/Military Expenditures　　207

Appendix 7 - Social and Socioeconomic Militarization:
　　Praetorian and Spartan Indices (1990-94 Means)　　210

Appendix 8 - Financial Militarization ME/GNP and ME/CGE　　212

Appendix 9 - Military Capabilities (1996-97)　　214

Sources　　217

ACKNOWLEDGEMENTS

This book has evolved from a series of Country Militarization studies originally funded by the Africa and Middle East Branch of the Canadian International Development Agency (CIDA). As a part of that original project, the Agency also supported a field trip by the author to the Canadian Embassy and High Commissions in Egypt, Zimbabwe, and Kenya, in order to provide a field reality-check against the literature sources which constituted the basis of the original studies.

During those visits, the CIDA Counselors at the Embassy and High Commissions provided invaluable insights and input themselves, but also went to great lengths to arrange interviews with other agencies both inside the Embassy and High Commissions, including senior Foreign Service Officers and Canadian Forces Attachés, and with outside agencies, including an official of the Egyptian Foreign Office, a representative of the Danish International Development Agency in Cairo, and United States Military Attachés in Nairobi—all of whom were generous with their time and advice.

The partial correlations programs used in the study were written by my son, Michael A. MacDonald.

The staff of Carleton University Press have been most helpful during the two major revisions which the manuscript underwent while I was responding to the criticisms of Douglas G. Anglin, whose perspective is different from mine, but whose scholarly challenges drove me to revisions which have resulted in a far better work. I am also indebted to John Flood, the General Editor, Douglas Campbell, the copy editor, and Jennie Strickland, whose cheerful patience made the process of the technical preparation of the manuscript a much less painful process than I had feared.

I am particularly indebted to Wayne Primeau, Senior Project Manager with the Africa and Middle East Branch of CIDA, and an old personal friend, whose patience and constant encouragement throughout the evolution of the manuscript is really the reason that it exists today.

LIST OF ACRONYMS

ABE	Armoured Brigade Equivalent
ADATS	Air Defence Anti-tank System
ADE	Armoured Division Equivalent
ANC	African National Congress
APC	Armoured Personnel Carrier
CAR	Central African Republic
CCSBMDE	Conference on Confidence- and Security-building Measures and Disarmament in Europe
CDE	Conference on Disarmament in Europe
CGE	Central Government Expenditures
CIDA	Canadian International Development Agency
COIN	Counter-insurgency
CSCE	Conference on Security and Cooperation in Europe
DANIDA	Danish International Development Agency
DND	Canadian Department of National Defence
DRP	Demobilization and Reintegration Program
FGA	Fighter/Ground Attack Aircraft
FIBUA	Fighting in Built-up Areas
FIS	Front Islamique de Salut
FNLA	Frente Nacional de Libertação Angola
FORD	Forum for the Restoration of Democracy
FRELIMO	Frente de Libertação de Moçambique
FSU	Former Soviet Union
FY	Fiscal Year
GCC	Gulf Cooperation Council
GNP	Gross National Product
IBE	Infantry Brigade Equivalent
IDE	Infantry Division Equivalent
IGADD	Inter-governmental Authority on Drought and Development
IFV	Infantry Fighting Vehicle
IMF	International Monetary Fund
IS	Internal Security
KANU	Kenyan African National Union
LDC	Less Developed Country

MBT	Main Battle Tank
ME	Military Expenditures
MOC	Military Occupation Code
MPLA	Movimento Popular de Libertação de Angola
NATO	North American Treaty Organization
O&M	Operations and Maintenance
OAU	Organization of African Unity
ODA	Official Development Assistance
OECD	Organization for Economic Cooperation and Development
PI	Praetorian Index
PLA	Palestine Liberation Army
PLO	Palestine Liberation Organization
POLISARIO	Frente Popular para la Liberacion de Saguia el-Hamra y Rio de Oro
PRC	People's Republic of China
RENAMO	Resistancia Nacional Mozambicana
RPF	Rwanda Patriotic Front
SADF	South African Defence Force
SI	Spartan Index
SIPRI	Stockholm International Peace Research Institute
SPLA	Sudanese People's Liberation Army
TOW	Tube-launched/Optically-tracked/Wire-guided
UDI	Unilateral Declaration of Independence
UNHCR	United Nations High Commission for Refugees
UNITA	Uniço Nacional para a Independencia Total de Angola
UPC	Ugandan People's Congress
USSR	Union of Soviet Socialist Republics
WEI/WUV	Weapons Effectiveness Index/Weighted Unit Values
WMEAT	World Military Expenditures and Arms Transfers
ZANU	Zimbabwe African National Union
ZAPU	Zimbabwe African People's Union

THE CONCEPTUAL MODEL:
THE PURPOSE OF MILITARY FORCES

Recently, increasing concern has been expressed about the size of military expenditures in certain developing countries, especially those receiving Canadian development assistance. It is felt that these countries may be spending more on their security forces than is necessary. In addition, it is feared that these countries may be increasing their military-related expenditures by redirecting funds that, without Canadian or other development assistance, might have been used for social or economic purposes. To respond to these concerns, development agencies must be able to determine the level of militarization in each recipient country, and to conclude whether such a level is either reasonable or excessive within the context of that country.

The objective of this program of research was to gather and analyze relatively reliable information from unclassified sources concerning the internal and external security policies and activities of a number of African and Middle East countries in order to determine justifiable security requirements and acceptable levels of military expenditure for each country. The Africa and Middle East Branch of the Canadian International Development Agency, which funded the research, selected the ten countries represented in this study.

THE MODEL-BUILDING APPROACH

International Monetary Fund Managing Director Michael Camdessus, in a July 1991 address to the United Nations Economic and Social Council meeting in Geneva (an excerpt of which was published in *Finance and Development*, September 1991), cited the benefits to be gained in terms of a decline in "unproductive spending"; this could be achieved by a reduction in military spending to the worldwide average of 4.5% of GNP recorded in 1988, by those states whose spending lay above that figure. This suggests that the International Monetary Fund analysis had, perhaps, taken the approach that a set percentage of GNP devoted to military spending (in this case 4.5%) would provide a model for judging the appropriateness of military spending. This study rejects such an approach as excessively simplistic. There is no prima facie validity in any given model of military spending that does not take into account the particular international and national context of the country in question. Indeed, history suggests that 4.5% might be dangerously low in some cases, while 1% could be excessive in other cases. Accordingly, the approach taken in this study was based on a conceptual framework that began by posing the question as to the taxonomy of purposes that military forces (and their budgets) are characteristically called upon to fulfil. Essentially there are four—two of which are related to their specific military characteristics as the principal national structure for the use of armed force, and two of which are essentially non-military in their application.

The key legitimate military purpose is that of *national defence*—the use of armed force to protect the nation against the incursion of a foreign aggressor. Ancillary purposes may include the use of the nation's military forces in coalition expeditions outside the nation to respond to a violation of regional security, or the use of forces in a variety of international peacekeeping or peace enforcement activities. There are, of course, aggressor states that seek an illegitimate use of their military forces to threaten or actually invade the territory of their neighbours.

The second purpose is that of *internal security*, the protection of the legitimately constituted national authority against the use of armed force by opposition forces within the country—the purpose described in the National Defence Act of Canada as the "Aid to the Civil Power" role. This role must be considered with some care in analysis. While at one end its purpose is the protection of the constitutional authority of the state, at the other and illegitimate end it constitutes the use of repressive force to maintain in power a government that has itself lost its legal and constitutional authority. Such a use is characteristic of the "Police Army." Indeed, an army may also take on the characteristics of a "Praetorian Army," which sees for itself an active role in the making and unmaking of governments by means of a military coup, and in exercising a controlling influence on policy within such a government.

The third purpose constitutes a non-military use of military forces— the use of military forces for *ceremonial purposes* as well as for national prestige. Normally such purposes can be accomplished by national defence forces without any significant additional expenditure, since most military forces make use of ceremony as a routine part of their normal activities.

The fourth purpose is also a non-military use of military forces. Here the focus is on the use of military forces to foster a variety of economic and social *national development roles* (what in the Canadian context is referred to as "Assistance to the Civil Authority") that do not involve the use of armed force. We can think, for example, of the traditional use of the United States Corps of Military Engineers to oversee and manage a variety of inland waterways projects, an activity that takes advantage of their engineering expertise, but does not degrade their military function as battlefield construction engineers; a uniquely Canadian activity has been the deployment during the winter of an artillery howitzer in Rogers Pass to control the development of avalanches by firing on snow and ice buildups to trigger small slides before enough mass has built up to generate a major avalanche. More recent examples have been attempts to make use of military weapons and equipment manufacturing activities to enhance the development of a national industrial strategy in high-technology sectors of the civilian economy, and such terms and concepts as "spin-offs," "technology transfer," and "socio-economic benefits" have entered the vocabulary of those arguing for such objectives in national development. Other objectives have traditionally included regional development, education and manpower training, reduction of unemployment rates, particularly among youth and young adults, and the social integration of minorities and the disadvantaged. Whether such objectives are most efficiently achieved through the military budget is an economic research issue that has yet to be satisfactorily resolved. In any event, most developing countries do not have significant defence industry sectors.

The basic model-building approach of this study has sought to determine an appropriate level for national defence forces, and to ascertain additionally from organizational analysis the extent to which national military forces might be being used for internal security purposes, as well as for national development purposes.

RESPONSE TO EXTERNAL THREATS: THE NATIONAL DEFENCE MODEL

Military planners legitimately charged with responsibility for national defence normally undertake a strategic threat/risk assessment to determine those nations that might conceivably attack them. Traditional geostrategic threat assessment relies on a conceptual model that views threats as a function of intentions and capabilities. Threat assessments normally examine the national interests of neighbouring states in order to determine whether there are differences appearing to be incapable of resolution by peaceful means—whether there is a sufficient casus belli. However, since in practical terms intent is not always easy to determine, such analysis tends to focus on an assessment of capabilities based on Balance of Power analysis.

At the broadest or grand strategic level, and following the theoretical models of de Mesquita (1981) and others, such analysis argues three determinants of strategic power: the capacity to meet an immediate military contingency with the "forces in being," or existing military capacity, including weapons systems and military personnel strength; the capacity to sustain a "long war," which is dependent on the capacity to expand military manpower, in turn based on the size of the population; and sufficient economic strength to sustain and expand military capacity. At the level of military strategy, risk assessment is characteristically based on a balance of power analysis that compares domestic military capability to that of the potential aggressor. The consequence is a military recommendation to the political authority of a force structure and weapons inventory adequate to deter the potential aggressor. Military planners are conservative, and will usually try to include a "safety" increment in their force structure. Since the political authority is usually the focus of competing claims on the public purse, its leaders will normally attempt to reduce military expenditures below what the military planners deem prudent—sometimes sharply so. However, a force structure adequate to national defence will normally exceed that which might be deployed on peacekeeping missions or expeditionary forces.

This paper has included in the potential threat set those countries that share borders with the country under analysis. For capability analysis the force structures of the threat set have been aggregated into a number of notional military formations (army brigades or divisions, air force squadrons, and naval warships) such that the balance of power can be more easily approximated.

RESPONSE TO INTERNAL THREATS: THE AID TO THE CIVIL POWER MODEL

Two different approaches have been taken in attempting to ascertain the proportion of the military (and paramilitary) forces that are devoted to this function as well as their capability to respond to serious insurgencies. National defence forces can be used as the "agency of last resort" in democratic regimes without significant organizational changes, since light forces in particular are suited to counterinsurgency actions. However, where the total army personnel strength is significantly above that required to man the field operational units and formations of the army plus an increment to support and train them, it may be that they are organized to exercise an internal security role separate from the national defence role. Paramilitary forces separate from the military also can be used in such a role. Where the combined number of military internal security personnel together with paramilitary personnel is high, we can question whether their real purpose is the legitimate protection of the national authority, or rather the repression of dissent through the illegitimate use of armed force against their own population. We should note as a caution, however, that a legitimate government faced with a well organized attempt to overthrow it will have greater such forces than one that does not, and that context analysis is again appropriate in making such a judgment.

THE DEFENCE SUFFICIENCY HYPOTHESIS: DETERMINING A REASONABLE FORCE STRUCTURE

Following the analytical stages outlined above, a proposal can made be for a reasonable level of defence effort and for a force structure adequate to meet the legitimate security requirements of the state, and then this proposal can be compared to the level in place. As a methodological caution one should note that such analysis does not distinguish qualitative differences. More sophisticated analysis attempts to accommodate such differences, but the methodologies used in the military operations research field are still undergoing development, and depend to a considerable extent on the judgment of experienced military professionals. Such qualitative assessments can provide a better though by no means perfect assessment. This stage of analysis frequently leads to the question of the validity of the equipment acquisition policies of the states in question. Those states that had adopted socialist government forms when they became independent, and had looked to the Soviet Union and the People's Republic of China for inspiration, purchased military equipment based on Soviet designs either of USSR production or later PRC production, intended for the high-intensity battlefield of North West Europe. That battlefield was characterized by high force to space ratios, relatively flat terrain, and substantial logistics and maintenance capabilities. Since those characteristics are not a feature of the Sub-Saharan strategic region, the validity of such an equipment acquisition rationale is questionable. On the other hand, for the Saharan/Middle East strategic region a clearer case can be made to justify such policies.

FUNDING DEFENCE: THE MILITARY EXPENDITURE QUESTION

The analyst of military expenditures faces three tasks: to estimate how individual national military budgets are spent; to estimate how they are funded; and to estimate the cost of the Defence Sufficiency Budget. From a microeconomic perspective, military budgets can be subdivided into three major categories: equipment, personnel, and operations and maintenance (O&M) spending; NATO budget breakouts also include spending on civilian infrastructure that benefits military operations capacities. A difficulty with many Saharan and Sub-Saharan states is that not all military expenditures are included in reported annual defence budgets. Consequently, attention must be paid to various "off budget" devices that result in the under-reporting of true defence expenditures. The first is the purchase of military imports through supplier credit terms. A second is the inclusion of military expenditures in operating budgets of other government departments. A third is the use of conscripts paid less than prevailing wage rates, who are in effect required to contribute to the defence budget the difference between their conscript compensation and the prevailing wage. A fourth is the provision of official military assistance by foreign governments. A fifth has been the emergence of the military parastatal with significant activities in the civilian sector whose revenues can be used to reduce the apparent size of military expenditures.

Once the national breakdown into the three major components has been established it is possible to estimate the Defence Sufficiency Budget by taking the total number of personnel required to staff the Defence Sufficiency Force Structure and multiplying that figure by the component expenditure rates. Finally, by comparing the Defence Sufficiency Budget to current defence spending, it becomes possible to suggest a possible amount of central government expenditures that might be available for alternative purposes inside or outside the defence department. Since few developing countries have an indigenous defence industrial base, equipment spending has a foreign exchange implication. Analysis of military component costs (equipment, personnel, O&M), may suggest management reforms that might be undertaken to achieve greater efficiencies in the use of defence expenditures.

THE COMPARATIVE MILITARIZATION INDICATORS

Throughout, this study has emphasized the idea that military expenditures should be considered in the light of each country's regional strategic context. Donor countries, whose developmental aid expenditures are influenced by public opinion at home, will logically want to include a yardstick of comparison to their own contexts as well. Consequently, four quick comparative indices have been developed—two financial and two social.

The first financial index is the proportion of GNP spent on military activities (ME/GNP); this provides a picture of the militarization of the economy. It is difficult to capture all components of such expenditures. Consequently, two approaches have been used to calculate ME/GNP: the reported budget figure, and the adjusted figure, which attempts to include military equipment imports where they do not appear to be included in reported military budgets. The second is the proportion of central government expenditures devoted to the military sector (ME/CGE); this is a measure of the degree of militarization of the government. In some cases, particularly those involving Praetorian governments, the militarization of the economy can be relatively low, while at the same time the militarization of the government is rather high—a reflection of the fact that government priorities are directed to the maintenance of its own power rather than to the welfare of the population.

The first social militarization indicator, the Spartan Index, is the extent to which military forces make up a significant portion of the national population. To the reported military forces strength should be added the number of paramilitary personnel. Where the Spartan Index is significantly higher than that of the regional context there may be grounds for considering that we may be seeing a Police Army rather than a National Defence Army. The second indicator is the Praetorian Index, which rests on the idea that military forces may become financially privileged members of their society through their ability to take advantage of their monopoly of the use of force, and their ability to make and unmake governments, to gain an economic rent in the form of salary scales significantly in excess of those available to the general public.

NON-MILITARY USE OF THE MILITARY: THE NATIONAL DEVELOPMENT MODEL

This study has not attempted to address in depth the issues connected with the indirect benefits that accrue to a national economy through the existence of its military forces. These issues are complex, and current analysis has been clouded to some extent by the particular ideological perspectives of commentators, with the result that key variables are mentioned but sometimes omitted from the calculations of the studies. Certain indirect effects cited in other studies include labour market effects, human capital formation, infrastructure development, and industrial strategy benefits. Sometimes national military forces have been deliberately used as a means of reducing unemployment rates. Where conscript forces are large in proportion to the size of the relevant age cohorts the impact on nominal unemployment rates can be discernible. On the other hand, volunteer professional forces characteristically have such a low turnover rate that their impact on labour market unemployment rates can be expected to be minimal. To address the "military training as human capital formation" hypothesis would require detailed examination of military training curricula as well as a series of judgments as to the extent to which skills and knowledge useful in the civilian economy have been transferred. This issue has been the focus of some debate in the literature, particularly in the work of such as Deger (1986) and Ball (1988), who object to the concept, but their conclusions are not accepted as definitive. In part the difficulty lies in the extent to which military trades training can be held to develop skills transferable to civilian occupations. Of greater difficulty is the question of military training that does not have a direct civilian analogue, such as leadership training, but that may still be viewed as human capital formation; one is led to pose the parallel question as to whether much of the curriculum of public education, which is often referred to as "life skills development," is really human capital formation either.

Industrial strategy elements can take several different forms. The simplest is an import substitution approach whereby licences are gained to assemble and test military equipment in the purchasing country and thereby to substitute local labour inputs for some of the labour component of the equipment's value; simultaneously, of course, there will be a labour market impact through the creation of new jobs. A slightly more sophisticated approach is to negotiate a licence that includes an export dimension—either through the fabrication of sub-assemblies or assemblies that are returned to the licensing manufacturer, or through direct export sales on the part of the licensed country. More sophisticated yet is the actual manufacture of parts in the licensed country, which allows the creation of additional value added. A further stage may involve the creation of some of the design work in the licensed country, and this, in turn, may evolve to a total design responsibility. Within this range of possibilities there is a spectrum of increased value added in the licensed country. Moreover, as the value added becomes more sophisticated there is a degree of human capital formation that takes place in the development of the technical skills required to handle each incremental move up the value-added ladder; the "spin off" argument suggests that some of this human capital may eventually move out of the defence industry into civilian industries—an argument that is often made in the more technically sophisticated economies of the developed world. In addition one should, perhaps, add to the human capital concept the development of business capabilities, in that the personnel who manage the business acquire the abilities to manage more complex processes and to add value to their accounting, marketing, and personnel management capabilities.

Cases have been noted of the direct use of military forces for national infrastructure construction purposes, a practice undertaken by some developing countries (as well as developed ones) and those in which "civic duties" have been cited as part of the activities undertaken especially by conscript forces.

2

MODELLING ISSUES

NATIONAL DEFENCE BALANCE OF POWER MODELLING: MILITARY BALANCE OF POWER MODELLING

The issue of how to model qualitative differences in combat power is complex and has been the subject of extensive debate in the military operations research literature. Early models simply summed the numbers of major equipments by category. Subsequent work attempted to make static qualitative differentiations by a number of methods. One was the selection of a "standard" and its use as a comparative reference in assessing other equipments. The basic model used for comparing main battle tanks, for example, argued that the combat power of a main battle tank was a function of three principal factors: firepower, armour protection, and mobility. The operationalization of that simple model, of course, led to much more complex algorithms, such as those of the Weapons Effectiveness Index/Weighted Unit Values (WEI/WUV) variety, and an extensive debate as to their validity. In essence that debate has concluded (Huber, 1990) that while earlier static combat power models of the nature of the WEI/WUV are superior to simple "bean counts," or weapons inventories, they are not conclusive.

Moreover, a technical review of the unclassified (and extensive) military operations research literature has noted that many of the models used for capabilities analysis were developed using Delphi techniques, and are thus heavily influenced by the accepted practice of the military culture of origin of the officers making the judgment. The Delphi methodology is based on responses from a panel of knowledgeable persons, who are physically isolated, then posed a technical question within their area of expertise. The individual responses are aggregated and means calculated, then fed back to all members of the panel, who are asked the same question again. Respondents are given an opportunity to hold to their initial response, or to modify it in light of responses from the remainder of the panel. The new results are again provided as feedback to the panel. At some point, after a number of iterations, the aggregate responses will stabilize. It should be emphasized that the Delphi method is not a simple mean of the initial responses. Delphi analysis is very dependent upon the composition of the panel, a factor that creates the military culture effect evident in national preferences regarding main battle tank design.

The military operations research field has since moved to large computer simulation models that can include such variables as terrain, particularly in the area of potential military campaigns. However, some comments with respect to qualitative analysis are at times appropriate. Such comments might include inferences and conclusions drawn from a variety of factors. WEI/WUV-type analysis is one. Logistics capabilities is another. The capacity of command staffs to integrate air and ground operations or even to integrate the operations of the three ground combat arms of infantry, armour, and artillery is another. The results of the Gulf War drive home the lesson that technology differences, particularly in electronics and aircraft avionics, are extraordinarily important combat multipliers. And as a final observation in this short and not exhaustive list of qualitative factors, we would normally expect to find that, other things being equal, professional troops will defeat either conscripts or reservists in equal numbers. Moreover, if we examine the latest developments in arms control, exemplified in the Conventional Forces in Europe Agreement between NATO and the nations of the former Warsaw Treaty Organization, we discover that the world of arms control is still lodged in the simple "bean count" model, since the critical elements of verification theory have not advanced to the point of being able to cope with the issue of qualitative arms control. As a consequence, this study is comfortable with the use of comparatively simple "bean count" algorithms, which are conceptually broadly consistent with the state of current arms control agreements practices.

In this study, notional armoured division equivalents (ADEs) are based on a 300 main battle tank inventory, the average divisional holdings of armoured divisions of the six major powers. Armoured Brigade Equivalents (ABEs) are based on 100 main battle tanks. Notional infantry divisions (IDEs) are assumed to hold no main battle tanks. No distinction has been made between "heavy" infantry divisions, which are equipped with armoured personnel carriers, and "light" infantry divisions, which usually travel on foot, since most "heavy" infantry will be found in armoured divisions. Since armoured and mechanized divisions characteristically contain a mix of tank and infantry brigades/battalions, mechanized infantry brigades of armoured divisions have been included in the Notional Infantry Division construct on the basis of a three-brigade division. Where two figures are shown for infantry divisions the second represents additional divisions formed on mobilization of reserves. Since the notional ADE figure is based on tank holdings, no distinction is made between regular and reserve divisions.

A key observation from the Gulf War was the combat multiplier impact of Western night-fighting target acquisition devices for main battle tanks, which gets us back into the qualitative issues already referred to, and which had previously caused some considerable modification to the combat power calculus used in WEI/WUV scoring analysis, particularly in flat, open terrain conditions. Iraqi T-72s, which in firepower and armour protection are not markedly inferior to Western tanks, were destroyed because Western tanks could see them in the dark and they could not see Western tanks. No attempt has been made to quantify such advantages. This example also points out the effect of terrain conditions in influencing battle outcomes.

Notional aircraft squadrons are assumed to hold 16 aircraft. Since some air forces are organized on a 24-aircraft model, the number of squadrons shown here may be larger than shown in *The Military Balance*. Where two figures are shown, the second indicates aircraft in store that could be deployed on mobilization provided adequate warning time were available. Fighter aircraft have avionics packages designed for air-to-air combat with air-to-air missiles. Fighter/ground attack aircraft (FGA) usually carry guns that allow them to engage in air-to-air combat, but do not usually have extensive avionics packages or missiles; this usually places them at a substantial disadvantage against a fighter aircraft. Modern FGAs can usually carry bomb and air-to-ground missile loads equivalent to those of older light bombers. A straight quantitative analysis of aircraft inventories can be dangerously misleading, since succeeding generations of aircraft designs represent very significant increments in air combat power; this is particularly the case with the avionics packages. A rough rule of thumb seems to be that each succeeding design generation achieves a doubling or even trebling of the combat power of the preceding generation of aircraft. The Chinese have attempted to upgrade older Soviet designs with the addition of more modern avionics packages, primarily Western in origin; such modifications appear to achieve about a 20-40% increase in combat power. A second qualitative difference lies in the state of training of pilots, which is highly dependent on the number of flying hours that they are able to get. Flying hours are expensive in fuel and maintenance requirements, and Western air forces have increasingly substituted simulator training for part of them. Since simulators are also expensive, few Third World countries have acquired them. The pattern of the Arab-Israeli wars has been that the state of training of pilots has been a critical combat multiplier advantage for Israel. No attempt has been made to quantify this advantage.

Naval forces are less significant in the African context than air and land forces, both from a strategic and from a combat power perspective. Consequently, an extensive naval power analysis has not been attempted. There are comparatively few major surface combatants (aircraft carriers, cruisers, destroyers, frigates, or corvettes) in evidence. Nor are there many submarines, and those found are conventionally powered. The bulk of naval craft are really patrol craft of the inshore and offshore variety, with little real seakeeping capability or endurance, and include missile boats, and patrol craft over 100 tonnes. Supply ships are not included.

AID TO THE CIVIL POWER MODELLING

Where counter-insurgency (COIN) operations are conducted in societies that are predominantly urban and/or have relatively high population densities, there appears to be little change in the normal military organizational or equipment structures used, and the operational doctrines employed appear to be a combination of standard police work doctrines and those used in what the military refers to as "FIBUA" or "fighting in built-up areas." Where this is the case this study has indicated that there is no specially designed COIN force structure, and it may be assumed that COIN operations will be carried out by the regular military. Where counter-insurgency operations are conducted in societies that are more predominantly rural, where population densities are lower, and where there is a significant proportion of forested areas and difficult terrain, COIN forces adopt more specialized organizations, equipment holdings, and operational doctrines. Such specialized COIN force structures have been identified where they appear to exist.

The basic requirement for ground counter-insurgency operations is for highly mobile lightly armoured forces with moderate firepower. These are similar to the requirements for traditional reconnaissance units. Armoured cars with a main armament in the 20mm to 90mm range provide adequate firepower, and wheeled armoured personnel carriers (APCs) and wheeled infantry fighting vehicles (IFVs) to transport the infantry component are quite suited to these types of operations. The notional COIN battalion is calculated to be equipped with 60 armoured cars and/or wheeled APCS/IFVs, and this study has arbitrarily concluded that armoured reconnaissance battalions are suited to COIN operations. While fighters and FGA aircraft can be used in COIN operations, the term "COIN aircraft" is usually used to describe less capable propeller-driven aircraft and light attack jets. More recently the use of armed and attack helicopters has become a feature of such operations, and they have been included with fixed-wing COIN aircraft under the rubric of attack squadrons. The notional squadron is 16 aircraft. Separate are troop-carrying assault helicopters, which are used to deploy infantry—though the United States prefers to use the term "air cavalry." This study refers to them as transport squadrons but does not include fixed wing transport aircraft in them. The notional COIN transport squadron is set at 16 aircraft.

SOCIAL BALANCE OF POWER MODELLING

At its simplest, Social Balance of Power can be modelled by comparing total population size. A somewhat more sophisticated model might compare the size of the populations of males within the prime military age group of 17 to 45 years of age, though experienced officers will question the stamina of the over-40s and thus their capability of meeting the requirements of an army's field force, the most physically demanding role. The rising technology levels of modern weapon systems place an increasing premium on the level of education of military personnel. Consequently, a social balance of power assessment of military forces that might expect to be engaged in sustained high-intensity operations should include some consideration of national levels of education, particularly in science and technology. For developing countries whose weapons inventories are less complex, this element of social balance of power assessment is arguably less important. In any event, the development of a reliable measure of inter-country comparison of technological education levels is complex. Accordingly, even though its limitations are acknowledged, the simplest measure—population size—is used, since the social balance of power appears less significant than the combat balance of power in the modern strategic context.

ECONOMIC BALANCE OF POWER MODELLING

The simplest measure of the economic balance of power is a comparison of GNPs to provide a rough estimate of the relative power of national economies. It was striking to observe the magnitude of the year-to-year changes in this measure, caused by changes in exchange rates, which do not necessarily reflect equivalent changes in economic activity measured in local currency terms. This phenomenon is particularly marked in the Sub-Saharan African analysis. Presumably some form of purchasing power comparison might be added to produce a modified GNP figure, which could be then used for balance of power analysis. Since a significant portion of the changes in exchange rates reflects differences in national inflation rates, such a measure would require frequent updating in order to maintain its reliability. De Mesquita (1981) uses a somewhat more complex measure, which includes relative shares of the total system (the set of countries included in the balance of power analysis) steel production and industrial fuel consumption. Following the direction of this measure would logically require the development of some form of electronics/technology measure to encompass the enormous impact of technology on military potential in the last decade. This study is content to accept the weakness of the simple comparison of GNPs measure.

ECONOMIC MODELLING OF MILITARY EXPENDITURES: MACROECONOMIC MODELLING

Traditional "military burden" cross-country comparative modelling tools have been based on the reported military expenditures as a percentage of GNP (ME/GNP), and as a percentage of Central Government Expenditures (ME/CGE). This measure is limited, in that not all military expenditures are consistently reported. This issue has been partially addressed by more fully including military imports in reported defence budgets and has resulted in an "adjusted" ME/GNP, where the partial correlation tests have led to the conclusion that imports are treated as "off budget" items. An additional factor complicating cross-country comparisons of military spending is the impact of variations in exchange rates which, given fluctuating inflation patterns, can vary widely from year to year; this study has been struck by the variability of this factor when database updates have been required as a consequence of year-to-year changes in *World Military Expenditures and Arms Transfers*.

MICROECONOMIC MODELLING: SUBDIVIDING THE MILITARY BUDGET

Microeconomic modelling with respect to the components of military budgets is still a difficult and underdeveloped field of analysis, particularly on a cross-country comparison basis. Military budgets can conceptually be broken into four categories: capital costs for equipment, the construction of facilities, personnel costs, and operations and maintenance (O&M) costs. Appendix 2 provides a more detailed NATO-driven breakdown of these categories that separates research and development costs from procurement. Most less developed countries (LDCs) do not provide a detailed reporting of these categories, so a series of modelling assumptions has been made.

The most reliable dataset is that provided by the sixteen NATO nations, which is contained in Appendix 4. One approach would be the use of the NATO dataset as a means of developing a surrogate for estimating patterns applicable to other parts of the world. A first assumption was that the four southern-tier NATO countries, Turkey, Greece, Portugal, and Spain, would provide the closest model we might use to estimate LDC proportions. It was discovered, however, that the NATO southern-tier means were similar to the NATO continental northern-tier means, and that the significant difference was to be found between the NATO states that used conscription-based forces as opposed to those (Britain, Canada, and the United States—referred to as NATO West) that have used professional volunteer-based forces.

Area	Equipment	Personnel	O&M	Infrastructure
NATO North Mean	16.9	52.6	24.9	5.4
NATO South Mean	15.9	54.6	24.4	4.2
NATO West Mean	23.3	40.6	33.2	2.5
Overall NATO Mean	18.0	50.6	26.6	4.3

As a result of this analysis, an initial heuristic was developed to estimate the proportions of the defence budget by assuming that non-capital spending divides on the basis of one third devoted to O&M, and two thirds to personnel, and by ignoring infrastructure spending. This produced an expected division in the following range:

Capital	10-19%
Operations and Maintenance	27-30%
Personnel	54-60%

Data from National Estimates for 1992-93 was obtained for two Sub-Saharan African states—Namibia and Zimbabwe. The data for Zimbabwe fitted the derived model quite closely, with capital spending of 20.1%, personnel spending of 53.7%, and O&M spending of 26.0%; the spending for 1991-92 was similar, with capital at 18.8%, personnel at 54.2%, and O&M at 27.0%. Thus the ratios between personnel and O&M spending were the expected 2:1. That for Namibia did not fit the pattern as well, with the ratio between personnel and O&M expenditures being 2.6:1 in 1991-92, and 3:1 in 1992-93, instead of the expected 2:1. The difference may be due to the fact that the Namibian forces were in the process of being formed and were not fully operational. Consequently they would have a lower O&M expenditure. In the end the 1/3-2/3 algorithm was rejected on the basis that it was an artificial construct that was no different mathematically than simply using the entire PO&M figure.

CAPITAL COSTS

The NATO ratio between the equipment and infrastructure components of the capital budgets has been about 5:1 to 6:1, a figure characteristic of mature defence establishments. The North American states have had a higher ratio, but this may be the result of their not being able to count as much infrastructure as dual use and eligible for inclusion in the NATO infrastructure category. The Zimbabwe ratios were 3:7 and 4:6, the consequence of a national air defence radar system building program with heavy construction costs. Since there may be sharp differences between mature defence establishments and those that are not, no algorithm was developed to include estimated infrastructure costs in the model.

Since few developing countries maintain indigenous defence industries, Military Import figures have been used as a surrogate for equipment spending for Sub-Saharan African states, with the exception of South Africa; in some cases, particularly in the Middle East, there are local defence industries, and attempts must be made to estimate the total equipment spending. The Military Imports figure also allows the estimation of the proportion of the defence budget spent within the state. While there has been considerable rhetoric with respect to the benefits of "defence conversion," there is a need to examine the actual economic impact of such withdrawals of military activity; the results to date of such macroeconomic analysis have been mixed and must still be regarded as inconclusive.

This, however, led to a new modelling problem, in that military imports have frequently been found in certain years to exceed the entire defence budget of certain states, or at least have substantially exceeded what would be expected on the basis of NATO means. In some cases these arms transfers have been received as military aid, and no financial obligation has been incurred. In other cases they have been purchased on credit terms the details of which have not been disclosed. While arms transfers in the 1960s were frequently in the form of aid given to achieve foreign policy objectives, particularly in the case of the USSR and the United States, in more recent years transfers have been on credit terms. Appendix 3 provides a list of total remaining military debts incurred for purchases of equipment from the former Soviet Union as of December 1991; it is unclear whether these debts are denominated in current rubles (in which case they would be much reduced through the de facto exchange rate decline in the ruble) or in a fixed ruble-local currency exchange rate. Some creditor balances have been later cancelled; the case of the cancellation of U.S. credit balances with Egypt following the Gulf War, which was seen by many analysts as a quid pro quo for Egyptian participation as a key Muslim member of the coalition forces, is a case in point. Hewitt (personal comment to the author) questions whether these military equipment debts will ever be repaid, which leads to the question whether they should be included in military expenditures at all. This study takes the view that until they have been cancelled they represent a claim against the state and as such should appear on a national income/expenditure statement and national balance sheet.

Published analysis within the Canadian defence community has argued that Canada should allocate about 25-30% of its defence budget to equipment spending to stay abreast of military technological development, given the overwhelming impact of military technology as a combat multiplier; the Canadian analysis, however, reflects a need for "catch-up" spending to compensate for the long period in which Canadian equipment spending was as low as 9% of the total defence budget. Britain and the United States allocate about 25% to equipment spending, but the NATO continental states allocate less—about 17%. Thus 10-20% of the reported defence budget is probably about the most that a normal developing country can afford to spend; if it is spending more than this it is probably making use of supplier credits or debts that are treated "off budget" and that should be added back in to get a clearer picture of actual defence expenditures. Countries in regions with a perceived high external threat level, such as the Middle East for example, will usually be found to be spending more than this proportion on equipment purchases.

Since this study was particularly interested in the use of the Praetorian Index (PO&M per uniform/GNP per capita), a number of regression analysis models were experimented with to estimate whether Military Imports were treated as "in budget" or "off budget." In a first iteration total military expenditure was set as the dependent variable and military imports as the independent variable. In a second iteration, military expenditure (the dependent variable) was lagged by one, two, or three years to allow for the case where payments for imports are made over several years; alternatively, military imports were lagged to accommodate the third case, in which the importing state appears to pay in advance for military imports. A multiple regression model was considered, but rejected, on the basis that there is a significant problem with the *World Military Expenditures and Arms Transfers* (WMEAT) dataset (or any dataset dealing with African countries) in that many datapoints are missing for many countries. Ultimately a partial correlation model was used, where the impact of changes in GNP, CGE, and the prior years' military expenditures were accommodated as the basis for the judgment to be made. Some care must therefore be taken with extrapolations from the Praetorian Index—while it is intuitively a very powerful interpretative tool, the methodological basis for its numbers has limitations with respect to this study.

PERSONNEL COSTS

Attempts at cross-country organizational comparison of personnel costs can be misleading, since per soldier costs vary widely, depending on whether conscript or volunteer systems are used. Conscript systems characteristically pay soldiers below the prevailing composite average wage level and are cheaper per soldier—a de facto tax borne by that portion of the conscriptable cohort enrolled in the forces. Another difficulty lies in the extent to which prevailing wage rates in the country in question are a determinant of military wage rates, or whether the military has been able to make use of economic elites within the country as wage referents. In many cases the proportion of conscripts to professionals are reported. Usually the conscript proportion is higher in the army than in the air force or navy. This is consistent with the higher technological level of the latter two, which requires longer training periods, making the use of professionals more economical. In terms of the financing of military expenditures, the existence of a "Conscript Premium" is noted, which reflects at least qualitatively the existence of this form and the existence of a higher level of real military expenditures than that which is reported.

Another complicating factor is the impact of varying levels of national wealth and their effect on prevailing local wage levels. While one might attempt to use some form of purchasing-power yardstick in developed-world comparisons, that approach is less comfortable for developing-world comparisons, even if such a measure could be found. A different approach might equate military spending per soldier to a composite average industrial wage, but the extent of the subsistence economy in developing countries leads to doubts as to the validity of that approach.

SOCIAL MILITARIZATION MODELLING ISSUES
THE MILITARIZATION OF SOCIETY: THE SPARTAN INDEX

This study was initially concerned with the proportion of the population contained within the military sector. An indicator termed the "Spartan Index" was constructed, which is the number of military personnel per 1,000 population. A number of subsidiary issues had to be dealt with. One was the question of paramilitary forces and another was that of reservists. Since paramilitary forces are full-time forces available to the central government, this study has included them within the social militarization concept. Many countries use a conscription system in which recruits undergo twelve to eighteen months of military training and then serve as reservists with varying commitments for annual military refresher training. The average maximum annual reserve duty seems to be about 30 days, which is somewhat less than the period (43 days in 1994) put in by active Canadian volunteer reservists. Since mobilization of reserves is economically disruptive, they are usually not available to the central government except in emergencies. Accordingly 1/12 of a person year has been calculated for each reserve member in the Spartan Index calculation.

Yet another issue was the question of the proportion of the military appearing to be devoted to paramilitary or internal security duties. An analysis of a sample of 32 Sub-Saharan African states (excluding Chad, Equatorial Guinea, and Mozambique because of unreliability of statistics) was based on the hypothesis that regular military personnel found outside the operational (or combat) units would be either employed in traditional support and training roles, or assigned to what were essentially internal security (IS) duties. The problem was to find some sense of what the usual patterns might be. A beginning was made when assumptions as to the personnel strength of units and formations were simplified: it was assumed that a company-sized unit (which would include an artillery battery and an armoured or engineer squadron) would hold about 100 personnel. A battalion-sized unit was estimated to contain about 450 to 600 personnel, depending on whether Soviet/Chinese or Western organizational models were being used. A Soviet/Chinese model "regiment" was estimated at 2,000 personnel, and a Western model brigade at 3,000 personnel. Current NATO strengths will be larger than these, but the smaller figures were selected on the expectation that the equipment intensity of Sub-Saharan states is lower and that therefore the numbers of personnel devoted to maintenance and logistics would be smaller. It was found that a sub-sample of 15 of the 32 countries had 35% or less of their army personnel outside the operational (combat) units; a different sub-sample of 13 of the 32 states had 60% or more of their army personnel outside of the combat units. This led to the hypothesis that these two sub-samples represent the "National Defence" army on the one hand, and the internal security or "Police Army" on the other. There is an alternative "Military Inefficiency" hypothesis for such discrepancies.

However, in the interest of avoiding the use of artificial constructs with limited prima facie validity, a simple algorithm of military plus paramilitary plus 1/12 of reserves is used as the basis of the Spartan Index.

THE FINANCIAL DIMENSION OF SOCIAL MILITARIZATION: THE PRAETORIAN INDEX

The conceptual hypothesis is that a "Praetorian" military will take advantage of its power to make and unmake governments to give itself an "economic rent" in the form of excessive pay and compensation schedules. The concept was operationalized as a measure based on non-capital expenditure per soldier as a multiple of GNP per capita, since that seems to better capture the military burden concept and since GNP per capita ratios are more readily available in developing-world economic statistics than are reliable composite average industrial wage rates. A reservation in that approach is the extent to which dependency ratios are similar in the countries under comparison, since that will impact on GNP per capita values. The study began with the NATO norms for the subdivision of defence budgets. If the total estimated personnel, operations and maintenance (PO&M) spending is divided by the number of uniformed personnel, a

PO&M spending per soldier figure could be established. The range for NATO countries for such a PO&M multiple was from 2.25 to 4.65, with a mean of 3.22; the personnel spending alone ratio varied from 1.5 to 3.1, with a mean of 2.15.

Area	Index
NATO West	5.09
NATO South	3.11
NATO North	2.72
NATO Overall	3.39

The actual personnel spending per uniformed position is clearly a more accurate figure, since operations and maintenance spending varies considerably among NATO countries. However, these figures are not available in the standard data sources for developing countries. While we could use the NATO mean divisions as the basis of estimating the division between personnel spending and O&M spending, such a derived figure offers no additional mathematical rigour. Consequently the PO&M figure was chosen.

As the study progressed, an additional feature of the Praetorian Index was observed that suggested that it had a predictive capability. When tracked historically there seemed to be an interesting apparent correlation between sharp upward jumps in the Index and subsequent violent civil strife or civil war in the country in question. It appeared, however, to be the sharp jump rather than the absolute level of the Index that was the better violence predictor.

MILITARY AS NATIONAL DEVELOPMENT MODELLING

Appendix 1 provides the list of National Development tasks assigned to the Canadian Armed Forces by the Defence Structure Review of 1975. It is particularly useful in fleshing out the "Assistance to Civil Authority" concept cited earlier.

NATIONAL INFRASTRUCTURE BUILDING

As noted, this study has been limited to the direct application of military forces for national infrastructure-building purposes. Accordingly the concept was operationalized by examining the proportion of military engineers in the national army structure. Where the proportion exceeds the normal proportion in most armies of about 5-6% of the total, it could be hypothesized that the army in question may have a national infrastructure-development purpose. In addition, the existence of "civil duties" has been noted, including those that are included within the terms of reference of paramilitary forces, but the methodology of this study has not been able to quantify those effects.

MILITARY MANPOWER AND NATIONAL LABOUR FORCE STRATEGIES

Labour market impacts of military forces are derived from the proportion of military forces to the total labour market and from transfers between the two. One question to be considered is whether the dependent variable should be considered to be employment rates or unemployment rates. Since governments are more politically concerned about unemployment rates, that is preferred as the dependent variable. Western military forces use a combination of conscript and professional forces. Conscript forces withdraw predominantly young males from the labour market for the conscription period—usually eight months to two or three years. Depending on the size of the conscript cohort, there may be a greater or lesser effect on labour market supply, and thus on unemployment rates. Conscript forces can have a significant effect, particularly where conscription is also used as a means of staffing paramilitary forces, as is the case in Egypt. The professional military component represents a much smaller effect on the overall labour market, for two reasons: the salary expense of professional forces is a severe limit on their size, and their annual turnover is smaller. The expected annual turnover of Western professional military forces represents about 8-12% of the total of such forces; the portion of the turnover that is retirement-driven is perhaps 3%, and the total impact on the labour market will therefore be somewhat less than the total turnover rate. Consequently, professional military forces are unlikely to have significant impacts on labour markets. Some indication is made of the size of the expected impact of military forces on the local labour market and on unemployment rates where such a policy objective is believed to exist.

Ball (1988) expresses strong reservations about the claim that military forces contribute to human capital formation in the civilian sector, on the basis of both the limited degree to which there are clear civilian analogues of military trades, and the limited size of the annual turnover rate. Testimony provided to the Canadian Special Joint Committee of the Senate and House of Commons with respect to Canada's Defence Policy has provided an analysis of the current proportions between MOCs in

Canada. An examination of this list indicates the proportions of military occupations that have and do not have clear civilian analogues (see Appendix 5). An initial examination of those figures suggests that approximately 71% of the MOCs in the Canadian Forces have reasonably clear civilian analogues. Since the Canadian Forces are representative of high-technology Western militaries, the direct applicability of these ratios to less developed states can be questioned. Nonetheless, Ball's strong reservations may be on somewhat shaky ground.

On the issue of annual turnover rates, however, Ball is on surer ground. In professional military forces the small annual rates of turnover would render skill transfer of relatively little significance on a national scale—though perhaps of greater significance with respect to a specific occupation, such as aircraft pilots, for example. The much higher annual rates of turnover of conscript-based forces would, in theory, permit a significant degree of transfer, but once again the question requires a close examination of specific individual training curricula. Paramilitary forces training curricula or "national service" curricula, or the employment patterns of conscripts used in military parastatals, may provide different bases for conclusions than those drawn from the military training curricula per se. No attempt has been made to quantify this variable, but the issue has been noted where applicable.

INDUSTRIAL STRATEGY

An industrial strategy policy objective has been noted where it is believed to exist. Of particular interest is the military parastatal that produces for both the military and the civilian sectors in both the agricultural and consumer/industrial products sectors.

THE OFFICIAL DEVELOPMENT ASSISTANCE (ODA) FUNGIBILITY ISSUE

The fungibility issue concerns two questions: whether the provision of ODA permits recipient states to spend more on their military sector than they would if all central government expenditures had to be funded internally; and whether the size of ODA receipts relative to CGE allows donor states the leverage to require the recipient state to reduce its military expenditures as a condition of continuing to receive ODA. The Organizational Behaviour literature of the Management schools has examined the leverage question with respect to non-profit and quasi-public sector agencies in North America and has found that leverage tends to be exertable at around the 15% level; whether this observation can be transferred to sovereign states is, of course, moot.

3

NORTHWEST AFRICA

THE REGIONAL STRATEGIC CONTEXT

In the early part of the study period, the key contentious strategic issue was that of the control of the former Spanish Sahara, an issue that initially set Morocco and Mauritania against Algeria and the Frente Popular para la Liberacion de Saguia el-Hamra y Rio de Oro (POLISARIO). A variety of diplomatic manoeuvres resulted by 1984 in a realignment that effectively saw Morocco and Libya opposed to Algeria, Tunisia, and POLISARIO, with Mauritania's alignment not entirely clear. By 1989 it appeared that this issue had declined as an acute regional concern and, while not resolved, it seems unlikely to result in overt military conflict between the regional states.

The rising security concerns in the region appear to be driven by internal socioeconomic problems in Algeria, Morocco, and Tunisia, all of which stem from population growth that is outstripping economic growth, with the result that unemployment levels are rising. In Algeria and Tunisia the result has been an increase in Muslim fundamentalism; Algeria's military responded by a coup that prevented the Front Islamique de Salut (FIS) from being able to capitalize on its electoral success. In Morocco, Islamic fundamentalism seems less influential, perhaps in part because of King Hassan's claim to descent from the Prophet, and the leadership of the populist protest movement appears to be drawn from the trade union sector.

These events suggest that the security concerns of all states will be focused internally rather than externally, and that the issue of the Western Sahara will be less disruptive of regional inter-state relations than in the earlier part of the 1980s.

THE REGIONAL SOCIO-ECONOMIC BALANCE OF POWER (1990-94 MEANS)

Country	Population (millions)	GNP ($US billions)	ME ($US millions)
Algeria	26.6	41.0	963
Morocco	27.2	28.1	1,368
Libya	4.7	29.8	2,415
Tunisia	8.4	14.1	429
Mauritania	2.1	0.9	36

THE REGIONAL MILITARY BALANCE OF POWER, 1996

Country	Fighter Squadrons	FGA Squadrons	Armoured Division Equivalents	Infantry Division Equivalents
Algeria	8.1	3.1	3.2	6.0
Morocco	0.9	4.1	1.7	9.9
Libya	13.1	10.3	7.4	6.6
Tunisia	0	0.9	0.3	1.7
Mauritania	0	0	0.1	2.1

Libya's military personnel totals are inadequate to man the equipment inventory levels held. Consequently these figures should be viewed with considerable scepticism.

MILITARIZATION LEVELS

Country	Financial: Economy ME/GNP %		Financial: Government ME/CGE %		Spartan Index		Praetorian Index	
	90-94	85-89	90-94	85-89	90-94	85-89	90-94	85-89
Algeria	2.3	2.9	6.8	7.7	6.9	7.5	4.2	1.5
Libya	8.1	17.1	16.1	21.9	18.6	21.8	3.8	5.4
Mauritania	4.0	6.7	NA	24.2	9.2	6.7	6.1	8.4
Morocco	5.3	6.9	15.3	17.5	12.4	12.8	6.8	7.1
Tunisia	3.0	3.2	9.3	10.9	6.5	6.4	7.2	6.4
Mean	4.54	7.36	12.3	16.44	10.72	11.04	5.62	5.76

MILITARY EXPENDITURE LEVELS AND TRENDS

Military expenditures in this region as a percentage of GNP peaked around the 1982 period and have generally declined since. Expenditures on the import of military equipment showed a parallel decline in this period. These patterns are consistent with a declining external security orientation, which would see lower equipment imports, but an increased internal security concern, which would see increases in expenditures on personnel, and in operations and maintenance costs. Algeria and Libya appear to adopt pay as you go patterns for military imports; Morocco makes use of supplier credits; Tunisia appears to have prepaid in advance in the early 1980s; Mauritania seems to rely on foreign military assistance for military imports. All use the conscript premium in addition to reported budget expenditures in the financing of their military sectors; however, the proportions vary fairly sharply from country to country, with Algeria appearing to make significantly greater use of the conscript premium than the other states.

THE SOCIAL IMPACT OF MILITARY EXPENDITURES

The Northwestern Sahara states (except Libya) are less heavily socially militarized than the Northeastern Sahara/Middle East states—which reflects the much less threatening external environment. However, all states in this region rely on large paramilitary forces and appear to allocate internal security duties to their military forces as well—a phenomenon consistent with a much higher level of threat perception with respect to internal forces of dissent and their capability to threaten their governments.

The Praetorian militarization index scores have been comparatively low, which suggests that the military forces in the region have not been able to secure the economically privileged status that is characteristic of the Sub-Saharan regions. A sharp rise in Algeria's Praetorian score took place in 1989 following the move to market reform in 1988 and the ensuing riots and civil unrest. Such sharp rises in the Praetorian index either are consistent with moves to ensure the loyalty of the military, or represent an increase in operations expenditures, and in either case appear to be early signs of impending violent civil strife.

THE MILITARY AS NATIONAL DEVELOPMENT FACTOR

The military forces of the Northwestern Sahara region appear to be focused on security concerns, both internal and external, rather than on national development.

CASE STUDY 1: MOROCCO

STRATEGIC THREAT ANALYSIS

A geostrategic Threat Analysis for Morocco should normally consider three areas:
- threats of direct military confrontation with bordering states, Algeria and Mauritania,
- guerrilla warfare with irredentist movements in Moroccan controlled territories, and
- the possibility that a civil war or insurrection in a neighbouring country will spill over into Morocco territory either through combatant forces making use of Morocco territory, or through the movement of refugees fleeing from that civil war or insurrection.

THE NEIGHBOURING STATES AS MILITARY THREATS TO MOROCCO

Mauritania is a state with no history of conflict with Morocco and no significant military capability. Mauritania and Morocco cooperated in the initial division of the Western Sahara territory upon the withdrawal of the Spanish. The financial strain of attempting to counter Algerian support of the POLISARIO forces eventually proved too much for Mauritania, and it withdrew its claim to the southern third of the Western Sahara. Moreover, Mauritania's small forces are concentrated at the moment along the border with Senegal. Mauritania represents no conceivable strategic threat to Morocco.

On the other hand, *Algeria* has a history of conflict with Morocco and has a significant military capability. The principal source of conflict between Algeria and Morocco has been the former Spanish territories in the Western Sahara. Prior to the Spanish withdrawal from those territories, Algeria, Mauritania, and Morocco had combined to press the Spanish to leave. To a considerable extent Morocco and Algeria were interested in gaining control of the extensive phosphate deposits in the northern part of the territory. There was, as well, an independence movement in the territory, POLISARIO, which began guerrilla operations against the Spanish in 1974.

When the Spanish indicated that they intended to surrender the territory, the erstwhile allies broke up, with Morocco, supported by Mauritania, arguing that the territory should be returned to its "homelands" (Morocco and Mauritania), and POLISARIO, supported by Algeria, that it should be given its independence. A United Nations resolution had taken the position that Spain should determine the wishes of the people of the Western Sahara, and that those people should have the right of self-determination. The Moroccan "Green Invasion" by 200,000 civilians some six miles into the Spanish Sahara led to an agreement between Spain and Morocco to cede the territory to Morocco and Mauritania. A further United Nations resolution recognized the "interim administration" of Morocco and Mauritania. POLISARIO, supported by Algeria, refused to accept the Moroccan/Spanish agreement and launched a vigorous guerrilla war from bases around Tindouf (to which Morocco also made claim) in Algeria. The cost of the guerrilla war drove Mauritania to withdraw its claims in 1978 and recognize POLISARIO as the legitimate government, whereupon Moroccan forces seized the southern third of the territory, which had been under Mauritanian control. Libya also supported POLISARIO at this time.

Moroccan diplomacy in 1983-84 concluded an agreement with Algeria by which Morocco relinquished its claim to the Tindouf region in hopes of ending Algerian support of POLISARIO. In addition, Morocco concluded a "Unity" agreement (The Treaty of Oujda) with Libya, which resulted in Libyan support being withdrawn from POLISARIO. However, the treaty did nothing to improve Morocco-Algeria relations, since Libya maintained a claim to a part of southern Algeria. The 1983 Maghrebi Treaty of Fraternity and Concord between Algeria and Tunisia, extended to Mauritania in 1984, together with the Treaty of Oujda, caused a split in Northwest Africa, with Morocco and Libya on one side and Algeria, Tunisia, Mauritania, and POLISARIO on the other. Indirect talks between POLISARIO and Morocco in 1986 were inconclusive. However, the training of Moroccan forces by the United States in anti-guerrilla warfare coupled with improved air resources, plus a series of extensive earthworks along the Algerian border led to Moroccan success in containing POLISARIO forces by mid-1988 and a further round of equally inconclusive talks with POLISARIO. From 1991-92 to 1995 the United Nations has made moves to attempt to hold the long delayed referendum approved in 1974 to determine the wishes of the inhabitants of the Western Sahara. Morocco, however, has continued to throw a series of roadblocks in the path of the referendum and shows, in fact, no evidence of being willing to surrender its control of the rich phosphate deposits of the region.

The 1990 municipal election victory of the FIS in Algeria, followed by its victory in the first round of the 1991 parliamentary elections, led to a coup by the Algerian army in January of 1992, which was followed by an internal focus on the problem of containing the growing FIS insurrection. The assassination of President Boudiaf reinforced this, and the crisis continued into 1995 without signs of resolution, when the large voter turnout for the late-1995 election of General Liamine Zeroual suggested declining popular enthusiasm for the violent confrontation. Consequently, at the moment there does not appear to be any direct threat of Algerian action against Morocco, and direct Algerian support for POLISARIO appears to have been reduced because of the internal Algerian crisis.

GUERRILLA WAR WITH POLISARIO

The POLISARIO guerrilla campaign can be expected to continue as long as it enjoys Algerian support and sanctuary. While the current military administration in Algeria seems unlikely to increase that level of support while it is still concerned with containing the FIS campaign, there is equally no clear evidence that Algeria intends to evict POLISARIO from its support area around Tindouf. We can, therefore, expect that POLISARIO operations will continue at a low level, which continues to tie down a considerable number of Moroccan troops and to impose a significant burden on the Moroccan economy.

CIVIL WAR SPILLOVER

Spillover from civil war is not a threat with respect to Mauritania, but Algeria may be a different case. While the Algerian military is at present in control in Algeria, the long-term effects of the military coup against the results of the 1991 elections remain uncertain. The assassination of the military-appointed President Boudiaf resulted in increasingly harsh repressive measures by the military government of Algeria and was matched by a violent urban guerrilla campaign by FIS supporters. Attacks on foreigners are continuing and are having an economic effect that continues to influence the political position of the government. Given the concern of the Moroccan government about the threat of Islamic fundamentalism in that country, it seems unlikely that Morocco would offer a sanctuary to Algerian FIS rebels similar to that provided to POLISARIO by Algeria.

SUMMARY

It would appear that Moroccan military expenditures are driven by two perceived requirements: the force level needed to contain the POLISARIO guerrilla war, which continues to enjoy Algeria's tacit support, and the need to be able to deter the threat of an Algerian invasion of Moroccan territory. The POLISARIO guerrilla war is effectively under control. However, the longer-term Algerian military buildup, whose real focus remains unclear, has required a parallel increase in Moroccan force levels. In effect, there had been an Algerian-Moroccan arms race under way in North West Africa.

THE MILITARY BALANCE OF POWER, 1996-97

THE LOCAL STRATEGIC CONTEXT
(RANKED IN ORDER OF ESTIMATED TOTAL COMBAT POTENTIAL)

Country	Air Force				Army			Navy	
	Fighter Sqns	FGA Sqns	COIN Attack Sqns	COIN Transport Sqns	ADEs	IDEs	COIN Bns	Subs	Ships
Algeria	8.1	3.1	3.8	3.9	3.2	6.0	9	2	6
Morocco	0.9	4.1	3.2	5.5	1.7	9.9	22	–	3
Mauritania	–	–	0.4	–	0.1	2.1	4	–	–

Mauritania, with light equipment of French origin, is of no significance in the regional power balance. Algeria, with a mixture of older and newer Soviet equipment, has a powerful offensive capability. Morocco's equipment (predominantly French, with some U.S. and Austrian models) is of good quality, but its focus is more defensive than offensive.

Allowing for equipment quality differences between Algerian and Moroccan forces (though not for differences in training and leadership), there are trends in the balance between Algeria and Morocco that should be worrying to the Moroccan General Staff. The Algerian air force has for some time enjoyed an advantage over Morocco, currently estimated to be about 2.2 to 1 in fixed-wing aircraft and 2.5 to 1 in attack helicopters. Moreover, whereas the Moroccan air force is designed essentially as a FGA ground-support force, Algeria's fighter capabilities render it an air-superiority air force. Consequently, we would expect that in a war between the two, Algeria would win the air superiority battle and would then be able to use its ground attack aircraft and particularly its attack helicopters as powerful combat multipliers for its ground forces. The army balance of power is of even more concern. Prior to 1992 Algeria enjoyed an estimated combat power advantage of 1.2 to 1 in main battle tanks and 1.5 to 1 in artillery. During and after 1992 Algeria took delivery of 300 T-72 main battle tanks, 175 armoured self-propelled howitzers, and 50 multiple rocket launchers; Morocco took delivery of 100 Kurassier tank destroyers/light tanks and 240 M-60 tanks during the same period. The effect of these deliveries was to increase the estimated combat power advantage of Algeria to about 1.8 to 1 in main battle tanks and to about to 1.8 to 1 in artillery. While the Moroccan army has greater manpower than the Algerian army, it would appear that much of it is tied down in garrison operations in the Western Sahara against the POLISARIO forces.

The deployment pattern of the Moroccan forces also presents some considerable difficulties. As a consequence of the war with POLISARIO, perhaps as much as 80% of the Moroccan forces have been deployed (tied down?) in the south, including the Western Sahara. Slightly over 15% have been deployed along the border with Algeria, and somewhat less than 10% in the Northwest Atlas region—effectively the garrison of the capital region. The consequence of the POLISARIO war is a high level of strategic vulnerability vis-à-vis Algeria. A concept of operations for the Algerian forces in a war with Morocco, therefore, might be to concentrate first on the destruction of the Moroccan air force, then to launch an attack into northern Morocco through the more weakly defended border areas with the intent of forcing the southern Moroccan forces to make the long move north and then subjecting them while on the move to a series of attacks by the Algerian air force with the object of destroying the Moroccan armour in a series of defeats in detail. The remainder of the campaign would then be a series of mopping-up actions.

POLISARIO CAPABILITIES

Total POLISARIO forces are estimated at around 3,000-6,000 with perhaps 4,000 active. Their equipment is a mix of weapons captured from Moroccan garrisons and those supplied by Algeria. The weapons supplied by Algeria include some main battle tanks (T-55s and T-62s) and armoured infantry-fighting vehicles (BMP-1s and Cascavel EE-9s), some field artillery (122mm howitzers and BM-21 MRLs), and some air defence missiles (SAM-6s, SAM-7s, and SAM-9s). They enjoy sanctuaries on Algerian territory. As a consequence Morocco is constrained from being able to defeat them decisively, since that would require an invasion of Algerian sovereignty. The effect is to require Morocco to tie down substantial forces in the Western Sahara in an essentially passive defensive role which, given the mobility and firepower of the POLISARIO forces, offers the prospect of a series of small defeats in detail. The acquisition of attack helicopters and FGA, as well as U.S. training in anti-guerrilla operations, tipped the operational balance in favour of Moroccan forces. The POLISARIO acquisition of air defence missiles from Algeria, particularly SAM-6s, tipped the balance back somewhat.

POLISARIO does not have the capability of defeating Morocco in the field. Its strategy is to force Morocco to pay an excessive cost over the long run and to demoralize the Moroccan forces to such an extent that Morocco eventually gives up and withdraws. The pattern is familiar to anyone who has read Mao Zedong's works on guerrilla warfare. However, the openness of desert terrain and the efficiency of the Moroccan anti-guerrilla forces, particularly in the air, has meant that to this point the Morocco-POLISARIO war has settled into a stalemate. If POLISARIO is to be successful in driving Morocco out of the Western Sahara an increased level of Algerian military support will be necessary.

A DEFENCE SUFFICIENCY FORCE STRUCTURE FOR MOROCCO

If Moroccan national policy objectives continue to include retaining possession of the Western Sahara—which seems to be the case—then the current military force structure seems to be the minimum that prudence would dictate. The dominant strategic threat comes not so much from POLISARIO, since the Moroccan forces have demonstrated quite clearly that they can contain that guerrilla war and can probably do so indefinitely, as it does from the larger Algerian force structure. This is particularly the case in the light of the late 1980s-early 1990s Algerian military buildup, which has sharply altered the Morocco-Algeria balance of power in favour of Algeria. Since Algeria's purpose in this military buildup seems unclear, it is prudent on the part of Morocco to maintain its force structure at least at the current level, even though that represents a severe economic burden.

A strong case can be made, on the basis of the Algerian threat, for the acquisition of additional Kurassier tank destroyers in order to upgrade the eight mechanized infantry regiments to mechanized brigade status.

Moreover, the substantial Algerian air threat provides argument for the acquisition of air defence missiles of greater capacity than available in the three Chapparal batteries; the capabilities of the ADATS (Air Defence Anti-Tank System) would seem particularly well suited to Moroccan needs. The size of the Algerian fighter capabilities provides a strong argument for additional Mirage F1s in the Moroccan air force. No attempt has been made to quantify the cost of these additions to the equipment inventory of the Moroccan forces. They would be considerable, particularly in the case of the ADATS missiles and additional Mirages.

MILITARY EXPENDITURES: ANALYSIS OF VARIABLES

THE LOCAL STRATEGIC CONTEXT
(BORDERING COUNTRIES IN ORDER OF GNP)

Country	1994			ME/GNP		MI/ME	
	GNP $US millions	ME $US millions	ME/GNP %	1990-94 %	1985-89 %	1990-94 %	1985-89 %
Algeria	40,510	1,335	3.3	2.3	2.9	13.5	68.1
Morocco	30,200	1,228	4.5	5.3	6.9	8.3	14.6
Mauritania	969	36	3.7	4.0	6.7	NA	27.7

Appendix 6 concludes that Algeria's arms imports are included in reported military expenditures, but that those of Mauritania and Morocco are not. Accordingly, adjusted figures are used for the two latter states. All three use the conscript premium to reduce the effective cost of their military establishments. However, Morocco's forces are predominantly volunteer, so that the financial leverage obtained through the use of the conscript premium is less than that of Algeria, where about half are conscripts. While this reduces the personnel costs of the Algerian forces, and allows them to spend a higher proportion of ME on equipment, it has been counterbalanced by the higher O&M costs associated with the anti-FIS campaign, such that since 1990 Algerian spending on military imports has decreased substantially.

TRENDS IN THE REGION

Morocco had been reducing military expenditures as a percentage of GNP over the previous ten-year period. Algeria had been following a similar policy in the early 1980s but military expenditures rose in constant dollar terms (though continuing to decline as a percentage of GNP) from

1985, and took a sharp jump upward in 1989 in both constant dollars and percentage of GNP. This increase in Algerian military expenditure appeared to affect Morocco, whose defence expenditures as a percentage of GNP turned upward in 1989. Algerian ME turned downward in 1990-91. This may have represented a shift of financial resources from the military to the paramilitary sector, in that paramilitary force strength more than doubled in 1991 in response to the campaign of violence by FIS supporters, but appeared to be rising again in 1995.

The financial evidence suggests that an arms race between Morocco and Algeria may have begun in the late 1980s, and that it has been interrupted by Algeria's internal security problem. Financial data suggests that Morocco was responding to the Algerian buildup rather than the other way round.

SENSITIVITY ANALYSIS: THE EXISTING MOROCCAN SPENDING PATTERN (MEAN 1990-94)

Spending Category	Budget Share %	$US per Position	Foreign Currency $US millions	Local Currency $US millions	Total $US millions
Equipment	8.3	629	123	0	123
PO&M	91.7	6,996	0	1,368	1,368
Total	100	7,626	123	1,368	1,491

CHANGE EFFECTS

- Changing Equipment spending
  by 1% of Budget $14,910,000   (Foreign Currency)
- Changing Personnel strength by 1,000
  – Change in Equipment spending $629,000   (Foreign Currency)
  – Change in PO&M spending $6,996,000 (Local Currency)
  – Total change in Military
    spending $7,626,000
- Changing the Praetorian
  Index by 1 $202,500,000 (Local Currency)

THE DEFENCE SUFFICIENCY BUDGET

The Moroccan force structure is not excessive given the local strategic context, and force reductions in the absence of an arms limitation treaty between Morocco and Algeria is unfruitful. A reduction of the Moroccan

Praetorian Index (6.8) to the mean of the other two states (5.25) could decrease PO&M spending by $314 million.

IS MOROCCO SPENDING TOO MUCH ON ITS MILITARY?

This study makes no conclusion as to the legitimacy of the Moroccan national policy decision to retain control over the Western Sahara. Given that decision, the force structure of the Moroccan military is not excessive in comparison to that of Algeria. A case can be made that the equipment inventory of the Moroccan forces should continue to be upgraded (at considerable expense). Morocco's military expenditures represent a significant economic burden, however, and Morocco's level of social militarization is substantial. The higher Praetorian index may suggest a possible area for defence spending reductions—though since the Praetorian Index used in this study does not discriminate between personnel and O&M spending it may be that the higher Moroccan Index simply reflects the higher O&M spending associated with the anti-POLISARIO campaign.

SOCIAL MILITARIZATION ANALYSIS

PRAETORIAN AND SPARTAN INDICES
(1990-94 MEANS)

Country	Praetorian Index	Spartan Index	Total Regular Personnel
Algeria	4.2	6.9	129,380
Morocco	6.8	12.4	195,500
Mauritania	6.1	9.2	13,640

These three countries are quite heavily socially militarized in Western or Sub-Saharan African terms, though not by North East Africa/Middle East terms. It appears that the Moroccan-POLISARIO war in the former Spanish Sahara is the principal cause of the militarization level in Morocco and Mauritania, with Algeria having provided both a refuge and a marshalling area for POLISARIO in the Tindouf area, as well as weapons and logistics support. Algeria, and to a somewhat lesser extent Morocco, is also responding to concerns over the rising level of support for violent Moslem fundamentalism, which in turn seems to be strongly linked to rising levels of unemployment, as economic growth in those states fails to keep up with rising populations. Praetorian militarization in Mauritania and Morocco is similar to that in North East Africa/Middle East and considerably lower than in Sub-Saharan Africa, though higher than NATO norms. There seems no doubt that the military is an economically privileged component of society, but the size of the differential is considerably lower than that found in Sub-Saharan Africa.

DEVELOPMENT ISSUES

THE MILITARY AS NATIONAL DEVELOPMENT AGENCY

No evidence was found of Morocco's forces being used for infrastructure-building purposes. Interestingly, though, two thirds of the Algerian conscripts' period of service is devoted to civil projects. Since there is no significant indigenous defence industrial base, nor any evidence of building military equipment under licensing arrangements, it appears that Moroccan military procurement does not play an industrial-development role.

Though Morocco maintains an eighteen-month conscription system, most of the Moroccan forces are volunteers. Characteristically, the turnover rate for such a professional volunteer force would range from 3% to 12% annually. Given that part of the force is based on conscripts, we would assume that the experienced turnover rate would lie in the upper end of this range. An estimated maximum turnover figure of 23,400 would amount to 8.6% of the annual cohort of males aged 18-22. Without an examination of the actual training curriculum for Moroccan soldiers it is impossible to estimate the amount of human capital formation that would take place as a consequence of military service.

THE ODA FUNGIBILITY ISSUE

With 1994 ODA at 46.7% of military expenditures it would seem that Morocco is in a fungible situation but that with ODA at only 7.1% of 1994 CGE the degree of donor leverage may not be sufficient to induce Morocco to reduce its military spending.

4

WEST AFRICA

THE REGIONAL STRATEGIC CONTEXT:
INTER-STATE ISSUES

The overwhelming predominance of Nigeria within the regional balance of power context is strikingly clear from the following tables. That predominance is evident in all the classical elements of strategic power analysis: available military forces with a true offensive capability (armoured forces backed by fighter/FGA air power), an economy that can provide the financial and economic force to sustain that military power, and a population that can generate additional military forces should the need arise. Not shown is the similar Nigerian preponderance in naval forces. While this study does not assess the logistics and maintenance capability of the forces under consideration, it would not likely alter the regional power balance. It is fortunate, given the realities of the regional power balance, that Nigeria has shown few signs of hegemonic intent with respect to its neighbours, and, indeed, has followed a policy of leadership in peacemaking initiatives—although Nigeria's deepening internal political conflicts may well be a contributing factor to its relative external calm. In any event, Nigeria has over a period of ten or so years followed a pattern of reducing its military capabilities—a move that, given its strategic power advantage, has been financially quite sensible.

The continuing presence of French military forces, which in Côte d'Ivoire and Senegal amount to garrisons, has allowed France to play a post-colonial role in helping governments of which it approves to remain in power. Whatever the political rationality of such intervention it, too, has had the useful effect of encouraging regional governments to maintain relatively low levels of military forces and consequently a relatively low level of military expenditures.

THE REGIONAL SOCIO-ECONOMIC BALANCE OF POWER (1990-94 MEANS)

Country	Population (millions)	GNP ($US billions)	ME ($US millions)
Nigeria	92.2	39.1	368
Côte d'Ivoire	13.3	5.7	87
Ghana	16.2	4.9	37
Senegal	8.2	3.7	89
Burkina Faso	9.6	1.8	54
Mali	8.6	1.8	34
Niger	8.4	1.5	17
Guinea	6.2	3.0	47
Benin	5.0	1.4	26
Togo	4.0	1.0	29
Chad	5.2	0.9	56
Mauritania	2.1	0.9	36
Sierra Leone	4.4	0.7	22
Liberia	2.6	NA	36
The Gambia	0.9	0.4	13
Guinea-Bissau	1.0	0.2	8

THE REGIONAL MILITARY BALANCE OF POWER, 1995-96

Country	Fighter Squadrons	FGA Squadrons	ABEs	IBEs
Nigeria	–	3.6	2.0	7.7
Mali	0.7	0.3	0.2	2.0
Guinea	–	0.5	0.4	2.3
Guinea-Bissau	–	0.2	0.1	1.7
Togo	–	0.3	–	2.2
Côte d'Ivoire	–	0.3	–	1.4
Mauritania	–	–	0.3	6.3
Ghana	–	–	–	2.3
Chad	–	–	0.6	NA
Senegal	–	–	–	3.0
Burkina Faso	–	–	–	2.9
Sierra Leone	–	–	–	2.3
Benin	–	–	–	1.3
Niger	–	–	–	1.0
The Gambia	–	–	–	0.7
Liberia	–	–	–	NA

INTRA-STATE ISSUES

The West African regional context is one of militarily weak states whose primary focus has been internal rather than external. With few exceptions, the dominant military model appears to have been that of the Praetorian state, in which the military is a highly privileged economic elite whose principal activity is the making, controlling, and unmaking of governments—or the protection of an entrenched political elite. Paradoxically, one positive impact of such a military model is a relative lack of interest in external wars (and high levels of military expenditures), since they represent too high a risk to the future of the Praetorians themselves. Opposed to the Praetorian model has been the populist reform model, which has emerged in Ghana under Rawlings and for a short period in Burkina Faso under Sankara. The two diverged, however, with Rawlings' administration moving toward the position of one of the least militarized states in the region, whereas Sankara launched the region's one war.

As in other parts of Africa, the immediate post-colonial attraction to Marxist-Leninist economic models brought with it the influence of Chinese/Soviet models with respect to military organization structures and equipment philosophies; these are particularly reflected in Guinea, Guinea-Bissau, and Mali. The Soviet/Chinese influence led to the sales of Soviet/Chinese-built military equipment designed for the NATO/Warsaw Pact high-intensity armoured war on the North European plain; it is not well suited to the geography of West Africa, and is a colossal waste of scarce resources for the states induced to buy it.

MILITARIZATION LEVELS:
MILITARY EXPENDITURE LEVELS AND TRENDS

The overall trend of military expenditure has been downward during the ten-year period—in some cases quite substantially so. As with most Sub-Saharan countries, supplier debt has been a major source of financing real military expenditures. The use of the conscript premium to help finance the defence budget is also characteristic of most of the West African countries—Ghana is an exception. With the end of the Cold War, and with former Warsaw Pact countries and China needing to use military exports to earn hard currency, Sub-Saharan countries of doubtful debt repayment capacity will experience increasing difficulty in gaining military supplier credits. There should be a further downward impact in these expenditures, particularly if ODA-granting countries increase their opposition to military imports. Since West Africa is a comparatively peaceful region in terms of inter-state conflict, such a cut in military equipment imports should have little impact on regional security.

Country	Financial: Economy ME/GNP %		Financial: Government ME/CGE %		Spartan Index		Praetorian Index	
	90-94	85-89	90-94	85-89	90-94	85-89	90-94	85-89
Liberia	NA	4.0	NA	14.0	NA	3.5	NA	12.8
Chad	3.5	4.0	6.4	13.8	5.6	4.8	6.9	11.3
Mauritania	4.0	6.7	NA	24.2	2.6	3.2	6.2	8.9
Guinea-Bissau	3.6	15.8	8.2	29.4	8.9	9.7	5.0	3.1
The Gambia	3.5	4.1	17.4	32.5	1.4	1.2	32.2	8.9
Burkina Faso	3.0	3.8	17.6	26.5	1.5	1.4	29.8	32.3
Togo	3.0	3.2	11.6	10.5	1.6	2.0	20.3	10.8
Sierra Leone	3.0	1.1	14.4	6.3	1.2	1.0	23.4	16.7
Senegal	2.4	2.7	8.3	14.2	1.4	1.8	17.8	16.9
Mali	1.9	4.7	14.6	15.8	1.8	1.9	25.8	28.6
Benin	1.9	2.3	15.4	20.4	1.6	1.9	20.3	22.4
Guinea	1.6	3.4	7.1	21.8	3.1	3.6	8.9	6.7
Côte d'Ivoire	1.5	1.9	NA	NA	1.2	1.4	27.9	21.1
Niger	1.1	1.7	5.6	8.5	1.1	0.9	24.0	22.9
Nigeria	0.9	1.9	4.2	9.1	1.0	1.3	8.9	9.2
Ghana	0.8	1.3	4.7	9.0	0.8	1.3	16.0	10.2
Means	2.38	3.91	10.42	17.07	2.32	2.6	17.09	15.18

THE SOCIAL IMPACT OF MILITARY EXPENDITURES

With the exception of Guinea-Bissau and Chad, the overall level of Spartan militarization in the West African countries is comparatively low. However, the Praetorian Index level is very high.

THE MILITARY AS NATIONAL DEVELOPMENT FACTOR

Only in Burkina Faso has there been any substantial indication of the possible use of military or paramilitary forces in national infrastructure construction. There is also no indication of the use of military equipment purchases as part of an industrial development strategy through the use of licensed manufacture. The overall size of the military forces in each of the West African states, with the possible exception of Guinea-Bissau and Mauritania, suggests that they have little impact on local labour market unemployment rates. In addition, the relatively small sizes suggest that, even though the use of conscript-based forces is common, there will be relatively little impact on national human capital formation; in any event, such a judgment would also depend on an examination of the conscript training curriculum.

CASE STUDY 2: BURKINA FASO

STRATEGIC THREAT ANALYSIS

A geostrategic Threat Analysis for Burkina Faso should normally consider three areas:
- threats of military confrontation with other states with which Burkina Faso shares borders, or that, though geographically distant, have the capability to threaten Burkina Faso. These include Benin, Côte d'Ivoire, Ghana, Mali, Niger, and Togo,
- the possibility that a civil war or insurrection in a neighbouring country will spill over into Burkina Faso territory either through combatant forces making use of Burkina Faso territory, or through the movement of refugees fleeing from that civil war or insurrection, and
- threats to Burkina Faso's internal political stability and armed resistance to the civil authority, possibly aided by the government of one of the neighbouring countries.

THE NEIGHBOURING STATES AS MILITARY THREATS TO BURKINA FASO

Four of the six neighbouring states, *Benin, Côte d'Ivoire, Niger,* and *Togo*, can be eliminated as strategic threats on the basis that they have little or no significant military capacity or casus belli. There is no significant history of border disputes with any of them. All are militarily weaker than Burkina Faso and particularly so in the three critical areas required to mount effective offensive operations—air power, heavy armour, and adequate artillery resources. Benin and Niger have no combat aircraft of any kind. While Côte d'Ivoire and Togo possess Alphajets, these aircraft are essentially jet trainer aircraft with a limited light ground attack capability; they are no match for the Burkina Faso MIG-21s. The presence of a French marine regiment in the most economically powerful of the four, Côte d'Ivoire, implies a degree of French influence over that state's strategic policy, and French post-colonial policy in West Africa has been to discourage inter-state warfare. Moreover, the rail linkage between Côte d'Ivoire and Burkina Faso heightens their mutual economic relationship. The heavy French economic support of Benin argues a similar influence. Togo remains distracted by its internal troubles and the difficulties with Ghana over the presence of cross-border refugees and opposition political forces in the neighbouring country.

Ghana is a state with some capability but no significant history of conflict with Burkina Faso. Its ground forces are stronger than those of the four states already discussed, but still weaker than those of Burkina Faso in light armour, though stronger in infantry and artillery. Ghana lacks any air combat capability, and its ground forces would be vulnerable to attack by Burkina Faso's MIG-21s. Moreover, there existed a strong cooperative linkage between Ghana and Burkina Faso during the period of the Sankara regime in Burkina Faso and the Rawlings administration in Ghana. Sankara acknowledged valuable political, diplomatic, and military assistance from the Rawlings regime and the two leaders undertook a number of cooperative measures to control smuggling and facilitate trade, and began talks about a common currency. The overthrow and execution of Sankara in 1988 by the successor Campaoré regime does not appear to have led to a significant breakdown of relations with Ghana. In any event Ghana's attentions have been directed internally toward economic growth and development and the impact of cross-border refugee migration from Togo.

Mali is the only neighbouring state with some capability and a significant history of conflict with Burkina Faso—a long-standing dispute over the location of the border in the Agacher region based on the question of which maps showing the colonial borders were definitive. The disputed region amounted to about 800 square miles rich in manganese deposits. Burkina Faso was technically the aggressor in the brief war of December 1985, when it sent its troops to occupy a number of Malian villages before being driven back. Mali responded by bombing some Burkina Faso villages, and about forty people were killed before neighbours involved in the West African Non-Aggression and Aid Agreement intervened to secure a truce. Eventually the issue was settled by the World Court with a ruling giving about half the disputed territory to each. Mali has a slight advantage in air combat power.

CIVIL WAR OR CIVIL WAR SPILLOVER

The countries of West Africa, with the exception of Liberia and Nigeria (and now Sierra Leone), have seen governments normally change by means of military coups rather than protracted civil wars. Civil war spillover is thus not a likely contingency. Massive migrations of refugees into Burkina Faso seem unlikely, though lesser movements are possible. There is no history of general uprisings in Burkina Faso, but rather one of successive coups by military factions. Consequently the prospects of a traditional civil war seem unlikely, and a defence against a coup by military malcontents a much more likely prospect given the history of the country.

SUMMARY

Burkina Faso's local geostrategic context is not particularly threatening. It would appear that a military force structure broadly similar to that of its neighbours is all that is really required for security from what must be viewed as a comparatively weak external threat context. Such a force would appear to be about one brigade and a half squadron of aircraft.

THE MILITARY BALANCE OF POWER, 1996-97

THE LOCAL STRATEGIC CONTEXT
(RANKED IN ORDER OF ESTIMATED TOTAL COMBAT POTENTIAL)

Country	Air Force					Army	
	Fighter Squadrons	FGA Squadrons	COIN Attack Squadrons	COIN Transport Squadrons	ABEs	IBEs	COIN Battalions
Mali	0.7	0.3	–	0.4	0.2	2.0	2
Togo	–	0.3	0.7	0.1	–	2.2	2
Burkina Faso	–	–	0.3	0.2	–	2.9	1
Côte d'Ivoire	–	0.3	–	0.3	–	1.4	0.3
Ghana	–	–	0.3	0.3	–	2.3	2
Benin	–	–	–	0.2	–	1.3	1
Niger	–	–	–	–	–	1.0	2

Burkina Faso's army contains 19 "battalions" of various arms, but the manning levels are reduced much below normal. The logistics capability to support even the notional 2.9 IBEs is doubtful. Its equipment, a mix of French and Soviet/Chinese, is light in nature, and reasonably well suited to the geography of the country. **Benin**'s army is equipped with a mix of light equipment of Soviet and western design. **Côte d'Ivoire**'s army is composed of light forces with French equipment. A French Marine regiment is stationed in the country. The six Alphajets of the air force are really COIN aircraft. **Ghana**'s army uses Western light equipment of high mobility. The air force jets are really COIN aircraft. **Mali**'s equipment is predominantly Soviet, with some Chinese, and includes obsolete main battle tanks of World War II vintage whose maintenance must be a nightmare. The air force uses Soviet aircraft and has some theoretical air combat capability. **Niger**'s army is composed of light forces with French equipment. **Togo**'s army is equipped with a mixture of light equipment from various sources. The multiplicity of vehicle types must create considerable maintenance problems. The air force has six Alphajets that are really COIN aircraft.

Apart from Burkina Faso and Mali the other states in the region seem well balanced in combat capabilities. None has a significant offensive capability, which would require heavy armour and significant field artillery supported by fighter aircraft and FGA or ground attack helicopters, and the forces of each of these states can be viewed as genuinely defensive in nature. Burkina Faso and Mali are significantly more heavily armed. Their equipment holdings represent two different philosophies. Mali prefers obsolete main battle tanks and light tanks, which impose a considerable burden in terms of maintenance and fuel consumption. Burkina Faso prefers armoured cars, whose guns are the equal of Mali's tanks but whose armour protection is weaker; their advantage is highly superior mobility over the road networks that parallel the border between the two countries. With the 1994 retirement of Burkina Faso's MIG-21s, Mali has an absolute edge in air power, but otherwise Mali and Burkina Faso are sufficiently closely matched in combat power that neither is likely to be able to prevail. Such was the case in the Agacher war, in which Burkina Faso was the aggressor. In any event, Mali's attention is diverted by its ongoing problems with its Tuareg population in the north, which is suspected of receiving Libyan aid. Consequently there is little likelihood of Mali initiating a war with Burkina Faso. In terms of COIN capabilities, Burkina Faso more strongly resembles the remainder of the states in the region than it does Mali.

UNUSUAL FEATURES OF THE BURKINA FASO MILITARY FORCE STRUCTURE

One highly unusual feature of the Burkina Faso force structure is the presence of the 45,000-strong People's Militia, which *The Military Balance* shows as paramilitary forces. This force includes both men and women in the 20-35 age group; they serve part-time for a period of two years and perform both civil and military duties. The force, assuming a complete turnover at the end of the two-year period of service, constitutes approximately 16% of the average two-year cohort in this age group. This curious structure seems to be the product of former President Sankara's interest in Marxist-populist "revolutionary" concepts. Given Sankara's interest in Libya's Gadaffi, it may be that the People's Militia concept is modelled on that of Libya and ultimately on the Maoist concept of the "Peoples' War," in which the entire population is mobilized to resist an invader, as the ultimate element of national defence. It may be linked too to the localized Committees for the Defence of the Revolution (CDRs), which Sankara established.

If that is correct the People's Militia may have been intended to serve several purposes. The first would be to provide a "volunteer" labour pool that could be used in such infrastructure projects as the extension of the railway from Ouagadougou to Tambao, a project whose American and Japanese financial support was withdrawn. The second might be as an element of social control reminiscent of the pattern adopted in the People's Republic of China, particularly during the Red Guards period. The third might be as a reserve military manpower pool that could be used to flesh out existing skeleton army units to full war establishments. The fourth might be to artificially reduce local unemployment rates, since the People's Militia constitute about 2.25% of the total population in the 20-35 age group.

A second unusual feature is the presence of many skeleton units and formations in the Burkina Faso force structure. There are five infantry "regiments," each consisting of three "battalions" containing a single company of five platoons, instead of the usual three companies found in the Warsaw Treaty/Chinese organizational model. Each battalion thus contains five platoons of infantry instead of the nine that one would expect. The artillery and armoured "battalions" have two platoons instead of the six expected. One explanation could be that the People's Militia is expected to provide a mobilization pool to allow the army to bring its regular regiments up to full strength. An attraction of such a structure is that an artificially high number of senior appointments can be justified to command the large number of skeleton units. If, for example, the 25 infantry platoons were organized into full-strength battalions, we would find only three regiments and nine battalions instead of five regiments and fifteen battalions—40% of the senior officer appointments would thus have to be eliminated. However, even the three regiment/nine battalion figure is questionable, since it is unlikely that it can be manned. If staffed using the Soviet/Chinese model of about 2,200 positions per combined arms regiment we would expect it to require a total force of about

9,000 positions, including the supporting infrastructure. The Burkina Faso army strength is about 7,000 positions. Moreover, the equipment holdings are insufficient for the larger force.

A DEFENCE SUFFICIENCY FORCE STRUCTURE FOR BURKINA FASO

The existing Burkina Faso military force manning level is not particularly excessive in terms of the surrounding local strategic context. However, the organizational structure is inefficiently organized, perhaps in order to provide an excessive number of senior command positions. In turn this top-heavy rank structure contributes to the highly excessive socioeconomic militarization—even by West African norms. Since Burkina Faso's army is likely organized on Soviet/Chinese organizational models, an army of two combined arms regiments each of three infantry, one armoured car, one artillery, and one logistics battalion would be adequate. These battalions are smaller than Western ones, and the total strength of the Soviet/Chinese regimental form is about 2,200 positions. To this would be added an infrastructure increment for a total establishment of about 6,000 positions, or about 1,000 positions fewer than present. The eliminated positions would include redundant senior officers and their staffs, with a resultant improvement in the army's Praetorian Index. No change in the 200 positions in the air force or the 1,500 positions in the Gendarmerie (included in the army figures) is proposed. The total force proposed would total approximately 7,700 positions—a reduction of 1,000 positions or approximately 11% of the mean 1990-94 manning level. In 1994 the manning level of the Army was reduced to 5,800 positions, or 200 less than recommended here. However, 2,450 of those positions were transferred to the paramilitary Gendarmerie, which is also part of the Army—the reduction is assessed as cosmetic rather than real.

MILITARY EXPENDITURES: ANALYSIS OF VARIABLES

Appendix 6 concludes that only Burkina Faso appears to include military imports in reported expenditures. All states except Ghana make use of the conscript premium, though Burkina Faso appears to use a volunteer professional military while restricting conscripts to the part-time People's Militia. The general level of military expenditures as a percentage of GNP in 1994 is not very high in comparative terms, and the regional trend has been downward in the previous decade. In most cases this has come from reduced imports of military equipment, suggesting a decreased emphasis on inter-state conflict.

THE MILITARY EXPENDITURES BALANCE
(BORDERING COUNTRIES IN ORDER OF GNP)

Country	1994			ME/GNP		MI/ME	
	GNP $US millions	ME $US millions	ME/GNP %	1990-94 %	1985-89 %	1990-94 %	1985-89 %
Côte d'Ivoire	5,445	61	1.1	1.5	1.9	0.0	11.9
Ghana	5,319	41	0.8	0.8	1.3	3.2	37.9
Mali	1,838	34	1.8	1.9	4.7	13.1	47.7
Burkina Faso	1,824	48	2.6	3.0	3.8	15.5	29.8
Niger	1,507	14	0.9	1.1	1.7	0.0	43.0
Benin	1,481	34	2.3	1.9	2.3	4.6	26.6
Togo	929	25	2.7	3.0	3.2	3.4	20.5

SENSITIVITY ANALYSIS: THE EXISTING BURKINA FASO SPENDING
PATTERN (MEAN 1990-94)

Spending Category	Budget Share %	$US per Position	Foreign Currency $US millions	Local Currency $US millions	Total $US millions
Equipment	15.5	1,034	8.4	0	8.4
PO&M	84.5	5,460	0	45.8	45.8
Total	100	6,675	8.4	45.8	54.2

CHANGE EFFECTS

- Changing Equipment spending
  by 1% of the Budget $542,000   (Foreign Currency)
- Changing Personnel strength by 1,000
  – Change in Equipment spending $1,034,000   (Foreign Currency)
  – Change in PO&M spending $5,460,000   (Local Currency)
  – Total Change in Military
    spending $6,494,000
- Changing the Praetorian
  Index by 1 $1,518,000   (Local Currency)

THE DEFENCE SUFFICIENCY BUDGET

With 1,000 positions cut, and a decrease in the Burkinabe Praetorian Index (29.8) to the West African mean (18.2), the following would result.

Mean 1990-94 Budget without changes	$54,200,000
– Decrease in Personnel (local currency) spending	$5,460,000
– Decrease in Equipment (foreign currency) spending	$1,034,000
– Decrease in Praetorian multiple	$17,609,000
Total Decrease	$24,103,000
Mean 1990-94 Budget with changes	$30,097,000

IS BURKINA FASO SPENDING TOO MUCH ON ITS MILITARY?

The answer to our question is Yes. The Burkinabe military has taken advantage of its monopoly on the use of force and its controlling influence in government to become economic rent-takers by inflating military salaries and creating an excessive number of headquarters and superfluous senior appointments. A real rather than cosmetic reduction of 1,000 positions plus a cut in the Praetorian Index to the West African mean could be achieved without weakening the Burkinabe defence capability, and would result in savings of $24.1 million in defence spending—a sum equal to 1.3% of mean 1990-94 GNP, or 5.9% of mean 1990-94 ODA.

SOCIAL MILITARIZATION ANALYSIS

PRAETORIAN AND SPARTAN INDICES (1990-94 MEANS)

Country	Praetorian Index	Spartan Index	Total Regular Personnel
Burkina Faso	30.2	1.5	8,120
Côted'Ivoire	29.0	1.2	7,800
Niger	23.5	1.1	4,100
Benin	20.5	1.4	4,430
Mali	19.4	1.8	7,430
Ghana	14.8	0.8	5,000
Togo	10.7	1.6	5,560

Burkina Faso's high Praetorian Index indicates that its military constitutes a highly privileged elite, even in terms of the regional context. It seems that the Burkina Faso military takes advantage of its monopoly on the use of force to exact a heavy economic rent. The use of a conscript premium appears restricted to the People's Militia rather than being used for the regular force, though it appears that one de facto purpose of the People's Militia may be to justify a larger senior officer structure than is necessary and that this may contribute to the larger than normal Praetorian Index characterizing the Burkinabe forces. It appears that the Burkina Faso military has also executed a series of military coups to maintain control of the government. Burkina Faso's Spartan militarization lies in the middle range, relative to its neighbours, largely as a result of the People's Militia strength. However, this may understate the actual situation, given what appears to have been the ideological aim of the Sankara administration in the original creation of the force and the role that it may play as an element of local social control. It is not clear how the successor Campaoré and Konare administrations have treated the People's Militia.

DEVELOPMENT ISSUES

THE MILITARY AS NATIONAL DEVELOPMENT AGENCY

The "civil duties" aspect of the part-time People's Militia has been noted. That force may have been used to supply the "volunteer" labour used in the attempt to extend the railway line to Tambao when American and Japanese financial support was withdrawn. However, since there is no significant indigenous defence industrial base nor any evidence of building military equipment under licensing arrangements, it is unlikely that Burkina Faso military procurement plays an industrial development role.

Burkina Faso appears to use a professional volunteer system for its regular force. Turnover rates for such forces characteristically range from 3% to 12% annually. With an economically privileged elite, turnover should lie in the bottom end of that range. Even at the top it would amount to around 1,000 annually, or about 1.25% of the annual cohort of males aged 18-22. Thus it is unlikely that the Burkinabe regular military has a significant impact on unemployment rates or on civilian human capital formation. Conscription is used for the part-time People's Militia. It is doubtful, without access to the details of that program, to argue that the training program for this part-time force would amount to a significant amount of human capital formation.

THE ODA FUNGIBILITY ISSUE

With mean 1990-94 ODA at 897% of the defence budget fungibility is clearly possible. With mean ODA at 133% of CGE it appears that donors have a great deal of potential leverage available to them.

CASE STUDY 3: MALI

STRATEGIC THREAT ANALYSIS

A geostrategic Threat Analysis for Mali should normally consider three areas:
- threats of military confrontation with or intervention by states with which Mali shares borders,
- the threat of insurrection or civil war within Mali, and
- the threat of a coup against the established government.

THE NEIGHBOURING STATES AS THREATS TO MALI

Of the seven neighbouring states, three, *Mauritania*, *Senegal* and *Côte d'Ivoire*, can be excluded as strategic threats on the basis of their having little or no capability and no significant history of conflict. None possesses a heavy armoured capability of any kind, and except for Côte d'Ivoire none possesses an air force equipped with fighter or FGA aircraft. Moreover, Mali's only rail link lies through Senegal. The presence of a French marine regiment in both Senegal and Côte d'Ivoire implies some French influence over their strategic policy and the pattern of French involvement in post-colonial West Africa has been to discourage interstate warfare. *Niger*, too, can be excluded on the basis of a lack of capability, though there is a slight history of conflict in the form of a border dispute, which was settled peacefully early in the Traoré administration. Niger has no heavy armoured forces or air force equipped with fighters or FGA.

While *Guinea* has some capability, there is no significant history of conflict or border disputes, and it can be excluded as a strategic threat. Though Guinea's army is somewhat stronger in towed artillery and heavy armor than Mali's, their air forces are relatively evenly matched. The advantage is insufficient to guarantee victory, and a prudent general staff could be expected to recommend strategic caution except in self-defence. Guinea's participation in the five-nation peacekeeping force deployed to Liberia under the aegis of the Economic Community of West African States suggests a preference for peaceful resolution of conflict on the part of the Guinean government.

Burkina Faso is a marginal strategic threat. A border conflict over the Agacher strip in 1985, during the Sankara administration, was resolved after thirty days of fighting by a truce mediated by Nigeria and Libya and ultimately a World Court decision. The coup that replaced Sankara with the more moderate Campaoré suggests the dispute is unlikely to recur. Neither side has a conclusive strategic advantage. Mali's air force is superior to that of Burkina Faso. The two armies represent different armour philosophies: Mali holds elderly main battle tanks and light tanks, whereas Burkina Faso prefers more modern wheeled armoured cars with superior firepower and mobility, though inferior armour protection.

Algeria is also a marginal strategic threat. A border dispute between Mali and Algeria was peacefully settled early in the Traoré regime. Algeria also mediated the 1990 fighting between the Malian government and Tuareg rebels. It seems likely that Algeria was motivated by a desire to defuse tensions on its southern border. There has been some suggestion that Libya supported the Tuareg rebels. If this is so, one Algerian motive to act as mediator might have been to frustrate Libya. Algeria certainly has the capability to intervene militarily in Mali if it chooses to do so. The power balance between the two is sufficiently wide that Mali could not defend itself, and given the size and technological capabilities of the two there are no circumstances under which Mali could achieve such a balance. However, Algerian action could have difficult foreign policy implications, and the current Algerian administration, which has profound internal distractions, seems unlikely to do so. Consequently, Malian security policy vis-à-vis Algeria must logically be directed along the modalities of cooperation, and the encouragement of good relations with Western states, who might be able to constrain Algerian behaviour.

THE INTERNAL SECURITY DIMENSION

A major ethnic fault line running through all of the South Saharan states is that between Berbers/Arabs and Black Africans. Libya has exploited this periodically by intervention on the side of the Arabs. In Mali this ethnic fault line lies between the Tuareg of the North and the Mandingo/Fulani of the Niger valley and the south who control the government. A similar fault line lies through Niger. There is some speculation that the Tuareg, with Libyan support, favour the establishment of an autonomous Tuareg region in the north of both countries. Attacks on government posts in both countries in 1990 resulted in the deaths of at least 400 Tuareg in Niger and 200 in Mali. Fighting ended with Algerian mediation that established a cease-fire line in early 1991, but fighting broke out again with a government attack on a Tuareg base in late 1994, and a Tuareg attack on Timbuktu in early 1995. The Tuareg rebel group, the Arab Islamic Front, declared a cease-fire in June 1995 that still appears to be holding. Taken together, the internal security dimension and the geostrategic context provide opportunities for external agencies to involve themselves in internal Malian affairs on the basis of ethnic connections with the Tuareg. This suggests another reason for the central Malian authorities to seek to resolve Tuareg grievances by means of political and economic reforms rather than simply through the use of force.

A second internal security dimension stems from the pattern of the army coup as a dominant method of changing government in Mali. The administration of Modibo Keita, which came to power on independence in 1960, was overthrown by the National Liberation Committee headed by Lieutenant Moussa Traoré in 1968. His administration, in turn, was overthrown by the army in March of 1991, shortly after Traoré had used his elderly main battle tanks to suppress pro-democracy demonstrations in January, and after the army had killed dozens of students who had attacked government offices in Bamako in early March. The election of Alpha Konare in 1992, conducted by the "Transitional Committee for the Salvation of the People," together with the arrest of five high-ranking army officers and the tracing of sums in Swiss bank accounts, provides some hope for a change from the military coup pattern.

SUMMARY

A defence capability to deal with the marginal threat from Burkina Faso would seem prudent. However, non-military policies are required to deal with the marginal threat from Algeria.

THE MILITARY BALANCE OF POWER, 1996-97

THE LOCAL STRATEGIC CONTEXT
(RANKED IN ORDER OF ESTIMATED TOTAL COMBAT POTENTIAL)

Country	Air Force				Army			Navy	
	Fighter Sqns	Bomber/ FGA Sqns	COIN Attack Sqns	COIN Transport Sqns	ADEs	IDEs	COIN Bns	Subs	Ships
Algeria	8.1	3.1	–	–	9.6	18.0	–	2	6+21
Mali	0.7	0.3	–	0.4	0.2	2.0	2	–	–
Guinea	–	0.5	–	0.2	0.4	2.3	2	–	0+9
Mauritania	–	–	0.4	–	0.3	6.3	4	–	0+11
Burkina Faso	–	–	0.6	0.1	–	2.9	0.2	–	–
Côte d'Ivoire	–	0.3	–	0.3	–	1.4	0.3	–	0+4
Senegal	–	–	0.5	0.1	–	3.0	2	–	0+10
Niger	–	–	–	–	–	1.0	2	–	–

The first number under "Ships" includes frigates and corvettes; the second includes patrol craft of various types. *Algeria*'s army is equipped for high-intensity warfare and can handle COIN operations with its main forces. *Burkina Faso*'s army contains 19 "battalions" of various arms, but manning levels are much below normal levels. The logistics capability to support the notional 2.9 IBEs is doubtful. The equipment is a mix of French and Soviet/Chinese and light in nature. *Côte d'Ivoire*'s army is composed of light forces with French equipment. A French marine regiment is stationed in the country. *Guinea*'s equipment is Soviet but obsolescent at best. *Mali*'s equipment is predominantly Soviet with some Chinese. *Mauritania*'s army is composed of light forces with a mix of Western and Soviet equipment; its COIN forces include two Camel Corps battalions. *Niger*'s army is composed of light forces with primarily French equipment. *Senegal*'s army is composed of light forces with predominantly French equipment. A French marine regiment is stationed in the country. Counter-insurgency operations appear to be of concern to a number of states in the region, judging from their acquisition of light aircraft and helicopters.

A DEFENCE SUFFICIENCY STRUCTURE FOR MALI

There is a marginal threat to Mali from Burkina Faso solely on the basis that the two states fought a short war in 1985; none of the other South-Saharan states seem to be motivated to go to war with Mali. The capabilities of the South Sahara states are reasonably similar—accordingly one could argue that the largest threat that reasonably might be encountered would be approximately a brigade group in size supported by a half squadron of fighter or FGA aircraft. Thus a force level of about one infantry brigade group equivalent plus a half squadron of fighter aircraft would be adequate to deal with any threat except that from Algeria. Interestingly, this is about the size of the Malian military capability. It appears to be organized on the Soviet model with two regiments (which are smaller than the Western brigade groups) each with one armoured battalion, two infantry battalions, one artillery battalion, and an air defence gun battery. In general support at what would be the divisional level in a Soviet organization is found an engineer battalion and an air defence missile battery.

However, Mali's military forces are not optimized to deal with insurgency actions against groups such as the Tuareg, since its force structure is based on Soviet/Chinese forms and equipments designed for high-intensity warfare in North West Europe. In COIN operations its tanks will impose a logistics difficulty in such a physically large country. What Mali needs for counter-insurgency operations are highly mobile light forces. Mali's wheeled APCs need a heavier firepower armoured car backup, a better helicopter capability, and COIN aircraft instead of MIG-17s.

There is no great requirement to alter the Malian force structure in its organizational models, but gradual equipment changes make sense. The World War II vintage T-34s must be maintenance horrors by this time and should be eventually replaced by armoured cars with a 90mm gun. The not quite as elderly PT-76 light tanks could go the same route. Since the Tuareg are not likely to acquire heavy armour of their own, the two battalions of Malian infantry mounted in wheeled armoured personnel carriers should be able to cope with that problem.

Mali's air force flies nine different types of aircraft plus two types of helicopter in its total holdings of 35 aircraft and three helicopters; this must be a maintenance and training nightmare for such a small force. The air force has, in effect, one squadron composed of two different combat aircraft: the very elderly MIG-17, and the somewhat less elderly MIG-21. Over time increasing age will phase out the five MIG-17s and there is no real requirement for their replacement, particularly since Burkina Faso appears to have retired its own MIG-21s. The eleven MIG-21s should eventually be replaced by about eight light COIN aircraft. Mali's COIN air capability, especially the helicopter component, which is more useful for

COIN operations, is weak. MIG-17s and MIG-21s are not particularly good COIN aircraft, and Mali's three helicopters have a limited lift and no ground attack capability.

The overall Malian force structure is adequate to deal with its security needs and is not excessive. No change is suggested in the manning level of the Malian armed forces.

MILITARY EXPENDITURES: ANALYSIS OF VARIABLES

THE LOCAL STRATEGIC CONTEXT
(BORDERING COUNTRIES IN ORDER OF GNP)

Country	1994			ME/GNP		MI/ME	
	GNP $US millions	ME $US millions	ME/GNP %	1990-94 %	1985-89 %	1990-94 %	1985-89 %
Algeria	40,510	1,335	3.3	2.3	2.9	13.5	68.1
Côte d'Ivoire	5,445	61	1.1	1.5	1.9	0	11.9
Senegal	3,711	65	1.8	2.4	2.7	8.4	15.4
Guinea	3,277	50	1.5	1.6	3.4	13.0	397.0
Mali	1,838	34	1.8	1.9	4.7	13.1	47.7
Burkina Faso	1,824	48	2.6	3.0	3.8	15.5	29.8
Niger	1,507	14	0.9	1.1	1.7	0	43.0
Mauritania	969	36	3.7	4.0	6.7	NA	27.7

None of these states appears to include military imports in reported expenditures. All use conscription.

TRENDS IN THE REGION

During the period from 1985 to 1994 military spending as a percentage of GNP has decreased in the region. While imports of military equipment represent a large portion of the defence budgets of Algeria and Guinea, they have decreased substantially since 1982-86. Imports for other states are within the normal expected range and capabilities of annual military budgets. With the end of the Cold War the previous pattern of arms imports on a long-term credit basis from Soviet/Chinese suppliers appears to have ended.

SENSITIVITY ANALYSIS: THE EXISTING MALIAN SPENDING PATTERN
(MEAN 1990-94)

Spending Category	Budget Share %	$US per Position	Foreign Currency $US millions	Local Currency $US millions	Total $US millions
Equipment	13.1	599	4.4	0	4.4
PO&M	86.9	3,985	0	29.3	29.3
Total	100	4,594	4.4	29.3	33.7

CHANGE EFFECTS

- Changing Equipment spending
  by 1% of Budget $337,000   (Foreign Currency)
- Changing Personnel strength by 1,000
  – Change in Equipment spending $599,000   (Foreign Currency)
  – Change in PO&M spending $3,985,000 (Local Currency)
  – Total change in Military
    spending $4,594,000
- Changing the Praetorian
  Index by 1 $1,512,000 (Local Currency)

THE DEFENCE SUFFICIENCY BUDGET

The Malian force structure is reasonable and the amount currently devoted to equipment purchases allows for modestly paced equipment modernization. The Praetorian Index is excessive, however. With no change in numbers but with a decrease in the Praetorian Index (19.4) to the West African mean (18.2):

Mean 1990-94 Budget without changes	$29,300,000
– Decrease in Equipment (foreign currency) spending	$ 0
– Decrease in PO&M (local currency) spending	$1,814,000
Mean 1990-94 Budget with changes	$27,486,000

IS MALI SPENDING TOO MUCH ON THE MILITARY?

The answer to our question is Yes. The Malian military, in comparison to its Sub-Saharan neighbours, is exacting an economic rent from the economy of about $1,814,000 annually.

SOCIAL MILITARIZATION ANALYSIS

PRAETORIAN AND SPARTAN INDICES
(1990-94 MEANS)

Country	Praetorian Index	Spartan Index	Total Regular Personnel
Burkina Faso	30.2	1.5	8,120
Côte d'Ivoire	29.0	1.2	7,800
Niger	23.5	1.1	4,100
Mali	19.4	1.8	7,430
Senegal	17.3	1.5	10,430
Guinea	8.8	3.1	9,700
Mauritania	6.1	9.2	13,640
Algeria	4.2	6.9	129,380

Mali's Spartan Index is comparatively low. However, Malian paramilitary forces are larger than the military forces, which suggests that the government is more concerned with the control of its own population than with external threats, an inference reinforced by the high Praetorian Index. The fact that both the 1968 and 1991 coups were led by the military suggests that officers have played a role in government beyond that solely of defence, and that the recent moves toward democratic electoral processes are still tentative.

DEVELOPMENT ISSUES

THE MILITARY AS NATIONAL DEVELOPMENT AGENCY

No evidence has been found that Mali's forces have been used for infrastructure development. Nor is there any evidence of an indigenous defence industrial base or the use of licensing arrangements to build military equipment locally. Consequently, it is unlikely that Mali's military procurement plays any significant industrial development role. The conscript term is two years and the annual intake would be about 2,875, probably staggered on a quarterly or semi-annual basis to even the impact on the training system. This represents about 3.5% of the annual cohort of males in the 18-22 age group of about 86,000. The small size of Mali's forces suggests a minuscule impact on unemployment rates or human capital formation.

THE ODA FUNGIBILITY ISSUE

With mean 1990-94 ODA receipts at 1,445% of Military Expenditures for the period there has been ample opportunity for the Malian government to divert its own spending toward the military sector. There is also considerable leverage available should donors choose to use it to encourage Mali to reduce its military spending in the direction suggested, since 1990-94 ODA/CGE amounts to 180%.

5

CENTRAL AFRICA

THE REGIONAL STRATEGIC CONTEXT:
INTER-STATE ISSUES

The Central African region is a set of comparatively small and militarily weak states sandwiched between two of the three largest states of Sub-Saharan Africa—Nigeria and Zaire. Fortunately, neither state has displayed any significantly aggressive intent toward its neighbours to this point. Indeed, Nigeria, the regional great power, has been reducing the size of its military forces. With the exception of Chad and the Central African Republic, the region is shielded from outside interference by the geographical boundaries of the two large states. In addition, France has continued to maintain military garrisons in Chad, Gabon, and the Central African Republic. Consequently, as in West Africa, France has been able to play a post-colonial role in helping governments of which it approves to remain in power. As in West Africa a corollary of the French presence has been the encouragement of regional governments to maintain comparatively low levels of military forces.

Other than Chad, which has had an ongoing confrontation with Libya, the northern portion of the region is comparatively quiet. A border dispute between Cameroon and Nigeria has not yet escalated to a major military confrontation. The south, however, is less secure. An acute concern is the future of Angola, which particularly concerns Congo, whose socialist-oriented government has considerable sympathy for the MPLA (Movimento Popular de Libertação de Angola). Another concern is the future of the Mobutu administration in Zaire, which looks increasingly shaky.

THE REGIONAL SOCIO-ECONOMIC BALANCE OF POWER (1990-94 MEANS)

Country	Population (millions)	GNP ($US billions)	ME ($US millions)
Nigeria	92.2	39.1	368
Zaire	40.2	7.1	193
Cameroon	12.4	6.1	103
Chad	5.2	0.9	56
Central African Republic	3.0	0.9	22
Congo	2.4	1.4	67
Gabon	1.1	4.0	123
Equatorial Guinea	0.4	0.1	NA

THE REGIONAL MILITARY BALANCE OF POWER, 1996-97

Country	Fighter Squadrons	FGA Squadrons	ABEs	IBEs
Nigeria	–	3.6	2.0	7.7
Zaire	–	0.5	0.6	10
Congo	–	1.4	0.4	1.3
Cameroon	0.3	0.3	–	5.3
Gabon	–	0.6	–	1.3
Central African Republic	–	–	–	2.0
Chad	–	–	0.6	NA
Equatorial Guinea	–	–	–	0.3

INTRA-STATE ISSUES

The predominant concerns in the region are related to internal security, with Gabon, Equatorial Guinea, and Congo devoting considerable resources to internal security roles.

MILITARY EXPENDITURE LEVELS AND TRENDS

The consequence of the generally stable local strategic context has been a declining pattern of military spending, with the exception of Zaire and the Central African Republic, where spending increases appear, judging by the sharply higher Praetorian Indices, to be related to internal security issues. The financing pattern of military expenditures has been broadly similar to that of West Africa, with extensive use of supplier credits.

MILITARIZATION LEVELS

Country	Financial: Economy ME/GNP %		Financial: Government ME/CGE %		Spartan Index		Praetorian Index	
	90-94	85-89	90-94	85-89	90-94	85-89	90-94	85-89
Congo	5.3	6.5	13.0	15.0	7.2	7.2	11.8	15.3
Chad	6.4	13.8	20.7	43.4	5.6	4.8	7.4	11.5
Gabon	3.2	4.9	9.8	11.9	8.7	8.1	7.2	11.6
Zaire	3.0	2.7	18.5	18.4	1.5	1.5	40.1	27.4
Central African Republic	2.4	1.1	NA	4.2	2.1	2.1	19.8	9.4
Cameroon	1.7	1.8	8.2	8.7	1.1	1.1	23.1	26.3
Nigeria	0.9	1.9	4.2	9.1	1.0	1.3	8.8	9.2
Equatorial Guinea	NA	NA	NA	NA	8.4	1.7	NA	NA
Means	3.27	4.67	12.4	15.81	4.45	3.48	16.89	15.81

THE SOCIAL IMPACT OF MILITARY EXPENDITURES

The overall level of social militarization is not particularly high. The highest levels of social militarization are found in Congo, Equatorial Guinea, and Gabon, and primarily reflect the comparatively high levels of paramilitary and internal security forces in those three countries.

THE MILITARY AS NATIONAL DEVELOPMENT FACTOR

There is little evidence of the use of military forces in this region for infrastructure development. Nor is there any indication of the use of military equipment purchases through licensed manufacture as part of an industrial development strategy. The overall size of the military forces in most of the Central African states indicates that they will have little impact on local labour market employment rates. In addition the relatively small sizes, together with the infrequent use of conscript-based forces, suggest that they will have little impact on national human capital formation.

CASE STUDY 4: CAMEROON

STRATEGIC THREAT ANALYSIS

A geostrategic Threat Analysis for Cameroon should normally consider three areas:
- threats of direct military confrontation with other states with which Cameroon shares borders: Central African Republic, Chad, Congo, Equatorial Guinea, Gabon, Nigeria,
- guerrilla warfare with irredentist movements in Cameroon controlled territories, and
- the possibility that a civil war or insurrection in a neighbouring country will spill over into Cameroon territory either through combatant forces making use of Cameroon territory, or through the movement of refugees fleeing from that civil war or insurrection.

THE NEIGHBOURING STATES AS MILITARY THREATS TO CAMEROON

Two of the six neighbouring states have no offensive capability and no significant history of conflict and can be excluded as strategic threats. The primary purpose of the tiny forces of **Equatorial Guinea** is to maintain internal control of the country; moreover, the small size of both its population and its GNP renders it incapable of ever being a threat to Cameroon. It appears that the purpose of the **Central African Republic** (CAR) forces also is to maintain internal control of the country. Moreover, France maintains an infantry battalion group plus an air force base in the Central African Republic as part of its strategic capability to support French interests in Central Africa. Consequently, France can be expected to use its influence on the Central African Republic government to restrain it from foreign adventurism.

Congo's military, particularly its air force, has some capability; however, their primary focus seems to be internal control. A secondary focus, given the Marxist tradition in Congo's government and the sympathy felt by much of the population for the MPLA, may be the ultimate outcome of the Angolan civil war and the future of the Cabinda enclave. The border between Congo and Cameroon is relatively remote from the core areas of both countries and there do not appear to be any significant disputes about it. The only "incident" between the two countries was a violent football match riot and a few deaths in the late 1970s, but the resulting coolness was dealt with by a state visit by the Congo president to Cameroon and the signing of the usual diplomatic and cooperation agreements. Congo is not a credible strategic threat to Cameroon.

Chad's military forces are lightly armed and oriented to two ongoing problems: an internal factional struggle and the meddling of Libya, whose aim had been to control the Aouzou strip along the Chad-Libya border. France maintained a force of about 1,100 troops in the country as a counter to Libyan efforts. The continuing pattern of the Chadian factional struggle has been for the leader out of power to withdraw to areas close to Sudan or Libya, where Libyan support allowed him to mount an operation against the Chadian "government." If successful, the victorious rival discarded Libyan support in favour of an arrangement with France, and the cycle repeated itself, as it did in 1990 with the overthrow of the Habré government by the Deby faction. This pattern gives the various Chad factions an internal focus; they have no reason to contemplate foreign adventures. Chad is no direct strategic threat to Cameroon.

Gabon's military forces have a limited capability and a focus directed toward maintaining internal control. The role of the Presidential Guard in particular has this function. The presence of a French marine regiment was also a support to the government during the 1990 anti-government riots. Gabon is a wealthy small country interested in preserving its position rather than acquiring the territory of its poorer neighbours. It represents no strategic threat to Cameroon.

Nigeria has the military capability to invade and defeat Cameroon. A significant incident between the two countries took place in 1981 in a clash between Nigerian and Cameroonian coast guards off the Rio del Rey, where there has been a border delineation dispute for some time over the Bakassi peninsula and its oil deposits. The incident seemed satisfactorily resolved at that time with a Cameroonian apology and reparations, Nigerian repairs to the Cameroon embassy, and an agreement to resolve the border issue by an international tribunal. The issue flared up again in 1994, after which Cameroon took the matter to the Security Council and France sent a small detachment to Cameroon as a show of support. Cameroon bases its claim on a treaty signed in 1913 between Britain and Germany, which then controlled Cameroon. Nigeria has denied the validity of the 1913 treaty, claiming that chiefs in the area had accepted British protection but not British sovereignty, that the British had thus no power to cede the area to German control in 1913, and that the 1958 Geneva agreement on international boundaries had set the Rio del Rey as the boundary between the two countries—which would put the Bakassi in Nigeria. In the spring of 1996 fighting broke out again with casualties estimated at up to 100, though UN and OAU intervention led to a commitment by Presidents Biya and Abacha to meet in Togo to find a peaceful means of settling the issue, though further incidents occurred in December 1996. The ongoing Nigerian reduction of its military forces as part of the austerity program's reduction of public expenditures also suggests little real interest in initiating a war with Cameroon, particularly given the French mutual security pact with Cameroon and demonstration of support. However, the increasingly unstable situation in Nigeria might lead to an interest in a foreign confrontation as a means of diverting attention from political troubles at home. Thus, while Nigeria's military capacity warrants a careful watching brief, Nigeria does not appear to be a critical strategic threat to Cameroon at this point.

GUERRILLA WAR IN CAMEROON

Cameroon contains the same ethnic fault line as that which has caused trouble for many West African states: a Sudanic/Nilotic north adhering to Islam, constituting about 17% of the population, and a West African Negro south adhering to Christianity or traditional animist beliefs. The Ahidjo administration, which ruled for the first twenty-two years after independence, gave a prominent place to northerners. The succession of President Paul Biya, a Christian southerner, and the subsequent replacement of many of the old Ahidjo party "barons" by younger technocrats resulted in the 1984 attempted coup by the northern-dominated Presidential Guard. The army overcame the coup, and a series of purges, show trials, and executions led to criticisms by Amnesty International, among others. The 1992 election, won by President Biya under questionable circumstances, has not led to national reconciliation, and a recurrence of the north-south ethno-religious difficulties cannot be ruled out, particularly in view of the economic distress following the 1994 devaluation of the CFA franc and the consequent stress associated with structural economic reforms. There is a 3:1 French-English official language split and the principal opposition leader, Fru Ndi, is from the English-speaking west of the country, though his support crosses ethno-linguistic lines as an alternative to the Biya administration. The English-French division does not yet appear to be as important as the north-south split. The apparent emphasis on COIN capabilities within the Cameroon military forces seems to reflect the belief among those forces that what must be seriously prepared for is aid to the civil power rather than response to an external threat.

CIVIL WAR SPILLOVER

The chronic civil war in Chad has frequently resulted in the losing faction's leadership seeking refuge in one of the neighbouring states. Whereas Sudan has from time to time provided a base area for Chadian factions, Nigeria and Cameroon have simply provided an exit point. Consequently, since Cameroon does not provide a base area for Chadian factions there is no great incentive for Chadian winning factions to pursue their rivals into Cameroon.

SUMMARY

It does not appear that Cameroon is particularly threatened by its external strategic environment. Most of its neighbours are too weak or too remote to represent a serious threat to its sovereignty, and the one that has the military capacity appears to have little immediate interest in applying it in a hostile manner—particularly since it has substantial internal troubles of its own. Nor does the prospect of external civil war spillover seem to constitute a severe threat, since the ongoing war inside Chad does not seem likely to draw Cameroon into it. However, the possibility of internal ethno-religious strife within Cameroon is one that would be of concern to the Cameroon general staff.

THE MILITARY BALANCE OF POWER, 1996-97

Cameroon's equipment is primarily Western and based on a light armour concept. *Central African Republic*'s equipment is a mix of Soviet and Western designs; it is a weakly armed force. *Chad*'s army, though comparatively large in numbers, is only lightly equipped. *Congo*'s equipment is primarily elderly Soviet and Chinese designs optimized for the heavy armoured battle on the north German plain, with some French helicopters. *Gabon* has a mix of French and Brazilian equipment designs and is built around a mobile, light armour concept. For its size it is a well

THE LOCAL STRATEGIC CONTEXT
(RANKED IN ORDER OF ESTIMATED TOTAL COMBAT POTENTIAL)

Country	Air Force				Army			Navy	
	Fighter Sqns	FGA Sqns	COIN Attack Sqns	COIN Transport Sqns	ADEs	IDEs	COIN Bns	Ships	Patrol Craft
Nigeria	–	3.6	3.1	0.4	2.0	7.7	5.0	2	50
Cameroon	0.3	0.3	–	0.2	–	5.3	2.0	–	2
Congo	–	1.4	–	0.2	0.4	1.3	1.0	–	6
Gabon	–	0.6	0.8	0.3	–	1.3	0.3	–	3
Chad	–	–	0.3	–	0.6	NA	NA	–	–
Central African Republic	–	–	–	–	–	2.0	–	–	–
Equatorial Guinea	–	–	–	–	–	0.3	–	–	–

armed force. *Equatorial Guinea* possesses some elderly personnel carriers and small arms only. *Nigeria*'s forces represent a well balanced combined arms force organized on a traditional British model with a mixture of Soviet and Western equipment types.

The only state in the local strategic context that has the capacity to launch an offensive against its neighbours is the regional great power—Nigeria. Fortunately, Nigeria has been conservative to this point in the inter-state use of its considerable military potential and has not sought to use it to the detriment of its neighbours. Moreover, the government austerity program in Nigeria has led to large cutbacks in military expenditures and a decision to reduce the size of its armed forces. Apart from Nigeria none of the other states has the capacity to invade and defeat Cameroon. Moreover, Cameroon appears to maintain amicable relations with all of them.

A DEFENCE SUFFICIENCY STRUCTURE FOR CAMEROON

The equipment policy of the Cameroon forces is justifiable. The army's equipment represents the high-mobility, wheeled light armour philosophy that is suited for most Sub-Saharan military forces. The air force has a reasonable mix of COIN aircraft with a light ground-attack capability, which is also appropriate to Cameroon's requirements. The Navy's patrol craft are equally appropriate. The 1994 increases in both military (14,600 from 7,700) and paramilitary (9,000 from 4,000) force strength seems questionable, however, since the previous levels appeared perfectly adequate.

MILITARY EXPENDITURES: ANALYSIS OF VARIABLES

THE MILITARY EXPENDITURES BALANCE
(BORDERING COUNTRIES IN ORDER OF GNP)

Country	1994			ME/GNP		MI/ME	
	GNP $US billions	ME $US millions	ME/GNP %	1990-94 %	1985-89 %	1990-94 %	1985-89 %
Nigeria	41.3	324	0.8	0.9	1.9	22.4	74.7
Cameroon	5.3	102	1.9	1.7	1.8	3.0	9.2
Gabon	3.2	93	33.2	3.2	4.9	3.2	18.9
Congo	1.2	67	4.1	5.3	6.5	9.0	31.0
Central African Republic	1.0	30	3.2	2.4	1.1	0	0
Chad	0.9	64	7.1	6.4	13.8	45.4	70.7
Equatorial Guinea	0.1	2	1.8	NA	NA	NA	NA

There have been two trends evident in the region. The first has been a steady overall decline in military expenditures as a percentage of GNP. The second has been a decline in imports of military equipment as a percentage of the total military expenditures, suggesting a declining emphasis on the possibility of inter-state conflict in the region. A 1994 expansion of Cameroon's force strength may indicate a trend reversal or an increasing emphasis on internal security. Both Chad and the Central African Republic make use of conscript-based forces.

SENSITIVITY ANALYSIS: THE EXISTING CAMEROON SPENDING PATTERN
(MEAN 1990-94)

Spending Category	Budget Share %	$US per Position	Foreign Currency $US millions	Local Currency $US millions	Total $US millions
Equipment	3.0	349	3.2	0	3.2
PO&M	97.0	11,288	0	103.4	103.4
Total	100	11,638	3.2	103.4	106.6

CHANGE EFFECTS

- Changing Equipment spending
  by 1% of the Budget $1,066,000   (Foreign Currency)
- Changing Personnel strength by 1,000
  – Change in Equipment spending $349,000   (Foreign Currency)
  – Change in PO&M spending $11,288,000 (Local Currency)
  – Total change in Military
    spending $11,638,000
- Changing the Praetorian
  Index by 1 $4,479,000   (Local Currency)

THE DEFENCE SUFFICIENCY BUDGET

With no change in the level of equipment spending and no change in the number of military positions but with a decrease in the Praetorian multiple (23.1) to the Central African mean (16.9):

Mean 1990-94 Budget without changes	$106,600,000
– Decrease in Praetorian multiple	$27,770,000
Mean 1990-94 Budget with changes	$78,830,000

IS CAMEROON SPENDING TOO MUCH ON ITS MILITARY?

From one perspective the answer to our question is No. Cameroon spends less on the military sector as a percentage of GNP than any of its neighbours with the exception of Nigeria. Moreover, it has had the second lowest level of Spartanism in the area, though the Spartan Index doubled in 1994—an increase that appeared to come from the numbers of the forces allocated to each Military Region, suggesting an increased concern with internal security issues. From a second viewpoint the answer is Yes. Cameroon's level of Praetorianism is the highest in the area. This suggests that the Cameroon military occupies a position in Cameroon society of an excessively highly paid public sector elite—that the Cameroon military has become, in effect, economic rent-takers, rewarded for supporting an increasingly unpopular regime. What is particularly worrisome is that the Praetorian Index spiked sharply upward in 1993 from 24.8 to 30.9—a pattern which in Rwanda was a precursor of civil war.

A cut in the Praetorian Index to the Sub-Saharan mean would have resulted in savings of 26.1% in the mean 1990-94 Defence Budget—a sum equal to 0.5% of GNP or of 5.0% of mean 1990-94 ODA.

SOCIAL MILITARIZATION ANALYSIS

PRAETORIAN AND SPARTAN INDICES (1990-94 MEANS)

Country	Praetorian Index	Spartan Index	Total Regular Personnel
Cameroon	23.1	1.1	9,160
Central African Republic	19.8	2.1	3,578
Congo	11.8	7.2	10,700
Nigeria	8.8	1.0	80,360
Chad	7.4	5.6	24,630
Gabon	7.2	8.7	4,740
Equatorial Guinea	NA	8.4	1,304

The group Praetorian Index mean is somewhat lower than that for West African states. The higher value for Cameroon suggests that the Cameroon military enjoys a relatively high level of economic advantage in comparison to its citizens—the classic position of the military economic rent-taker. Indeed, Cameroon fits the pattern of the West African Praetorian states much better than that of most of its neighbours in Central Africa.

DEVELOPMENT ISSUES

THE MILITARY AS NATIONAL DEVELOPMENT AGENCY

There is no evidence that Cameroon's forces are being used for infrastructure building. Since there is no significant indigenous defence industrial base nor any evidence of building military equipment under licensing arrangements it appears that Cameroon military procurement does not play an industrial development role. The small size of the Cameroon military has a miniscule impact on national employment rates and on national human capital formation.

THE ODA FUNGIBILITY ISSUE

With mean 1990-94 ODA receipts at 525% of Military Expenditures there is ample opportunity for the government of Cameroon to divert its own spending toward the military sector. With ODA receipts at 43.1% of CGE there is significant leverage available to donors wishing to see Cameroon's military spending reduced.

6

SOUTHERN AFRICA

THE REGIONAL STRATEGIC CONTEXT:
INTER-STATE ISSUES

Southern Africa has been the region of the undeclared War of the South African Succession. The fundamental source of the problem lay in the struggle to achieve a sharing of power between the white minority and the black majority in South Africa. As the regional (or "frontline") states passed into post-colonial independence, the new governments offered various degrees of political and operational support to the African National Congress (ANC). The Republic of South Africa, the regional military great power, responded by mounting raids on ANC bases in a number of the frontline states (Botswana, Zambia, Zimbabwe) and by providing logistics and operational support to dissident and opposition groups in other states (Angola, with a brigade-sized expeditionary force supported by air, and Mozambique, where the support to Resistancia Nacional Moçambicana [RENAMO] was more logistical). The strategic context was complicated by the Cold War: the Soviet Union and China supported states that had adopted Marxist-Leninist forms of government. South Africa emphasized the threat of international Communism as a means of gaining Western support for or acquiescence to its actions against the frontline states.

The ultimate reaction of the frontline states varied. Botswana and Zambia, having effectively concluded that operational support of the ANC was too costly to their own security, withdrew from the struggle and in effect joined Malawi, which had declined to be a frontline state in the first place. Mozambique was effectively destroyed as a coherent state. Angola's civil war is ongoing, and with the end of Cuban and Socialist Bloc support for the Movimento Popular de Libertação de Angola (MPLA) and the withdrawal of Western support for União Nacional para a Independencia Total de Angola (UNITA), seems likely to continue as a stalemate. Zimbabwe, however, continued to expand its military capacity well beyond the level needed to respond to any threat from its neighbouring frontline states. One possible motivation was that Zimbabwe's continued active support of the ANC might lead to a raid in force by South Africa that a heightened Zimbabwean military capability could either defeat or make so costly in the loss of white South African lives that South Africa would be deterred. A more dangerous scenario might have anticipated a South African black-white civil war, with Zimbabwe intervening militarily on the ANC side.

Regional militarization levels reached their peak in the 1987-89 period. At that point President Botha of South Africa was replaced by President de Klerk, whose government, in effect, brought the undeclared war to its end and began the five-year period of peace negotiations that ended with the South African elections of 1994 and accession of the new ANC government. These developments have brought new hope that the War of the South African Succession has finally ended, and that a Southern Africa "peace dividend" can be cashed by all of the regional states. Whether that hope will be satisfied remains to be seen. Given the disproportion between the socio-economic and military power of South Africa and that of the other regional states it is clear that events in South Africa will have a critical impact.

THE REGIONAL SOCIO-ECONOMIC BALANCE OF POWER
(1990-94 MEANS)

Country	Population (millions)	GNP ($US billions)	ME ($US millions)
South Africa	41.7	116.8	3,783
Zimbabwe	10.6	5.0	241
Mozambique	15.7	1.0	141
Malawi	9.6	1.3	19
Angola	9.1	NA	NA
Zambia	8.7	3.2	60
Namibia	1.5	2.7	61
Botswana	1.3	3.5	218

THE REGIONAL MILITARY BALANCE OF POWER, 1996-97

Country	Fighter Squadrons	FGA Squadrons	ABEs	IBEs
South Africa	0.7	14.6	2.5	6.0
Zimbabwe	0.9	1.4	0.4	7.3
Angola	0.6	1.1	4.0	4.0
Mozambique	–	2.7	0.8	2.7
Zambia	0.8	0.8	0.3	2.0
Botswana	–	0.8	0.5	1.7
Namibia	–	–	–	1.7
Malawi	–	–	–	1.3

INTRA-STATE ISSUES

The future development of inter-racial and inter-tribal relations within South Africa remains the single issue most critical to the security of the whole region. The initial policies of the new ANC government have been conciliatory and prudent. However, if the rising economic expectations of the black majority are to be achieved, South Africa must either achieve an unusually high and sustained economic growth rate or some degree of income redistribution from the white and coloured populations to the black population; the scope of the problem may be seen in the fact that GNP per capita declined by 12.7% between 1988 and 1993 and increased a miniscule 0.1% in 1994. Similarly, there will be pressure for land redistribution, and the question whether such redistribution will be acceptable, especially to the Boer population, will be critical.

Other states still have major internal reconciliation issues to deal with between competing ethno-linguistic groups. Some, such as Zimbabwe and perhaps Mozambique, show evidence of progress; others, such as Angola, do not.

MILITARIZATION LEVELS

South Africa has an indigenous arms industry, and therefore arms imports cannot be used as an equipment spending analogue. Accordingly, equipment spending has been arbitrarily set at 20% of the reported South African defence budget. This is approximately the mean figure for the thirteen largest NATO states measured by GNP over the 1985-89 period.

Country	Financial: Economy ME/GNP %		Financial: Government ME/CGE %		Spartan Index		Praetorian Index	
	90-94	85-89	90-94	85-89	90-94	85-89	90-94	85-89
Angola	NA	36.8	NA	NA	12.1	11.6	NA	9.4
Mozambique	13.8	39.4	49.9	157.0	2.8	3.9	35.8	30.5
Botswana	5.6	4.4	10.7	9.2	5.4	4.1	10.8	10.3
Zimbabwe	4.9	6.4	12.6	15.2	7.0	9.2	8.5	9.3
Zambia	2.0	3.6	6.9	9.0	2.7	2.4	6.9	9.4
South Africa	3.2	4.1	10.0	12.6	5.2	6.0	14.7	12.3
Namibia	2.2	NA	5.7	NA	5.0	NA	4.4	NA
Mean	5.28	15.78	15.97	40.6	5.74	6.2	13.52	13.53

MILITARY EXPENDITURE LEVELS AND TRENDS

The consequence of the chronic state of undeclared war has been the highest regional level of financial militarization in Sub-Saharan Africa—approximately double the rate of Sub-Saharan Africa as a whole and close to the level experienced in Saharan Africa and the Middle East when off-budget purchases of military equipment imports are included.

The situation was complicated by the influence exerted by Soviet and Chinese advisors to purchase Chinese- and Warsaw Bloc-manufactured equipment for the armies of the Socialist-oriented African states. This equipment, designed for the high-intensity war between NATO and the Warsaw Pact, consists of older designs whose apparent simplicity carries with it considerable disadvantages in fuel consumption and the high maintenance required of all tracked vehicles. In the low force-to-space ratios characteristic of African geography, such equipment does not represent a cost-effective solution to the security problem. Moreover, the quantities purchased have amounted to a severe (and in some cases disastrous) financial burden on states with low annual incomes. The military futility of such purchases lay in the disproportion between the economies of the frontline states and that of South Africa. With a total economy of all six frontline states one fifth that of South Africa (or one sixth with the deletion of Botswana and Malawi), no matter how much they spent they could not match the South African financial potential.

These financial realities led some of the frontline states to abandon their earlier confrontation policies and to reduce their military expenditures in recent years. Others were effectively destroyed economically, and their expenditures dropped accordingly. Only Zimbabwe continued to attempt to compete with South Africa's financial and military power.

The use of supplier debt was particularly striking among the frontline states. The Soviet External Trade Bank (Vneshecon) reported that as of December 1991 the three frontline states of Angola, Mozambique, and Zambia had incurred a total debt to the Soviet union for military imports of 2.7 billion rubles, plus an additional 380 million rubles in accrued interest (in pre-inflation rubles). Such debt, including debts to other arms suppliers, amounted to about 50% of total military expenditures in the region. In addition, of course, a number of the regional states made use of the conscription premium to finance their de facto military expenditures.

THE SOCIAL IMPACT OF MILITARY EXPENDITURES

It is not surprising that this region became the most heavily socially militarized in Sub-Saharan Africa. A substantial portion of the social militarization level, however, was devoted to internal control of the resident populations, in the frontline states as well as in South Africa. The pattern of the military as economic rent-seekers was less consistent, however. The Praetorian scores were sometimes higher in states, like Malawi, that had avoided confrontation with South Africa than in those who had not.

THE MILITARY AS NATIONAL DEVELOPMENT FACTOR

Except in South Africa, there is no clear indication of the use of the military for either infrastructure construction or industrial development. South Africa certainly has developed a considerable arms industry, with 1994 export sales estimated at 850 million rand (*The Economist*, 29 July 1995) and employment at 50,000. It would appear that some elements of the new ANC administration subscribe to the theory that the industry offers the prospect for increased export sales and thus regard it as a key element of South Africa's future industrial base.

CASE STUDY 5: ZAMBIA

STRATEGIC THREAT ANALYSIS

A geostrategic Threat Analysis for Zambia should normally consider three areas:
- threats of direct confrontation with other states with which Zambia shares borders, or that, though geographically distant, have the capability to threaten Zambian territory. These include Angola, Malawi, Mozambique, Namibia, Tanzania, Zaire, Zimbabwe, and South Africa,
- the possibility that a civil war or insurrection in a neighbouring country will spill over into Zambia, either through combatant forces making use of Zambian territory, or through the movement of refugees fleeing from that civil war or insurrection, and
- threats to Zambia's internal political stability and armed resistance to the civil authority, possibly aided by the government of one of the neighbouring countries.

THE NEIGHBOURING STATES AS MILITARY THREATS TO ZAMBIA

Two states—*Malawi* and *Namibia*—can be excluded as military threats, since their military forces are insignificant in comparison to those of Zambia, their economic base is inadequate to the development of such a military capacity, and there is no significant history of confrontation that might lead to military action.

Angola can be excluded as a direct military threat to Zambia on the grounds that the civil war in Angola has completely occupied the forces of UNITA and MPLA such that neither has had the capacity to divert sufficient forces to threaten Zambia directly. During the earlier part of the civil war President Kaunda appeared to be attempting to avoid being seen too visibly to be taking sides. There have been suggestions that Zambia provided some support in 1975 to United States/South African efforts to assist UNITA. On the other hand, President Kaunda's 1983 visit to Washington included statements supporting the presence of Cuban troops in Angola and suggestions that the United States pressure South Africa to remove its military forces from Angola. The 1991 Peace Accord brought hopes for a conclusion to the war, but UNITA's refusal to accept the results of the 1992 Angolan election led to its continuation. The July 1994

Praetoria Summit, held at the behest of the United Nations, appears to have included attempts to detach Zaire's support for UNITA, and to bring President Mandela into the peacemaking process in some manner—a considerable advantage to the MPLA supporters if the South African military forces could be brought to intervene again in Angola, but this time on the MPLA side. If some form of power-sharing arrangement can be worked out between UNITA and MPLA, it seems likely that Angola's energies will be directed more to reconstruction than to foreign military adventures. Moreover, if a settlement between UNITA and MPLA can be achieved, one possible outcome could be the reopening of the Benguela rail corridor and its possible use as an alternate Zambian export route. If such were to be the case there would be a further economic incentive to avoid conflict. Consequently, it appears that Angola represents little strategic threat to Zambia.

The aftermath of the debilitating civil war has left the central government of *Mozambique* without the means to wage a war against Zambia even if it wanted to. Since Zambia had provided bases for Frente de Libertação de Moçambique (FRELIMO) during the early stages of the independence movement in Mozambique there appears to be little likelihood of FRELIMO animosity toward Zambia. Whether RENAMO harbours any ill will against Zambia remains to be seen, but it seems doubtful. Mozambique can be eliminated as a credible strategic threat to Zambia.

Tanzania is an economic partner of Zambia whose copper and other mineral exports are dependent on access to the sea. Four potential rail corridors exist. One is the Benguela line through Zaire and Angola, which has been damaged by the Angolan civil war and whose capacity is doubtful until that conflict is resolved. A second lies through Zimbabwe, Botswana, and South Africa, and was vulnerable to South African political and economic pressure. A third lies through Zimbabwe and Mozambique, and had been under severe South African and RENAMO pressure, which had disrupted traffic along it. The fourth, the Tanzara or TanZam line, lies through Tanzania to Dar-es-Salaam and, though having considerable problems with maintenance and efficient management, remained relatively less vulnerable to South African pressure. Since the handling of Zambian exports generates carriage fees and port fees for Tanzania, there is a substantial economic incentive for peaceful relations between the two countries. Moreover, there has been no significant history of confrontation between the two states, and in any event Tanzania's security concerns appear to be oriented much more to the problems of dealing with cross-border flows of refugees from Rwanda and potentially Burundi, than to the prospect of wars of aggression with its neighbours. Consequently, Tanzania does not appear to be a credible strategic threat to Zambia.

The problems of maintaining internal control within *Zaire* are sufficiently great to act as a significant bar to foreign adventurism. Zaire has been severely concerned with issues of internal cohesion, particularly between the Mobutu government and various opposition forces, which have tended to be concentrated in Shaba (Katanga) province and Kive province in the northeast. Opposition forces have found external sanctuaries in Angola and the area around and to the north of Lake Tanganyika rather than in Zambia, where the Kaunda administration had been less willing to provide sanctuary to those foreign opposition movements which might trigger difficulties with neighbouring states. Consequently, there does not appear to be any Zairean need to press Zambia as a consequence of its harbouring Zairean rebel forces. In any event, with the disruption of the Benguela rail line through Angola the alternative routes for the export of Zairean mineral exports from the Katanga area are either the connecting rail link through Zambia to one of the three lines already mentioned, or the rail-water-rail linkage through Ilebo, the Kasai River, Kinshasa, and Matadi, which requires two awkward transshipments from rail to river transport and back to rail. Consequently there is an economic incentive for peaceable relations between the two countries. Thus Zaire does not appear to be a credible strategic threat to Zambia.

Nor does *Zimbabwe* seem a very credible strategic threat to Zambia. During the period of the Rhodesian Unilateral Declaration of Independence (UDI) Zambia provided considerable support to the Zimbabwe African People's Union (ZAPU) rebel forces of Joshua Nkomo; however, ZAPU militants opposed to Nkomo were rounded up and deported to Rhodesia in 1971. Less support was given to the Zimbabwe African National Union (ZANU) forces of Robert Mugabe: ZANU militants were imprisoned in 1975 and the ZANU organization driven out of Zambia. Consequently, immediately after Zimbabwean independence in 1981 relations between Kaunda and Mugabe were cool, but improved after a state visit by Kaunda to Zimbabwe in 1981 to mend fences. Moreover, the support by both Kaunda and Mugabe for the ANC programs in South Africa made them de facto allies in that cause. Nor is there any strong suggestion of conflict between Mugabe and the successor Chiluba administration in Zambia. Moreover, the rail links through Zimbabwe, either to South Africa or through Mozambique, provide an economic incentive to

Zimbabwe to maintain peaceable relations, since it gains the income from transit fees derived from both Zambian and Zairean exports along this rail corridor. Consequently, there is no strong evidence of political differences that might lead to armed conflict between the two states. The impetus for the military buildup in Zimbabwe, which peaked in 1989, came from Zimbabwean concerns about the potential threat from South Africa rather than any intent to intimidate its other neighbours. The reported mutual defence pact between Zambia and Botswana and the continuing expansion of Botswana's forces, however, suggest that Zimabawe's forces may be of concern to its neighbours.

South Africa, nonetheless, has been the central security concern for Zambia. The decision by President Kaunda to allow the ANC to establish a headquarters in Lusaka led to raids by South African forces in 1985 and 1986. In the 1986 raid South African aircraft bombed a UNHCR (UN High Commission for Refugees) camp near Lusaka that the South Africans held to be an ANC camp. Similar raids at the same time were carried out in Botswana and Zimbabwe. However, with the 1989 passage of power from President Botha to President de Klerk the South African government reversed the period of military confrontation with the frontline states. That year saw the high point in South African military expenditures, and substantial cuts followed. The ANC electoral success in 1994 represents the culmination of the process that began in 1989. ANC spokesmen have suggested that the South African military industrial complex will be maintained, though with its purpose directed to arms exports. In addition there is an ongoing radical transformation of the South African Defence Forces (SADF), involving first the integration of the 90,000 SADF with the 28,000 from the military wing of the ANC, 6,000 from the African People's Liberation Army, and 11,000 from the former "independent" homelands. In August 1995 the South African defence minister, Joe Modise, announced that the integrated SADF would be reduced to 75,000 by 1999—a reduction of approximately 60,000 from the total of the various forces. In addition, the government has indicated a desire that the new SADF better reflect the ethno-linguistic balance of the country—which would make the reductions fall more heavily upon the white portion of the military. The 1995-96 defence budget was also to be reduced to approximately 2.2% of GNP from the 2.7% of 1993-94 and 1994-95.

It would appear that the most credible threat to Zambian security has been removed. However, there remain doubts as to whether the new South African government can meet the raised expectations of its supporters without significant levels of income and asset redistribution from the white, coloured, and Asian populations. On top of this are continuing tensions between the ANC and Inkatha, which represents a larger portion of the Zulu population than some analysts like to believe. Future South African civil strife cannot be entirely ruled out, and increasing Western distaste for direct military intervention, fuelled by events in former Yugoslavia, Somalia, and Rwanda, suggests that there would be little enthusiasm among Western publics for direct involvement, particularly if the conflict developed into a civil war. Given that the technical elements of the South African military forces (air force, armoured forces, artillery, and support services) have been in the past reserved for whites whose skills are not easily replaced, the outcome of such a civil war must remain in doubt. Consequently, a prudent Zambian General Staff must maintain contingency plans for the possibility that such a war might still occur.

Since Zimbabwean territory lies between South Africa and Zambia, it seems likely that any future military action by white South Africans against Zambia would take the form of raids similar to the 1985 and 1986 operations rather than a land invasion. Such raids might include FGA bombing or strafing attacks on locations suspected by white South African forces of harbouring ANC operations, or possibly an air-cavalry operation involving heliborne troops of up to battalion size. Such operations could be preceded by reconnaissance aircraft and accompanied by fighter aircraft providing protection to helicopters and FGA.

CIVIL WAR SPILLOVER

Three civil wars might be considered: those in Angola, Zaire, and Mozambique. In Angola, UNITA forces were strong enough to prevent an MPLA victory during the Cold War period, when each Angolan faction was receiving support from the Cold War adversaries. UNITA's refusal to accept the results of the post-Cold War elections led to the continuation of the Angolan civil war. The withdrawal of overt external support from both MPLA and UNITA suggests that UNITA will remain strong enough to deny success to the MPLA without being sufficiently strong to overcome them, and that the MPLA will be unable to drive UNITA into exile. In past Katanga-Shaba civil wars, dissident forces (an estimated 250,000 civilians after the 1978 conflict) have tended to withdraw into Angola rather than into Zambia. In part this seems to have been a consequence of MPLA support of Frente Nacional de Libertaçao de Angola (FNLA) rebels in Zaire which was, in turn, motivated by de facto Zairean support of UNITA forces in Angola. President Kaunda, in contrast, had pursued a policy of limiting the operations of dissident groups of neighbouring states located in Zambia where those operations could threaten relations with those states (with the exception of South Africa). It is unlikely therefore, that Zambia will have to deal with UNITA attempts to use its territory. The Mozambique civil war seems to have ended in 1992, with FRELIMO and RENAMO involved in lengthy negotiations that led to the elections of October 1994.

In summation, it appears that the threat of foreign war spillover into Zambian territory is not particularly high, though prudence argues for the maintenance of sufficient military forces to be able to deal with limited incursions. The military requirement in refugee control consists of having sufficient forces to back up police forces as the instrument of last resort. Zambian military forces adequate to deal with military contingencies would prove adequate for this purpose.

CIVIL WAR IN ZAMBIA

While there was a peaceful turnover of power from the Kaunda to the Chiluba administration as a consequence of an election that has been regarded as free from electoral abuses, more recent attempts to amend the electoral laws so as to prevent Kaunda from standing for election again have raised tensions. Nonetheless, it seems that the traditional conditions for the inception of civil war are not evident at this moment in Zambia.

SUMMARY

The local geostrategic context facing Zambian military planners is not particularly threatening. However, a watching brief on the unstable Angolan situation is in order, as well as on the situation in South Africa.

THE MILITARY BALANCE OF POWER, 1996-97

THE LOCAL STRATEGIC CONTEXT
(RANKED IN ORDER OF ESTIMATED TOTAL COMBAT POTENTIAL)

Country	Air Force				Army		
	Fighter Squadrons	FGA Squadrons	COIN Attack Squadrons	COIN Transport Squadrons	ABEs	IBEs	COIN Battalions
South Africa	0.7	14.6	1	4.6	2.5	6	5
Zimbabwe	0.9	1.4	2.6	0.8	0.4	7.3	3
Angola	0.6	1.1	2.1	2.4	4.0	4.0	2.1
Tanzania	1.5	–	–	0.6	0.2	5	–
Zaire	–	0.5	0.9	0.3	0.6	10	6
Mozambique	–	2.7	0.3	0.3	0.8	2.7	3
Zambia	0.8	0.8	2.2	1.3	0.3	2	1
Malawi	–	–	0.3	0.3	–	1.3	0.3
Namibia	–	–	–	–	–	1.7	–

South Africa's army is currently capable of mobilizing a corps of three divisions, each consisting of two composite brigades. The Full Time Force contains an airborne brigade, a special operations brigade, a mechanized brigade, and nine infantry battalions. The level of training and maintenance makes it effective and combat ready. *Zimbabwe's* equipment is a mix of British and South African equipment inherited at independence, and Chinese versions of elderly Soviet designs purchased since independence. Maintenance levels are a problem. *Angola's* equipment is predominantly of elderly Soviet design, and its maintenance must be difficult. MPLA forces have air superiority over UNITA, but their ground forces fare less well. Most of *Mozambique's* equipment, also of predominantly elderly Soviet design, is largely non-operative. *Tanzania's* equipment is of predominantly elderly Soviet and Chinese design, ill-suited to the local context. *Zambia's* equipment, too, is primarily of elderly Soviet design, suited for operations on the north European plain and of Soviet or Chinese manufacture. The Zambian air force is equipped with elderly fighters (such as the Chinese J-6, a version of the 1950s era MIG-19) and FGA (MIG-21MFs, whose design dates from 1969); its helicopters are of more modern designs and suitable for Zambian operational needs. Maintenance remains a problem. *Botswana* has been upgrading its capabilities with Leopard-1 main battle tanks, light tracked AFVs, and a recent purchase of former Canadian CF-5 FGA. *Malawi* and *Namibia* possess forces for internal security purposes that are lightly equipped.

A DEFENCE SUFFICIENCY STRUCTURE FOR ZAMBIA

At first glance Zambia seems surrounded by states with substantially greater military capabilities than it possesses and would therefore seem to be underarmed. However, a closer look at the strategic contexts of those neighbouring countries presents a quite different picture. Angola, though powerfully armed, is still involved in a civil war, which prevents it from contemplating wars with foreign countries unless they become directly involved with the civil war by providing military forces to assist one of the competing sides; once the civil war eventually runs its course we can expect the focus of the successor national government to be on reconstruction, one of the consequences of which will be the need to transfer resources from the military to the civilian sectors. Mozambique is on the verge of this post-civil war reconstruction phase. Tanzania's force level had been driven by the East African strategic context of its relationships with Kenya and Uganda, and the provision of aid to northern Mozambique; with that strategic theatre becoming less threatening, Tanzanian force levels are slated to decrease, because of the economic costs of maintaining a comparatively large military force level on a weak economic base. Zimbabwe's force level had been driven by its requirement to maintain an expeditionary force in Mozambique to protect its strategic economic interests in the rail corridors to Mozambique's ports and by its security concerns vis-à-vis South Africa, concerns that were ultimately the result of its policy decision to provide some degree of active support to the ANC in its campaign for black participation in government in South Africa. Zaire's force level is driven by internal concerns.

Zambia's security concerns could be readily satisfied by a division size force of about two manoeuvre brigades, plus a support brigade, including close support and air defence artillery, engineers, and logistics personnel. This force could be supported by an air capability of about one squadron of light FGA plus a mixed squadron of light anti-armour helicopters plus some troop-lift helicopters. Such a force is not significantly different from the existing Zambian military structure. It would require a strength of about 9,600 plus an additional 2,000 for the air force. A relatively inexpensive mobilization base could be provided by a reserve force of one light infantry brigade, two field artillery battalions—one close support and one general support—and two logistics battalions with a manning level of about 400 active force and about 4,000 reserves. The infrastructure would require an additional 3,500 active force plus 1,500 reserves. Any counterinsurgency requirement can be handled by this Defence Sufficiency Force.

The army's equipment is generally adequate to such a force, though the obsolete Soviet and Chinese main battle tanks might usefully be gradually replaced with wheeled armoured cars equipped with an anti-armour gun capability of about 90mm instead. Zambia has a substantial COIN aircraft inventory but, as is the case with their fighter and FGA, the aircraft are relatively elderly. It appears that the Zambian air force has retained its original jet aircraft (Aeromacchi MB326 light jets dating from the late 1950s) as it has added newer ones. Thus it has an unusually high total number of aircraft types in inventory (thirteen), which must represent considerable training and maintenance inefficiency, particularly since so many of them are quite elderly. Zambia does not appear to have a significant COIN requirement and the army capability seems perfectly adequate to meet it. The air force COIN capability seems excessive and could be gradually run down through normal attrition of older types.

Manning levels might be reduced without affecting the field force capabilities, by either greater efficiencies or the expansion of the existing reserve force capability as the regular force level is reduced.

Army	Active	13,500
	Reserve	5,500
Air Force	Active	2,000
Total	Active	15,500
	Reserve	5,500

MILITARY EXPENDITURES: ANALYSIS OF VARIABLES

Two trends are evident. The first is the overall downward trend in military spending as a consequence of the South African decision in 1989 to end the war and to initiate the process for the sharing of power with the black majority. The exceptions are Botswana, whose concerns seem unclear, Tanzania, whose concerns relate to Eastern African issues and will decline, and Angola, where the civil war continues. The second welcome trend is the substantial decline in military equipment imports both in absolute terms, and as a percentage of defence budgets.

THE LOCAL STRATEGIC CONTEXT
(BORDERING COUNTRIES IN ORDER OF GNP)

Country	1994			ME/GNP		MI/ME	
	GNP $US millions	ME $US millions	ME/GNP %	1990-94 %	1985-89 %	1990-94 %	1985-89 %
South Africa	119,500	2,899	2.4	3.2	4.1	0.6	1.0
Zaire	5,690	117	2.1	3.0	2.7	11.0	24.5
Angola	NA	NA	NA	NA	36.8	NA	76.4
Zimbabwe	5,086	188	3.7	4.9	6.4	12.6	15.2
Botswana	3,806	249	6.0	5.6	4.4	9.5	19.4
Zambia	3,232	44	1.4	2.0	3.6	10.1	42.3
Namibia	2,929	56	1.9	2.2	NA	0	NA
Tanzania	2,058	79	3.8	4.8	8.0	12.9	33.6
Malawi	1,252	13	1.0	1.5	2.7	19.4	30.6
Mozambique	1,195	104	8.7	13.8	39.4	30.5	75.0

SENSITIVITY ANALYSIS: THE EXISTING ZAMBIAN SPENDING PATTERN
(MEAN 1990-94)

Spending Category	Budget Share %	$US per Position	Foreign Currency $US millions	Local Currency $US millions	Total $US millions
Equipment	10.1	287	6.4	0	6.4
PO&M	89.9	2,554	0	57.0	57
Total	100	2,841	6.4	57.0	63.4

CHANGE EFFECTS

- Changing Equipment spending by 1% of the Budget $634,000 (Foreign Currency)
- Changing Personnel strength by 1,000
  – Change in Equipment spending $287,000 (Foreign Currency)
  – Change in PO&M spending $2,554,000 (Local Currency)
  – Total change in Military spending $2,841,000
- Changing the Praetorian Index by 1 $8,214,000 (Local Currency)

THE DEFENCE SUFFICIENCY BUDGET

An argument can be made that the Zambian military is overstaffed (in proportion to the operational forces currently maintained) by approximately 6,820 positions when compared to the 1990-94 mean of 22,320. If 6,820 positions were to be eliminated the following savings might be obtained:

Mean 1990-94 Budget without changes	$63,400,000
– Decrease in equipment (foreign currency) spending	$1,957,000
– Decrease in other (local currency) spending	$17,418,000
Mean 1990-94 Budget with changes	$44,044,000
Reduction in the Defence Budget	$19,356,000

IS ZAMBIA SPENDING TOO MUCH ON ITS MILITARY?

From a regional perspective the level of militarism in Zambia is comparatively low. Moreover, the threat/risk assessment is generally supportive of existing Zambian force structure levels as prudent within the existing local strategic context. While there is no clear evidence of overt hostility on the part of neighbouring states and considerable evidence that their own military force structure levels are driven by factors other than their relationship with Zambia, a good case can be made for the maintenance of the existing Zambian force structures until such time as overall force levels in the region are reduced. Since Zambia is already in the low group on the Praetorian Index there seems little opportunity for savings in that area. There appears to be, however, a degree of overmanning in proportion to the number of actual military field formations. Whether this represents the use of military forces in internal security tasks as a consequence of comparatively small paramilitary forces or, alternatively, the existence of military inefficiency is somewhat unclear. Savings could, however, be made in this area. The potential is estimated to be in the order of $19,356,000, based on the mean 1990-94 manning levels—a sum equal to 2.4% of mean 1990-94 ODA or 0.6% of 1990-94 GNP.

SOCIAL MILITARIZATION ANALYSIS

Within the regional context Zambia is not particularly heavily socially militarized, standing seventh on the Spartan scale and ninth on the

PRAETORIAN AND SPARTAN INDICES
(1990-94 MEANS)

Country	Praetorian Index	Spartan Index	Total Regular Personnel
Zaire	40.1	1.5	27,220
Mozambique	35.8	2.8	42,080
Angola	NA	12.1	16,200
Tanzania	22.9	2.2	34,600
South Africa	14.7	5.2	73,660
Malawi	11.3	1.2	9,910
Botswana	10.8	5.4	6,040
Zimbabwe	8.5	7.0	49,340
Zambia	6.9	2.7	22,320
Namibia	4.4	5.0	7,350

Praetorian scale. Zambia appears, however, to have a significantly higher proportion of its army devoted to internal security duties than some of its neighbours, since its field units plus 35% for the supporting infrastructure should contain considerably fewer personnel than its total reported strength. The numbers of military personnel in excess of this total are assumed to be employed on internal security duties rather than on national defence duties. An alternative "inefficiency" explanation would be that the Zambian military is overmanned and could maintain the same field force level at a lower manning.

DEVELOPMENT ISSUES

THE MILITARY AS NATIONAL DEVELOPMENT AGENCY

No organizational indicators have been found that would lead to the conclusion that the Zambian military forces are used to a significant extent in infrastructure development. Since there is no significant indigenous defence industrial base, nor any evidence of building military equipment under licensing arrangements, it is doubtful that Zambian military procurement plays an industrial development role.

Zambia uses a professional volunteer military system. Characteristically the turnover rate for such a force would range from 3% to 12% annually. It is suspected, given the evidence that the Zambian military represents an economically privileged elite, that the turnover would lie at the bottom end of that range. Even if it were to lie at the top end it would amount to somewhat under 2,000 annually, or about 2.5% of the annual cohort of males aged 18-22. Consequently, because of its relatively small size, the Zambian military is unlikely to have a significant impact on unemployment rates or upon civilian human capital formation.

THE ODA FUNGIBILITY ISSUE

With mean 1990-94 ODA receipts at 1,256% of Military Expenditures, there is ample opportunity for the Zambian government to divert its own spending toward the military sector. However, with ODA receipts for the same period equal to 87% of CGE, there is strong donor leverage available to counteract this possibility.

CASE STUDY 6: ZIMBABWE

STRATEGIC THREAT ANALYSIS

A geostrategic Threat Analysis for Zimbabwe should normally consider three areas:
- threats of direct military confrontation with other states with which Zimbabwe shares borders other than the Republic of South Africa (RSA),
- the threat of direct military confrontation with the RSA,
- threats to Zimbabwe's economy through the possible closing of rail links to export markets, and
- threats to Zimbabwe's internal political stability and armed resistance to the civil authority.

WAR WITH STATES OTHER THAN A WHITE-CONTROLLED REPUBLIC OF SOUTH AFRICA

This study does not consider *Botswana*, *Mozambique*, or *Zambia* credible threats. None has any real capacity to launch an invasion of Zimbabwe. They would each lose such a contest and therefore have little incentive to launch it. Indeed, a balance of power analysis clearly argues that Zimbabwe is a much more credible threat to them. In addition, in the case of Mozambique, Zimbabwe provided military support to the FRELIMO government in order to help protect the rail lines to Beira and Maputo.

War with the ANC government of South Africa seems equally unlikely. First, the Mugabe administration provided support to the ANC during the closing years of the move toward majority rule in South Africa. Second, the economic relationship between the two countries benefits South Africa through transfer charges derived from the rail and road links for Zimbabwe's exports, as well as their own trade. Third, South Africa needs to meet the rising expectations of economic improvement for its black population. An obvious move is to transfer resources from the military to the civilian sector, and the defence budget declined from 2.8% of GNP in 1994 to 2.3% of GNP in 1995, according to *The Military Balance* 1996-97, and will have declined further to about 2.1% in 1996. War between these two Southern African states makes no sense.

WAR WITH A WHITE-CONTROLLED REPUBLIC OF SOUTH AFRICA

The probability of a direct military confrontation with the RSA is dependent on the flow of events in South Africa itself. There are three possible scenarios. In the first the process of national reconciliation continues and the problem of developing a system of political equality while at the same time allaying the legitimate security fears of all parties proves successful. In that case it seems likely that the South African government would continue to transfer funds from the military to the economic sectors to raise black South African income levels, with the result that the latent military threat to Zimbabwe should continue to decline.

The second scenario is bleaker. In this the process of reconciliation fails, and a hard-line white government assumes power following a coup. Such a government might follow traditional policies against foreign governments giving aid to the ANC. The third scenario is bleaker still. In it political rivalry between the ANC and the Zulu-backed Inkatha based on traditional antipathies, together with economic fears among the Afrikaaner and Coloured populations over the prospect of asset redistribution to the black population as part of the ANC government's social policies, leads to violence along ethnic lines. As the violence escalates it could spill over into white areas and assume a very fluid and disastrous multi-faceted interracial dimension, which might drag in neighbouring states, including Zimbabwe.

Of the three scenarios suggested, the first still seems most likely—particularly on the basis of the absence of a dominant ethnolinguistic group poised to seize power now that Apartheid has failed. The early moderate and prudent policies of the new ANC-dominated coalition government provides further hope that the first scenario will emerge and that the Zimbabwe model of relative racial harmony rather than the model of some other African states will prevail. Nonetheless, a prudent Zimbabwean General Staff will be obliged to undertake contingency planning for such a worst-case scenario.

THE CASUS BELLI WITH AN AFRIKAANER-CONTROLLED RSA

It seems unlikely that a white-controlled government of the RSA would itself initiate a war of imperial conquest against Zimbabwe. The demographic consequence would be the addition of nine million black Africans to the RSA population and a further dilution of the white component. The economic consequence would be the addition of an additional nine million whose per capita income is below that of South African black population and whose administration would require the dilution of white and/or black South African income levels, with all of the implications for political unrest among both blacks and whites in South Africa that that implies. There seems no significant enthusiasm for such a strategic policy. What would seem more likely, and consistent with the RSA's past strategic behaviour, is that Zimbabwean active support of the ANC (perhaps by providing sanctuaries, logistics, weapons, or training support to ANC guerrilla forces) would lead to RSA action to either knock out the sanctuaries or to punish Zimbabwe in order to force it to withdraw its support.

AN RSA CONCEPT OF OPERATIONS

Characteristically, RSA action in the past took one or more of three forms: a raid in force against the sanctuaries, the support of rebel movements within black African states, or an attack against their economies. Action against Mozambique took all three forms. RSA support of RENAMO was directed both to guerrilla operations and to attacks on the economic infrastructure of Mozambique. An assessment of the RSA operations against Mozambique must conclude that it largely achieved its objectives and effectively destroyed the Mozambiquean government.

At the upper end of the scale of violence, a raid in force would start with the establishment of air superiority by a pre-emptive attack by RSA aircraft against the Zimbabwean air force. Such an operation would commence with RSA fighters sweeping Zimbabwean fighters out of the air, followed by FGA attacks against airfields to knock out other aircraft on the ground and to destroy refuelling, maintenance, and control structures and to damage runways. With the Zimbabwean air force neutralized or destroyed, the RSA FGA aircraft would attack the ANC sanctuaries and any Zimbabwean army units supporting them, followed perhaps by an air assault operation by helicopter-carried troops to secure objectives, linking up with mechanized and armoured ground forces. With the destruction of the sanctuaries and the mauling of the Zimbabwean forces, the RSA forces could withdraw and wait cynically for the international condemnation and hand-wringing to gradually wither away as Western media eventually found new objects to entertain them. Having learned its lesson, Zimbabwe could be expected, as other African states have learned, to avoid irritating the RSA.

A second RSA tactic was to take advantage of tribal rivalries to forment insurgency. In Zimbabwe this might involve support to Ndebele resistance movements through the provision of arms, logistics, training, and *agents provocateurs*. Given the historic Shona-Ndebele rivalry, the Mugabe-Nkomo ZANU-ZAPU difficulties, and the brutality of the North Korean-trained 5th Brigade in Matabeleland in 1983, such a tactic might be expected to have some credibility. Insurgency forces are usually lightly armed and follow the theoretical precepts of Mao Zedong of advancing when government forces withdraw and withdrawing when government forces advance, with the aim of cutting off the government from the countryside, wearing it down through a series of minor defeats in detail, demoralizing the government, and destroying its capacity to maintain control. Government brutality against the civilians in the area plays into the hands of the insurgents.

A third tactic might be the economic pin derived from the fact that Zimbabwe's critical foreign exchange-earning exports go to markets by rail. Most, perhaps 80%, go through the RSA, and the closing of the rail link would represent a severe economic strategic constraint on Zimbabwean behaviour. The occurrence of periodic droughts in Southern Africa also makes Zimbabwe dependent on rail lines for food supplies in times of crisis. The major alternative rail routes to the export market are through Zaire and Angola, the TanZam rail link through Zambia and Tanzania, and the two links through Mozambique to either Beira or Maputo. The Zaire-Angola route has been disrupted by the Angolan civil war, and if the RSA chose to resume support of the Savimbi forces, an additional pressure point against this route might be achieved. Renewed RSA support of RENAMO forces could bring pressure on the twin links through Mozambique. Finally, the TanZam route has experienced considerable track and locomotive maintenance difficulties such that it can be judged inadequate to handling both Zambian and Zimbabwean export traffic.

ZIMBABWE'S STRATEGIC OPTIONS

Accommodating the RSA is strategically the most sensible option from both a military and an economic viewpoint, but is politically the most difficult, since it would mean the abandonment of a democratically elected ANC government and of the successful enfranchisement of black South Africans. For a successful revolutionary leader such as Robert Mugabe such an option would be particularly difficult. The alternative—countering the portfolio of RSA tactical options—would be even more difficult, however.

If a strategic consultant were designing a Zimbabwean defence to counter the raid in force, and money were no object, the following recommendations would probably be made. Since the RSA would have the initiative, could choose the time and place of the raid, and would seek to neutralize the Zimbabwean air force as a first stage, the following elements are required. (Unfortunately, such a system is very expensive.)

- an early warning radar system along the southern boundary covering Mozambique to Botswana inclusive; and/or an airborne early warning and control aircraft with 24 hour/7 days a week capability,
- low-level ground-based air defence missile/gun systems to protect Zimbabwean Air Force airports,
- an effective but easy to maintain air defence fighter to deny the RSA control of Zimbabwean air space,
- highly mobile light armoured forces with sufficient firepower to deny RSA army forces the ability to cross easily into Zimbabwean territory, and
- an effective FGA or attack helicopter armed with modern anti-tank missiles that might be able to offset the RSA heavy armour (main battle tank) advantage.

The aim for COIN operations would be to produce highly mobile forces that could respond so quickly to insurgency operations that they would be able to catch insurgent forces and inflict enough casualties on them to wear them down in a series of small defeats:

- A COIN air force of light fixed-wing ground attack aircraft and/or attack helicopters would provide fire support and interdiction, together with troop-carrying assault helicopters able to quickly deploy light infantry in the area of the insurgent forces to cut them off and either capture or destroy them. The fixed-wing aircraft do not have to be jets, and propeller-driven aircraft may be a better choice, since their

slower speeds and lower fuel consumption may allow them to spend a longer time in the immediate area.
- A COIN ground force of light-armoured cars would provide firepower and wheeled light-armoured personnel carriers would provide infantry transport. Such a force, though slower than the airmobile force, would be larger and the tactical pattern would be one of a series of linkup operations with the heliborne light infantry.
- A political/economic operation would deal with the legitimate grievances of the local population in a conciliatory fashion to lessen support they might provide to insurgents. This would be the opposite of the actions of the 5th Brigade in Matabeleland.

The economic pin is harder to deal with. Zimbabwe would have little leverage against the closing of RSA rail lines other than the loss of profit to the RSA in carrying Zimbabwean exports—a weak strategic weapon. It is unlikely that the TanZam rail link could be expanded in the short run as an alternative, and even in the best of conditions it is lengthy and less economic. The Angolan rail route, even assuming a benevolent Savimbi, requires more maintenance and rebuilding than the TanZam link. It, too, is lengthy and less economic. The Mozambiquean rail lines are shorter, but the threat from a renewed RSA intervention might mean that Zimbabwean forces would be required to garrison the line—which during the civil war involved forces estimated at 3,000 to 8,000. Given the low force to space ratios involved, garrison forces would have to have very high mobility if they were to have much hope of protecting the line. A combination of light infantry, wheeled light armour, and light COIN aircraft, including helicopter-borne light infantry, would seem to fit the bill.

THE MILITARY BALANCE OF POWER, 1996-97

THE LOCAL STRATEGIC CONTEXT
(RANKED IN ORDER OF ESTIMATED TOTAL COMBAT POTENTIAL)

Country	Air Force				Army			Navy	
	Fighter Sqns	FGA Sqns	COIN Attack Sqns	COIN Transport Sqns	ADEs	IDEs	COIN Bns	Subs	Ships/ Patrol Craft
South Africa	0.7	14.6	1	4.6	2.5	6.0	12	3	12
Zimbabwe	0.9	1.4	2.6	0.8	0.4	7.3	3	–	–
Mozambique	–	2.7	0.3	0.3	0.8	2.7	–	–	3
Zambia	0.8	0.8	2.2	1.3	0.3	2	1	–	–
Botswana	–	0.8	0.9	0.4	0.5	1.7	0.3	–	–

What is striking about the strategic context is the dominance of the *South African* capability. The table does not really reflect the fact that the South African army is a well balanced general purpose force with excellent field and air defence artillery together with highly mobile mechanized infantry. A straightforward battle between the South African and Zimbabwean armies would result in a quick and total defeat for Zimbabwe.

The *Zimbabwean* air force has bought Chinese J-7 Airguard aircraft, an upgrade of the older Soviet MIG-21 with increased combat power at the expense of range. Qualitatively they are 30-40% superior to the Zambian and Mozambiquean air forces on a plane-to-plane basis. They are, however, inferior to the later generation Mirages of the South African air force, which have also been upgraded and are estimated to be about 80-100% superior to the Zimbabwean J-7s on a plane-to-plane basis. The purchase of Chinese J-7s has a certain logic. The J-7 is an agile light air defence fighter whose limited range would be less of a problem in operations in Zimbabwean airspace. With enough warning to get airborne it could be expected to destroy some attacking RSA Mirages such that the raid would not be costless. It appears that earlier plans were for 48 J-7s to form the air defence capability but that by 1992 the lessening threat from South Africa led to a decision to cap the force at 14. Zimbabwe's close air support capability consists of 11 30-year-old Hawker Hunters plus 11 BAE Hawks. Given the weakness in air combat capability needed to protect them, their utility against a South African threat would be limited. In a Zimbabwean-South African war the air superiority battle would end with South African control of the air, which would allow the South African FGAs to be used as a combat multiplier in support of the South African army—already overwhelmingly superior to the Zimbabwean army. A marked deficiency in Zimbabwe's ability to respond to a South African pre-emptive strike lay in the lack of an air defence system to provide early warning of the approach of South African aircraft and to scramble, control, and vector Zimbabwe air defence aircraft to the threatened sector. In 1990, *Defence and Foreign Affairs Weekly* (February 19-25), reported that Zimbabwe was moving toward the purchase of a complete air defence system from China, including radar arrays and a complete command, control, and communications network. The 1992-93 Estimates of the Ministry of Public Construction and National Housing contained entries for an "Air Defence Project," consisting of Command Centres at Harare and Gweru, a Command Maintenance Centre, and Radars at Harare, Gweru, Chegutu and six other sites, plus twelve communications positions.

The Zimbabwean army holds two distinct sets of equipment. One consists of heavy tracked equipment purchased primarily from China and based on Soviet designs for high intensity war on the North European plain. The Chinese equipment is badly unsuited to Zimbabwe's actual needs and the money spent on it might have been better utilized. Its Chinese main battle tanks are few, slow, and expensive in fuel consumption, and lack the mobility to counter RSA forces. The second set consists of light armoured wheeled equipment inherited in part from the Rhodesian Defence Force, which seem a much better fit with Zimbabwe's actual requirements. Its field artillery is badly outranged by the excellent RSA guns. In attempting to counter an RSA raid in force Zimbabwe could expect to get badly beaten.

The critical strategic constraint on Zimbabwe's capability to defend itself against an Afrikaaner-controlled RSA is the strength of its economy. Not to put too fine a point on it, Zimbabwe cannot hope to successfully defend itself against an RSA raid in force under any circumstances. While it could probably contain an RSA-supported resistance in Matabeleland, the cost would be substantial. Similarly, while it could, in cooperation with Mozambique, mount a partially effective defence of the rail links to Maputo and Beira, that operation would be expensive. Should it have to deal with a revived RENAMO and an irredentist Ndebele rising simultaneously it might have considerable difficulty. Accordingly, the Zimbabwean military buildup from a 1983-84 post-ZANU-ZAPU force consolidation strength of 40,000 to a 1991-92 strength of 51,600, and the planned acquisition of 48 Chinese J-7 aircraft from 1986-90, must be viewed as an ineffective policy to effectively oppose the RSA, and excessive against a hypothetical Botswana/Zambia coalition.

A DEFENCE SUFFICIENCY STRUCTURE FOR ZIMBABWE

The comparative sizes of the Zimbabwean and South African economies ensure that there is no way for Zimbabwe to afford a credible defence against South Africa. Accordingly, attempts to build a force capable of engaging the South Africans does not seem to make any logical sense. Zimbabwean security vis-à-vis South Africa would be much better based on a willingness to avoid direct operational support of the ANC (though political support would appear possible) while at the same time attempting to mobilize political pressure from OECD states to ensure that South Africa refrains from direct operations against Zimbabwe. Accordingly, this Force Structure analysis rules out South Africa as an opponent.

Given that Zimbabwe had effectively entered into a coalition against RENAMO with Mozambique, the latter can, for the moment, be ruled out as a potential strategic threat. The remaining worst-case scenario would involve a Botswana-Zambia coalition against Zimbabwe which, given the Zambia-Botswana mutual defence pact, cannot be entirely ruled out, though it is unlikely. Such a coalition could at best mount a combined force of half an armoured brigade, four weak infantry brigades, a half-squadron of fighter aircraft, and a half-squadron of FGA aircraft. Given Zambian maintenance and logistics capabilities, the practical ability to fight a war outside its borders must be viewed as a fiction. A Zimbabwean Force Structure of a light armoured brigade and three infantry brigades plus an air force of two fighter squadrons and one FGA squadron would seem adequate to deal with this hypothetical threat. Such a force would probably require a personnel strength of about 15,000, plus another 5,000 in military infrastructure, for a total of about 20,000. Zimbabwe had provided 3,000-8,000 troops to assist Mozambique's operations against RENAMO forces and also, at times, to protect the Beira and Maputo rail corridors. With the end of the civil war this commitment is no longer required. However, since Mozambique's future is still somewhat cloudy, it seems sensible to maintain an interim capability to reconstitute this force. Such a cadre would be about 3,000 plus an additional 1,000 (35%) in supporting military infrastructure for a total of about 4,000. This structure could be handled within the force already recommended. If greater strategic insurance were felt necessary, then a brigade-sized reserve force might be constituted; the administrative and training increment required for such a force should again be capable of being handled by the force recommended. The 1996-97 air force personnel strength is about 4,000, which represents a sharp increase from the reported 1,200 of 1993-94. This may represent the manning of the new air defence radar establishment. The total number is not unreasonable, but the trend bears watching.

Continued purchases from the People's Republic of China of main battle tanks of Soviet design intended for high-intensity war on the North European plain, or of Chinese J-7 Airguard fighter aircraft, are unsuited to Zimbabwean security requirements and represent a waste of Zimbabwean foreign exchange.

Approximately 19,000 of the current military forces of Zimbabwe, together with at least 22,800 paramilitary forces plus the potential of an additional 20,000 in the National Militia, appear engaged in internal security activities. This seems excessive and the internal security role should be removed from the Zimbabwean Forces except as the agency of last resort. The Field Force structure suggested would be adequate for such purposes provided that one of the light infantry brigades was provided with helicopter lift for COIN operations. Accordingly, no allowance is made for additional internal security troops in the proposed Zimbabwe Force Structure. In summary, such a Zimbabwean Defence Force would require about 24,000 personnel on this model instead of the 43,000 it had in 1996, a 2,000 decrease from 1995.

MILITARY EXPENDITURES: ANALYSIS OF VARIABLES

THE MILITARY EXPENDITURES BALANCE
(BORDERING COUNTRIES IN ORDER OF GNP)

Country	1994			ME/GNP		MI/ME	
	GNP $US millions	ME $US millions	ME/GNP %	1990-94 %	1985-89 %	1990-94 %	1985-89 %
South Africa	119,500	2,899	2.4	3.2	4.1	0.6	1.0
Zimbabwe	5,086	188	3.7	4.9	6.4	19.1	25.1
Botswana	3,806	249	6.0	5.6	4.4	9.5	19.4
Zambia	3,232	63	1.4	2.0	3.6	10.1	42.3
Mozambique	1,195	104	8.7	13.8	29.4	30.5	75.0

The Appendix 6 Partial Regression Tests led to the conclusion that Military Imports were not included in Military Expenditures for Botswana, Mozambique, and Zambia. The Partial Regression Tests were consistent with military imports being included in military expenditures for South Africa and Zimbabwe. However, since South Africa maintains an extensive arms production industry, the MI/ME algorithm could not be used and an arbitrary 20% (the NATO average) was used as an estimate.

The Zimbabwe Estimates for 1992-93 included entries for vehicles, tools, and aircraft procurement amounting to 9.7% of the defence budget, which supports the conclusion from the regression models. However, a further examination of the Estimates found that a significant portion of defence spending was included in the Ministry of Public Construction and National Housing. These expenditures included sums allocated for FY1992-93 to the construction of the air defence radar sites as well as training areas and a variety of other military works and buildings. Had these items been included in the Defence Ministry Estimates the result would have been a de facto 15.8% increase in defence spending. With the inclusion of military construction spending, the division of the Zimbabwe defence budget into its three components for FY1991-92 would be as follows: personnel 54.2%, operations and maintenance 27.0%, capital 18.8%. This division is quite similar to that among NATO states and thus provides limited support for the theoretical proposition advanced in the modelling section in Chapter 2. The capital budget, in turn, was divided between construction at 69.7%, and procurement at 30.3%. The portion devoted to construction is substantially higher than recent NATO practice, but NATO practice rests on a much longer construction program which was, in effect, front-end loaded during the early Cold War. The previous table, derived from *World Military Expenditures and Arms Transfers (WMEAT)* figures, has not been adjusted to include the military construction figures. The effect of including them equally for 1990-94 figures would raise mean 1990-94 ME/GNP from 4.9% to 6.7%.

Regional military expenditures as a percentage of GNP have declined over the period following the end of the undeclared war with South Africa in 1989. Spending in Botswana alone runs counter to this trend. What is striking is the disproportion between the economies of Zimbabwe and South Africa, which allows South Africa to achieve a defence budget approximately 15 times that of Zimbabwe in absolute spending while carrying a defence burden (ME/GNP) only 65% as great. If Zimbabwe were to match South African spending in absolute terms it would have to carry a burden of 76% of GNP devoted to defence spending—an absurd notion. Zimbabwe cannot under any scenario devote sufficient financial resources to match South Africa's military. Turning to the largest of the other possible adversaries—Zambia—we note that the larger Zimbabwean economy could match 1994 Zambian military spending in absolute terms at a defence burden of 1.2% of the Zimbabwean economy, and a saving of 181 million dollars.

South Africa and Mozambique have made use of conscripts, though this may be less important in future. Botswana and Zambia have relied on volunteer forces. Though *The Military Balance* states that the Zimbabwean forces use conscripts, the Canadian Military Attaché in Harare reported this is not the case.

SENSITIVITY ANALYSIS: THE EXISTING ZIMBABWEAN SPENDING PATTERN (MEAN 1990-94)

Spending Category	Budget Share %	$US per Position	Foreign Currency $US millions	Local Currency $US millions	Total $US millions
Equipment	19.1	932	46	0	46
PO&M	80.9	3,948	0	195	195
Total	100	4,880	46	195	241

CHANGE EFFECTS

- Changing Equipment spending
  by 1% of the Budget $2,410,000 (Foreign Currency)
- Changing Personnel strength by 1,000
  – Change in Equipment spending $932,000 (Foreign Currency)
  – Change in PO&M spending $3,948,000 (Local Currency)
  – Total change in Military
    spending $4,880,000
- Changing the Praetorian
  Index by 1 $22,992,000 (Local Currency)

THE DEFENCE SUFFICIENCY BUDGET

With no change in the Praetorian Multiple, since the Zimbabwe Praetorian Index Level is the second lowest in the local context, or in the subdivision between equipment, personnel, and O&M spending, but with the proposed reduction of 22,900 positions:

Mean 1990-94 Budget without changes	$241,000,000
– Decrease in equipment (foreign currency) spending	$21,343,000
– Decrease in PO&M (local currency) spending	$90,409,000
Mean 1989-93 Budget with changes	$129,248,000
Reduction in the Defence Budget	$111,752,000
	(46% decrease)

Some concern may be felt about the labour market impact of a cut of 22,900 military personnel. With the professional volunteer model a normal (high) annual attrition of about 6,500 might achieve the reduction over about 3.5 years; a normal (low) attrition might take five years.

IS ZIMBABWE SPENDING TOO MUCH ON ITS MILITARY?

The answer to our question is Yes. Zimbabwe is spending more on its military forces than is required to meet its real national security requirements. Moreover, it is excessively socially militarized. There appear to be two reasons for this: an historically aggressive foreign policy vis-à-vis the RSA through its support of the ANC, plus a perceived need to provide long-term employment to members of its own independence military forces. The election victory of the ANC has largely eliminated the need for Zimbabwe to maintain such forces. In any event, the disproportion in respective economic strength ensures that no matter how much of GNP Zimbabwe spends on its military it can never match South Africa. Consequently, even under the condition of the former white-dominated government of the RSA, a non-provocative foreign policy was economically the most logical and beneficial strategic option for Zimbabwe. Such a policy would have envisaged the provision of political but not military support to the ANC, recognizing that the limitations of the Zimbabwean economy prevented it from ever hoping to match the military capacity of the RSA and that a more provocative policy simply would have made it vulnerable to RSA countermeasures. Similarly, the end of the civil war in Mozambique has removed a second threat to Zimbabwe's security concerns. While the rail lines through Mozambique represent a critical economic strategic interest of Zimbabwe, the need to maintain a continuing military garrison designed to exclude RENAMO from the rail corridors no longer exists.

The estimated annual savings based on the 1990-94 mean budget pattern are about $112 million. The 1995 announcement that Zimbabwe intends to reduce its military forces is thus consistent with the finding of this study, though the exact actual savings to be achieved remain unclear at this time. Further savings could come from reductions in Zimbabwe's excessively large paramilitary forces. This study has not attempted to quantify such a saving.

Zimbabwe's paramilitary forces, according to *The Military Balance*, include the National Militia. The actual status of this force is unclear. The term "militia" can refer to reservists (as in Canada) or police forces (as in much of southern and eastern Europe). They have been treated as paramilitary. Zimbabwe has the highest regular military index, which gives it the highest Spartan Index—some 50% greater than the mean of the neighbouring states. In part this appears to be the result of retaining the

SOCIAL MILITARIZATION ANALYSIS

PRAETORIAN AND SPARTAN INDICES
(1990-94 MEANS)

Country	Praetorian Index	Spartan Index	Total Regular Personnel
Mozambique	35.8	2.8	42,080
South Africa	14.7	5.2	73,660
Botswana	10.8	5.4	6,040
Zimbabwe	8.5	7.0	49,340
Zambia	6.9	2.7	22,320

members of the independence forces in the military. Because of their lack of marketable skills, these members might be expected to have difficulty re-entering civilian society.

DEVELOPMENT ISSUES

THE MILITARY AS NATIONAL DEVELOPMENT AGENCY

No evidence based on military organization and equipment analysis has been found that the Zimbabwean military performs any substantial national infrastructure development function. Nor is there any evidence of an indigenous defence industrial base, or the use of licensing arrangements to build military equipment locally. Zimbabwe's military procurement plays no significant industrial development role.

If the Zimbabwean forces are based fully on the professional volunteer model, and if they experienced the high end of the Western turnover model (which is unlikely, given the high unemployment rates in Zimbabwe and the fact that the military is economically advantaged), the annual turnover might amount to as much as about 6,500 annually. This represents approximately 6.5% of the annual cohort of males aged 18-22 and 0.5% of the total male population aged 18-32. The impact on human capital formation would depend on the curriculum content of the individual training program, and the degree to which military skills have analogues in the civilian economy. The low rate of turnover in the professional model suggests that its contribution to human capital formation would not be large. That of the mixed conscript/professional model could be more significant, given the comparatively large proportion of the annual male cohort involved. However, the excessively large size of the Zimbabwe forces appears related to the political and social objective of providing employment for former members of the independence forces who lack readily marketable civilian job skills. In this sense the Zimbabwe forces represent a form of public sector employment.

Media reports indicate that Zimbabwean military forces have been deployed in support of game wardens to combat poaching of game animals and elephants for ivory. They may also be being used in a border patrol function (which, strictly speaking, is a paramilitary rather than a civilian function).

THE ODA FUNGIBILITY ISSUE

With 1990-94 Official Development Aid at 201% of reported military expenditures the question as to whether the provision of official development aid has permitted Zimbabwe to maintain a higher level of military spending than would otherwise be possible is a legitimate one. With 1990-94 ODA at 9.8% of CGE donors have some leverage to address this issue.

7

EASTERN AFRICA

THE REGIONAL STRATEGIC CONTEXT:
INTER-STATE ISSUES

A quick review of the post-colonial history of East Africa leads to a picture of a relatively stable centre consisting of Tanzania and Kenya surrounded by a "ring of fire" of civil war, military threats, and floods of refugees that became the dominant factors in determining the security postures adopted by the two states. Kenya had to deal with claims on parts of its territory by Somalia, Sudan, and Uganda, and civil wars in Somalia, Ethiopia, Sudan, and Uganda. Tanzania's experience was hardly better, with an invasion by Uganda, and civil wars in Mozambique, Rwanda, and Uganda, and one developing in Burundi as well.

Policy differences between the market economy of Kenya and the centrally managed economy of Tanzania led, in turn, to the influence of advisors both economic and military from the two competing global power blocs—and thus to competing arms suppliers—and contributed to tensions between the two states. With the burnout of the civil wars in Somalia, Ethiopia, and Mozambique, and with the advent of an administration devoted to economic reconstruction and reduced military spending in Uganda, some elements of the regional threat context have been removed. Moreover, with the collapse of the Cold War and the move away from the centrally managed economic model in Tanzania, the ideological divide between Kenya and Tanzania seems to be shallower than before.

However, the conflict in Rwanda still smoulders, that in Burundi has the capacity for another bitter ethnic-based explosion, the departure of the failed United Nations peacekeeping mission in Somalia has allowed clan-based conflict to resume, and there are still worrisome tensions in Ethiopia. The threat posed by these conflicts, however, is not so much a direct military one as it is that of mass migrations of people fleeing from their own countries into the perceived sanctuaries of the neighbouring states. In addition to the problems of cross-border migration there is emerging a new concern based on the Sudan-Iran relationship and the increasing perception among the non-Islamic states of Sub-Saharan Africa of an Iranian-backed push to Islamicize Sub-Saharan Africa through its Sudanese client state, which alone appears on a trend to increase its store of heavy weaponry. Saharan analysts, however, see the Sudanese threat directed northward rather than southward. The place of the new states of Eritrea and perhaps Somaliland in the regional context is yet to be determined, though border incidents seemingly instigated by Sudan against Eritrea are worrisome.

On balance, however, opportunities for cuts in military force levels and spending, particularly for imported weaponry, which in itself would reduce threat levels and insecurity, seem to be encouraging.

THE REGIONAL SOCIO-ECONOMIC BALANCE OF POWER (1990-94 MEANS)

Country	Population (millions)	GNP ($US billions)	ME ($US millions)
Sudan	28.0	11.9	1,476
Ethiopia	51.2	4.7	415
Kenya	26.2	6.4	198
Tanzania	26.6	1.9	94
Uganda	18.0	3.9	90
Rwanda	7.9	1.8	130
Burundi	5.8	1.0	34
Somalia	6.6	0.9?	NA
Eritrea	3.0?	0.6?	NA

THE REGIONAL MILITARY BALANCE OF POWER, 1994

Country	Fighter Squadrons	FGA Squadrons	ABEs	IBEs
Sudan	0.6	2.4	2.8	26
Ethiopia	–	5.3	3.5	27
Tanzania	1.5	–	0.2	5
Kenya	–	1.1	0.8	2.7
Uganda	–	0.3	0.2	4
Rwanda	–	–	–	5
Burundi	–	–	–	1.7
Eritrea	–	–	?	?
Somalia	–	–	–	–

INTRA-STATE ISSUES

As in West Africa, two ethnocultural fault lines lie across the area. One is the division between the Bantu-speaking peoples of Central Africa and the Hamito/Nilotic-speaking peoples of the greater African Sudan. The second is the religious fault line dividing the Islamic north from the Christian/Animist south. These lines bear little resemblance in most part to post-Colonial boundaries, with the result that they can serve as sources of intra-state conflict, particularly where post-colonial leadership elites have politicized them. Thus intra-state conflict has been a greater source of grief for the region than has inter-state conflict.

MILITARIZATION LEVELS

Country	Financial: Economy ME/GNP %		Financial: Government ME/CGE %		Spartan Index		Praetorian Index	
	90-94	85-89	90-94	85-89	90-94	85-89	90-94	85-89
Sudan	12.4	5.1	268.0	106.0	3.7	2.7	39.1	16.1
Ethiopia	8.8	29.4	37.4	113.0	2.2	10.6	7.2	11.6
Rwanda	7.2	2.2	28.9	12.7	0.8	1.0	95.8	21.9
Somalia	NA	8.7	NA	84.4	2.4	13.7	NA	5.2
Tanzania	4.8	8.0	12.9	33.6	2.2	1.9	22.9	19.3
Burundi	3.5	4.6	18.3	29.5	1.5	1.6	23.2	23.8
Kenya	3.1	4.0	10.4	14.0	1.1	1.0	29.5	29.4
Uganda	2.3	5.3	12.4	54.2	3.4	2.6	6.4	11.1
Eritrea	NA	NA	NA	NA	NA	NA	NA	NA
Means	6.01	8.41	55.47	55.93	2.16	4.39	32.01	17.3

MILITARY EXPENDITURE LEVELS AND TRENDS

The economic burden of military spending, particularly when the hidden effects of debts incurred for imports of military equipment are included, has been substantial, with a Sub-Saharan regional military burden (ME/GNP) second to that of Southern Africa. However, the end of most of the regional civil wars and of the Cold War, and declines in regional tension, has led to declines in military spending in the more stable states in the area. This trend can continue if tensions in Sudan and the Great Lakes area can be contained.

FINANCING MILITARY EXPENDITURES

Two regional models for the financing of military expenditures emerged, partially as a result of the influence of the two economic models already alluded to. The centrally managed economic model (used mainly by Ethiopia, Somalia, and Tanzania) made use of substantial foreign supplier debts as well as the use of a conscript premium to finance a greater level of military spending than would be possible with the market economic model (exemplified by Kenya). Both economic systems relied at times on foreign military aid in the form of non-repayable grants, and at other times on the ability to include military related expenditures in other government departments.

The end of Cold War competition for influence will very substantially reduce the amount of non-repayable grants in the area, and should reduce the willingness of suppliers to make long-term military equipment debt capital available to countries whose ability to service those debts is open to question. The single exception is Sudan, whose apparent financial support from Iran has permitted it to continue to expand its military capacity. On balance, however, these financial constraints should reinforce the impact of lowered threat levels in further providing the impetus for reduced military expenditures in the area.

THE SOCIAL IMPACT OF MILITARY EXPENDITURES

With the exception of the states that are just emerging from protracted civil wars, the state of social militarization in the region is not particularly high, though higher than in Central or Western Africa. As the civil war states demobilize, this level of social militarization will decrease further. However, throughout the region (with the exception of Uganda) the military has become a relative socioeconomic elite, with Praetorian Indices estimated to be six to eight times that of the NATO South states. This raises the policy question as to whether the military of the countries in the region have become economic "rent-takers," who are able to take advantage of their monopoly on the use of military force to gain an economic benefit that would not otherwise be available to them. The pattern of Praetorian elitism is not quite the same as in West Africa, where these elites frequently make and unmake governments by military coups; East Africa's Praetorians are more likely to protect authoritarian governments than overthrow them.

THE MILITARY AS DEVELOPMENT FACTOR

With some possible exceptions there is little evidence of the direct use of military forces in economic development roles through infrastructure construction. There has been no evidence of building military equipment under license as a means of transferring equipment spending to the local economy, nor of increasing the number of more technologically advanced jobs as part of a national industrial strategy. In the non-warring states the absolute size of the military is too slight to have much impact on the labour market or unemployment rates. In those states that use the professional volunteer model, which is characterized by lower turnover and smaller size, the military can be expected to have a minor impact or none at all on national human capital formation; conscript-based armies may have an impact, depending on the curriculum content of the conscript training program. Interestingly, conscript-based armies may have a positive impact on enhanced social integration of differing tribal groups within the countries.

CASE STUDY 7: TANZANIA

STRATEGIC THREAT ANALYSIS

A geostrategic Threat Analysis for Tanzania should normally consider three areas:
- threats of military confrontation with states with which Tanzania shares borders, including Burundi, Kenya, Malawi, Mozambique, Rwanda, Uganda, Zaire, and Zambia,
- the possibility that a civil war or insurrection in a neighbouring country will spill over into Tanzanian territory either through combatant forces making use of Tanzanian territory, or through the movement of refugees fleeing from that civil war or insurrection, and
- threats to Tanzania's internal political stability and armed resistance to the civil authority, possibly aided by the government of one of the neighbouring countries.

THE NEIGHBOURING STATES AS THREATS TO TANZANIA

Of the eight neighbouring states, three—*Burundi, Malawi,* and *Rwanda*—can be excluded on the basis that their military capabilities are hopelessly inadequate to military confrontation with Tanzania, since none possesses an air force, nor an armoured offensive capability of any sort, and at best one eighth the infantry capability of Tanzania. None possesses as much as one third the population base of Tanzania, or half its GNP base.

Three more, Zaire, Zambia, and Mozambique, should be capable of exclusion on the basis that there does not appear to be any reason for them to form an intent to contemplate war with Tanzania.

Zaire's border with Tanzania lies in the middle of Lake Tanganyika, which limits the opportunity for direct confrontation. Zaire's strategic concerns seem to be directed to preventing the Angolan war from spilling over into Zairean territory, coping with the refugee flow from the Rwandan civil war, and preventing any irredentist movement from re-emerging in Shaba province. Provided that Tanzania does not attempt to provide support to any latent residual irredentist movement in Shaba province, and there is no evidence that such support is either given or contemplated, it seems difficult to conceive of any real reason for the two states to contemplate war. Moreover, a war between the two would be logistically very difficult, if not entirely impossible, to conduct. It would require either the development of heavy water transport on Lake Tanganyika or passage, either agreed or forced, through the territory of a third country.

Zambia's copper and other mineral exports are dependent on rail access to the sea. One rail corridor is the Benguela line through Zaire and Angola, which has been damaged by the Angolan civil war and whose capacity is doubtful. A second lies through Zimbabwe and Mozambique and is vulnerable to the still uneasy political situation in Mozambique. The third and best maintained lies through Zimbabwe, Botswana, and South Africa, but is vulnerable to future political developments in South Africa, particularly in the post-Mandela period. The fourth rail corridor is the TanZam line through Tanzania to Dar-es-Salaam which, though less well maintained, is relatively less vulnerable to political developments. Thus there is a substantial reason for Zambia to prefer peaceful and cooperative relations with Tanzania as a means of ensuring the security of a back-up rail export corridor. While a deliberate closing of the TanZam line as an act of economic aggression by Tanzania against Zambia might be conceived as a casus belli, the fact remains that such a move on Tanzania's part, since it would eliminate the opportunity to earn carriage and port handling fees, would be economically self-defeating. Finally, Zambia's effective military capacity has been in decline for some time.

Mozambique has had a long history of cooperative relations with Tanzania from the time that Tanzania provided support for FRELIMO forces during their campaign against Portuguese colonial rule. After the establishment of FRELIMO rule in Mozambique, both states had similar military and economic arrangements with Communist bloc countries and possessed a degree of shared values. Both similarly have turned away from Marxist economic philosophies and do not appear to have mutually hostile government ideologies. Moreover, the after-effects of the debilitating civil war in Mozambique makes any thought of its undertaking a campaign against another African state too strategically ludicrous to contemplate. Consequently, even the faint prospect of RENAMO forming a successor government to the current administration should not result in a strategic threat to its neighbours, since any government of Mozambique in the short (three to five years) or even the medium (five to ten years) term will simply not have the infrastructure to support a foreign war. Moreover, foreign arms sources, now that the Cold War is over, will want to be assured that Mozambique can pay for arms imports; this financial reality will further limit Mozambique's ability to import arms, even if it wanted to in order to launch a war against one of its neighbours.

Although *Kenya* does not appear to pose a real threat to Tanzanian security, it seems prudent to consider a Kenya-Tanzania conflict as a contingency to be guarded against. Historical grievances between the two do not seem to be a major potential casus belli. Indeed, in the aftermath of the breakup of the East African Community, Kenya obtained the bulk of the Community's assets, and Tanzania's closing of their border suggests that any historical grievance might run in the other direction. Nor does the initial ideological divide between Tanzania and Kenya, a major factor in the breakup of the Community, represent as significant a difference as it once did, with Tanzania's move away from radical socialist economic policies. Indeed, the signing in November 1993 of the Treaty for Enhanced East African Cooperation, known as the Arusha Agreement, which announced the establishment of a Tri-Partite Commission for cooperation in trade, industry, agriculture, energy, transport, communications, law, immigration, and security, argues that the predominant current modality is cooperative rather than confrontational. The November 1994 decision to establish a permanent secretariat in the old East African Community Headquarters in Arusha with a proposed budget of $400 million per year reinforces this pattern of cooperation.

The civil wars ongoing in Somalia and Sudan, and only recently concluded in Ethiopia and Uganda, have led to substantial movements (more than 500,000, including 400,000 Somalis, 80,000 Ethiopians, and 20,000 Sudanese by early 1993, according to the Europa publication *Africa South of the Sahara, 1995*) of refugee populations toward perceived safety in Kenya by mid-1992. Mixed among them may be armed elements of factions in those civil wars intent on the use of Kenyan territory to continue or resume operations against their own opponents who, in turn, may be willing to contemplate the invasion of Kenyan territory in hot pursuit. It seems reasonable that Kenyan strategic attention is far more likely to be directed against this very real threat than to the contemplation of an invasion of Tanzania. However, these developments, taken together with recent Kalenjin-Luo and Masai-Kikuyu violence in western Kenya, traditional Luo-Kikuyu contention, and the political rivalry between the Kenyan African National Union (KANU) and the Forum for the Restoration of Democracy (FORD) as a consequence of donor pressure to move from one-party rule to multi-party democracy, plus increasing economic uncertainty, all suggest the possibility of increasing political instability in Kenya. Under such circumstances, the development of an authoritarian government that might be led to foreign adventures as a means of diverting domestic attention cannot be entirely ruled out.

Strategic analysis of *Uganda* will continue to be coloured by the historical reality that the one African international war was between Tanzania and Uganda. Idi Amin's October 1978 invasion of 710 square kilometres of northwestern Tanzania and the pillage and terrorization of its occupants was a means of diverting domestic unrest. The successful Tanzanian counter-attack, a methodical infantry and artillery campaign, led to the capture of Kampala, the ousting of Amin, the restoration of Milton Obote's Uganda People's Congress (UPC), and the subsequent withdrawal of the Tanzanian army. However, Uganda remained in a chaotic state in which tribal rivalries played a major part, particularly among the Nilotic Acholis and Longos, who formed the majority of the army. Subsequent events in Uganda saw the development of the rebel National Resistance Army (NRA), the overthrow of Obote, a Longo, by Acholis led by Bazilio and Tito Okello, and the eventual acquisition of power by the NRA, led by Yoweri Museveni in 1986. Subsequent risings by Bagandan royalists, Nilotic remnants of the Okello-led army, and the Acholi-based Holy Spirit Battalion failed to overthrow the Museveni administration, which has since followed a policy of national reconciliation with considerable success, culminating in the elections of 1996. As a consequence of the lowered level of internal tensions, the Museveni government moved to reduce military expenditures and begin a major downsizing of military personnel strength in 1995 with ODA donor financial support for severance payments. In 1996 however, military spending turned up again as a consequence of increased tensions between Uganda and Sudan.

Nonetheless, Uganda has provided a conduit for support to Sudanese People's Liberation Army (SPLA) forces in southern Sudan, and to the Tutsi-dominated Rwanda Patriotic Front (RPF) invasion of Rwanda, a conflict followed by the genocidal massacres by the Interahamwe gangs and the final RPF victory. This Ugandan willingness to support opposition forces in neighbouring countries could be a concern, particularly since Tanzanian policy had been directed toward trying to encourage a peaceful settlement of the Hutu-Tutsi conflict. Consequently, it is not unreasonable to expect the Tanzanian General Staff, given the invasion of 1979 by the Ugandan army, their having observed the political chaos and civil war that followed, and the cooperative relationship between Uganda and the RPF, to view Uganda as a possible strategic concern, even though the recent politico/economic reconciliation in East Africa and demobilization in Uganda would suggest that a threat is not immediate.

In summary, then, a Tanzanian strategic analyst would wish to undertake contingency planning that could deal with a conceivable threat from either Kenya or Uganda. Of the two the threat from Uganda would represent a lesser military problem. That from Kenya would represent a more difficult military contingency. A two-front confrontation, though highly unlikely given the Kenya-Uganda common border and consequent mutual strategic nervousness, would be the most difficult strategic problem for Tanzania.

WAR WITH KENYA

One is hard pressed to find any convincing rationale for Kenya's launching a war against Tanzania. There are, on the other hand, many convincing arguments for Kenya's not doing so. Accordingly, this threat analysis rests solely on the capabilities argument and is not supported by the intention argument.

A strategic plan for a general war implies the defeat of the opposing forces, the dictating of peace terms, and perhaps the occupation of the defeated country to ensure that peace terms are complied with. A hypothetical Kenyan strategy might be based on a three-phase concept of operations: an air battle to secure air superiority, an armoured break-in battle to defeat the Tanzanian armoured forces, and a pursuit of the broken Tanzanian forces, ending with the capture of the Tanzanian capital and the surrender of the government. After a successful pre-emptive strike to knock out the Tanzanian air force, the remaining aircraft plus the anti-tank helicopters of the Kenyan air force would reduce the Tanzanian tanks, to allow a rapid armour-led punch through to Dar-es-Salaam by means perhaps of a two-pincer movement along the coastal plain from Mombasa and a simultaneous move through Arusha and Moshi and the rail line to Tanga. However, as the balance of power analysis in the following section indicates, Kenya does not possess a military capable of executing such a campaign. A failure to secure a quick victory would ensure at best a costly strategic draw which would, in fact, represent a strategic defeat in the long run.

A plan for a limited war or raid in force strategy might involve a border crossing, the seizure of a limited territory, and/or the mauling of one or more Tanzanian units. As a larger operation it might go so far as the air battle and/or armoured break-in battle already described without the march on Dar-es-Salaam. Once concessions had been extracted the raiding force might withdraw. Once again one would foresee a prudent Kenyan General Staff planner advising against the concept on the basis that its success cannot be guaranteed with a sufficiently high probability to justify the risk—not only the risk of failure of the operation itself, but also of escalation into a general war that would do little but bleed both states dry and expose them to attacks by others of their neighbours. From a capabilities argument it appears that Tanzania already possesses sufficient military resources to deny Kenya a guarantee of victory.

WAR WITH UGANDA

Three possible causes of a war with Uganda might be conceived. One is that the Tanzanian government might be seen to be actively supporting forces in opposition to the Ugandan government; however, while

Tanzania has frequently been the repository of exiles from its neighbours, there seems little or no evidence at the moment that it is providing such support and, indeed, the recent moves to re-establish aspects of the East Africa Development Council seem to clearly indicate the opposite. A second cause of war might arise if the government of Uganda, faced with strong internal opposition forces, were to seek to divert national attention to the threat of a foreign enemy; this does not appear to be the case at the moment, since the Museveni administration has emphasized internal political reconciliation and economic development and enjoys wide electoral support. Finally, there is the possibility that an out-of-control Ugandan army might cross over into Tanzanian territory with the intent to pillage; this seems a weak probability at the moment, particularly given the reductions in Ugandan military personnel through the provision of cash severance settlements to the demobilized forces. There is, at best, a very weak case for expecting war on the basis of an intentions argument.

Given the Ugandan weaknesses in combat aircraft and heavy armour, a Ugandan concept of operations would have to be based on a World War I campaign of a slow infantry and artillery advance, with its armour used essentially as close support assault guns rather than as an independent operation. Its air force would have to adopt an essentially defensive role designed to prevent attacks on the infantry advance. The analysis in the following "Balance of Power" section leads to the conclusion that this concept of operations would fail. The campaign would be a faster re-run of the campaign against Idi Amin. A guaranteed strategic defeat is hardly a viable option for Uganda. A cross-border raid, though potentially of nuisance value, could be easily contained and defeated given the comparative strategic mobility advantage of Tanzania, particularly were Tanzania to adopt a policy of "hot pursuit" into Ugandan territory to punish the raiding forces. In any event, such a raiding policy would run the risk of escalating hostilities with Tanzania. Since Tanzania possesses operational superiority at every step of the "ladder of escalation," such a policy is strategically stupid for Uganda.

A TWO-FRONT WAR AGAINST KENYA AND UGANDA

The critical question is whether there is a strategic conflux of interest sufficient to unite Uganda and Kenya in a coalition against Tanzania. There appears no rational argument for such a prospect. The classic coalition strategy would be to open a two-front war in which the Ugandan front would draw off sufficient Tanzanian forces to allow the Kenyan "quick war strategy" to succeed. However, given the Ugandan army's lack of strategic mobility and firepower, plus the great strategic depth possessed by Tanzania in the West, it appears that a steady-nerved Tanzanian General Staff could adopt an operational defensive in the West, based on an infantry and artillery force that the Ugandans do not have sufficient power to break. In short they would not have to divert air and heavy armour resources to the West and so weaken their defence in the East. A coalition war threat against Tanzania cannot be viewed as a serious contingency, both on the basis of lack of evidence of intent and on the basis of insufficient force capabilities on the part of the potential coalition partners to bring such a strategy to a sufficiently high probability of victory to warrant its costs.

CIVIL WAR SPILLOVER

Tanzania has sufficient military capabilities to deny its territory to rebel and opposition forces if it so chooses. However, Tanzania has had substantial flows of refugees from neighbouring civil wars in the past and can reasonably expect to receive more. The recent civil war in Rwanda is a case in point. Two responses to the refugee problem can involve the Tanzanian military: the support of local police forces in maintaining civil authority when controlling refugee movements; and the provision of relief supplies through military logistics capabilities to refugee populations until the civil authority can deal adequately with the problem.

THE MILITARY BALANCE OF POWER, 1996-97

THE LOCAL STRATEGIC CONTEXT
(RANKED IN ORDER OF ESTIMATED TOTAL COMBAT POTENTIAL)

Country	Air Force				Army		
	Fighter Squadrons	FGA Squadrons	COIN Attack Squadrons	COIN Transport Squadrons	ABEs	IBEs	COIN Battalions
Tanzania	1.5	–	–	0.6	0.2	5.0	–
Kenya	–	1.1	3.4	0.8	0.8	2.7+1	2
Zaire	–	0.5	0.9	0.3	0.6	10	7
Mozambique	–	2.7	0.3	0.3	0.8	2.7	1
Zambia	0.8	0.8	2.3	1.3	0.3	2+1	1
Uganda	–	0.3	0.3	0.4	0.2	4	–
Rwanda	–	–	0.1	–	–	5	NA
Burundi	–	–	0.4	0.1	–	1.7	2
Malawi	–	–	–	0.3	–	1.3	0.3

Where two figures are shown for IBEs the first represents the regular and the second the available reserve force. *Kenya* holds eight Hawk aircraft, which *The Military Balance* classifies as COIN aircraft; the version held by Kenya is really light FGA. The 10 F-5s should really be designated light fighters, on the basis of their Sidewinder missiles. They are superior to the fighters held by Tanzania. *Tanzanian* air defence artillery resources are not shown. The 20 SAM-3, 20 SAM-6, and 120 SAM-7 missile launchers of the Tanzanian air defence artillery could be expected to take a heavy toll of ground attack aircraft without anti-missile resources. Nor are the massive Tanzanian artillery resources shown. *The Military Balance*, however, suggests that not all of the Tanzanian equipment is fully serviceable. It does not appear that COIN activities per se are a particularly significant tasking for the Tanzanian forces. This stands in contrast to a number of the surrounding countries, such as Zaire. *The Military Balance* notes that the serviceability of much of Mozambique's equipment is in doubt. Only 10% of the armour is estimated to be serviceable.

If we make allowances for the qualitative differences in aircraft inventories we conclude that the most theoretically powerful regional air force is Mozambique's, though maintenance and serviceability problems heavily degrade its theoretical capability. Kenya's is about three quarters the theoretical combat power of Mozambique's. Those of Tanzania and Zambia are roughly equivalent and about half the theoretical combat power of Mozambique's. Uganda's air force is the weakest at about one ninth that of Mozambique. Though Kenya would be likely to win an air superiority battle with Tanzania, its air force could be very seriously damaged—perhaps reduced by two thirds. Given Kenya's concerns in the north, the losses to its air force would be too strategically damaging to be acceptable. Moreover, the use of Kenyan aircraft in a close air support ground attack role must be measured against the available Tanzanian army's air defence artillery resources. The missile launchers of the Tanzanian air defence artillery could be expected to take a toll of surviving Kenyan aircraft if they were used in a follow-on ground attack role.

In qualitative terms Kenya's armoured forces have the most powerful main battle tank combat capability. Zaire has about 75%, Mozambique about 50%, and Tanzania and Uganda each about 25% of Kenya's combat power. A traditional military rule of thumb recognizes Clausewitz's statement that defence is the stronger form of battle in that the attacker requires at least a three-to-one advantage in combat power if victory is to be ensured. The Tanzanian air defence artillery precludes the use of

Kenya's helicopters as a combat multiplier. The consequence is that Kenya does not have enough combat power to ensure victory in the armoured break-in battle stage. The long war of attrition, as opposed to the short war of the armoured battle, places a high premium on artillery and infantry resources. Here Tanzania holds a seven-to-one advantage in artillery and a two-to-one advantage in infantry brigades over Kenya. Even against a coalition of Kenya and Uganda, Tanzania holds a two-to-one advantage in artillery and three-quarters their combined number of infantry brigades. No allowance has been made for differences in the training and capabilities of soldiers, for field leadership capabilities of officers, the capabilities of general staffs to coordinate large formations in war, or for maintenance and logistics limitations.

WAR WITH KENYA

A war with Kenya, if initiated by Kenya, would have a logical concept of operations of three phases: the air superiority battle, the armoured break-in battle with close air support a critical combat multiplier, and the pursuit to Dar-es-Salaam. However, it is unlikely that a prudent Kenyan General Staff would willingly undertake that campaign, since failure would be highly likely.

The respective air forces are too closely matched in total combat power to make the Kenyan General Staff confident of the quick victory in the air superiority battle that is critical to a quick victory in the ground campaign. Though ultimate Kenyan success in the air superiority battle is likely, the attrition of combat aircraft would be too high to allow it to guarantee the success of the armoured battle. The Tanzanian air defence artillery's Russian SAM-3, SAM-6, and SAM-7 missile systems are capable of giving a significant level of protection to the Tanzanian armour, particularly against Kenya's slower armed helicopters, which would be crucial combat multipliers in the armoured battle that would open a land campaign. The attrition of Kenyan aircraft would be unacceptably high.

The Kenyan regular army is not large enough to guarantee a quick victory without the combat multipliers, and its reserves are essentially limited to bringing its regular brigades up to war establishments. Consequently, the concept of a quick strategic victory would have to be abandoned in favour of a slower and longer series of set piece battles—driving the Tanzanian army slowly back without being able to secure the crucial single victory that might win the war. The invasion of Tanzania would require substantial additional forces to garrison captured areas and to protect lines of communication with the forward troops. Given the former Tanzanian training relationship with the People's Republic of China, one could expect that Mao Zedong's concept of a guerrilla/people's war against the Kenyan lines of communication might be followed. The Kenyan army's weakness in artillery and infantry makes this sort of campaign highly likely to fail. This forced shift to the long attrition campaign would require the conscription of additional soldiers and their training, and a substantial shift to a war economy in order to support such an expeditionary force. Indeed, the Tanzanian war against Uganda, whose army at the time was much less capable than is the Tanzanian army now, has been estimated to have cost as much as $500 million; a Kenyan invasion of Tanzania, if the quick war strategy fails, would be much more costly. A long war could easily result in the economic exhaustion and defeat of the invader. In spite of the combat aircraft advantage of Kenya, Tanzania has more than enough combat resources to deny Kenya the quick victory essential to Kenyan success.

WAR WITH UGANDA

The concept of operations for a campaign against Uganda would have to involve a World War I-type infantry and artillery advance with the weak Ugandan armour limited to an assault gun supporting role and the weak Ugandan air force limited to an attempt to provide cover for the army. Tanzania would quickly win the air superiority battle and could subsequently devote its efforts to hunting out and destroying the limited Ugandan heavy armour, followed by attacks on the logistics line of communications. In the World War I-type campaign to follow, the massive advantage of the Tanzanian artillery, let alone the capabilities of its armour, would mean that Tanzania would quickly have the Ugandan forces at its mercy and the only question would be how quickly the surrender would take place. Tanzania has more than enough combat resources to defeat a Ugandan invasion.

WAR AGAINST THE KENYAN/UGANDAN COALITION

A concept of operations for a Kenyan/Ugandan coalition would involve a two-front campaign in which the Ugandan front's objective would be to draw off sufficient air power, air defence artillery, and heavy armour to allow the Kenyan front quick strategic strike to succeed. A successful Tanzanian counter would be to adopt a strategic defensive posture in the West based on an infantry and artillery structure of division size with perhaps a light armour battalion, and the older SAM-3s deployed against the less capable Ugandan air force. This would not weaken the resources available in the East sufficiently to alter the prospects of Kenyan success. Tanzania has enough resources to deny a coalition a strategic victory.

In summary, Tanzania has sufficient combat capability to defend itself against a hypothetical invasion attempt by Kenya or by Uganda alone or by Kenya and Uganda in coalition, provided that its equipment is in a serviceable state. While the air battle would result in a marginal win by Kenya, not enough air resources could be brought to bear on the armoured battle, with the result that that battle would essentially be a draw at worst. The artillery and infantry advantage would result in the defeat of a Kenyan or Kenyan/Ugandan invasion force.

A DEFENCE SUFFICIENCY STRUCTURE FOR TANZANIA

The hypothetical Kenyan threat is a division with one armoured brigade and two infantry brigades plus a weak artillery component of two close support (light) battalions. This would be supported by an armed helicopter squadron equipped with TOW anti-tank missiles plus FGA aircraft. A division-sized force consisting of an armoured brigade, two infantry brigades, and an artillery brigade (including a close support field artillery battalion, an anti-tank battalion, and an air defence artillery battalion), plus engineer and logistics support would provide adequate capability to deny victory to the potential Kenyan threat. Such a field force would require about 12,000 personnel plus a military infrastructure increment of 4,000, for a total of about 16,000.

The hypothetical Ugandan threat is four infantry brigades with limited heavy armour and limited (three light battalions) close support artillery. Ugandan demobilization plans in 1995 were described as a reduction of army strength by about half. This suggested a planned end state of about 20,000 to 30,000, a force strength that would require the number of brigades to be similarly reduced. Thus the threat would have been as little as three brigades. A second reduced division-sized force of one light armour battalion, two infantry brigades, one artillery brigade (a close support battalion, an anti-tank battalion, and an air defence battalion), plus engineer and logistics support would have provided an adequate defence capability to deal with the Ugandan threat. Such a field force would require about 8,000 personnel plus a military infrastructure increment of 2,000, for a total of about 10,000. Unfortunately, the 1996 decision to increase the Ugandan defence budget in response to the Sudanese-supported Lord's Resistance Army reversed this trend.

For rough planning purposes, a Tanzanian defence force dealing with the 1995 scenarios would have required about 26,000 personnel, instead of the mean of 48,440 it had in the 1990-94 period or the 34,600 of 1995. Since there does not appear to be a serious internal security threat in Tanzania at this time, a conclusion that is reinforced by the absence of any significant military or paramilitary forces assigned to such roles, the National Defence Structure cited could handle any aid to the civil power requirement. The existing equipment holdings of the Tanzanian armed forces appear generally adequate to equip the proposed defence sufficiency structure. Tanzania's infantry and artillery forces could be reduced substantially without degrading its ability to defend itself. Three infantry brigades could be demobilized and as many as 200 of the 345 light and field artillery pieces could be retired, though no reduction in medium artillery, in multiple-barrelled rocket launchers, or in air defence artillery missile systems is recommended.

The Military Balance 1995-96 reported Tanzanian plans to reduce its military forces strength to about 24,000, a figure consistent with the proposal of 26,000 in this analysis. However, early 1997 indications are that these reductions have been suspended in view of the deteriorating Great Lakes situation.

MILITARY EXPENDITURES: ANALYSIS OF VARIABLES

Appendix 6 concludes that arms imports are included in reported expenditures only for Burundi and Malawi. Accordingly, military expenditures have been adjusted to add arms imports for the other states.

Two trends were notable, one in civil war states and the other in the rest. The civil war states hit peaks in both military imports and expenditures, in 1987-88 in Uganda, 1989-91 in Rwanda, 1990 in both Ethiopia and Somalia, and 1991 in Mozambique, followed by sharp declines in all cases with the burnout of the wars. Of the others, Zaire and Kenya showed increases in ME/GNP, while the rest were stable or declining. Over the 1989-93 period Tanzania's equipment spending per soldier was greater than that of the much wealthier Kenya. The utility of much of the purchases is questionable other than to the profit statements of suppliers such as China's

THE LOCAL STRATEGIC CONTEXT
(BORDERING COUNTRIES IN ORDER OF GNP)

Country	1994		ME/GNP			MI/ME	
	GNP $US millions	ME $US millions	ME/GNP %	1989-93 %	1984-88 %	1989-93 %	1984-89 %
Kenya	6,565	198	2.3	3.1	4.0	12.6	34.7
Zaire	5,690	193	2.1	3.0	2.7	11.0	24.5
Uganda	4,414	66	1.5	2.3	5.3	4.9	44.2
Zambia	3,199	63	1.4	2.0	3.6	10.1	42.3
Tanzania	1,933	79	3.8	4.8	8.0	13.7	55.2
Malawi	1,328	13	1.0	1.5	2.7	19.4	30.6
Mozambique	1,019	104	8.7	13.8	39.4	30.5	75.0
Burundi	871	37	4.2	3.5	4.6	23.4	51.9
Rwanda	NA	194	NA	7.2	2.2	13.9	23.5

NORINCO. In 1989-90, for example, Tanzania added 30 T-62 (Soviet) main battle tanks, 80 85mm (Chinese) guns, and 20 122mm (Chinese) howitzers to its inventory. Tanzania already held 290 artillery pieces of various calibres (40 76mm howitzers, 40 85mm guns, 200 122mm howitzers, and 50 130mm guns), making its artillery the most powerful in the area.

SENSITIVITY ANALYSIS: THE EXISTING TANZANIAN SPENDING PATTERN (MEAN 1990-94)

Spending Category	Budget Share %	$US per Position	Foreign Currency $US millions	Local Currency $US millions	Total $US millions
Equipment	13.7	264	18	0	18
PO&M	86.3	1,662	0	93	93
Total	100	1,926	18	93	111

CHANGE EFFECTS

- Changing Equipment spending
  by 1% of the Budget $1,100,000   (Foreign Currency)
- Changing Personnel strength by 1,000
  – Change in Equipment spending $264,000   (Foreign Currency)
  – Change in PO&M spending $1,662,000 (Local Currency)
  – Total change in Military
    spending $1,926,000
- Changing the Praetorian
  Index by 1 $3,536,000 (Local Currency)

THE DEFENCE SUFFICIENCY BUDGET

With a reduction of 22,440 positions, and a reduction in the Praetorian Index from 22.9 to the East African mean of 20.5:

Mean 1990-94 Budget without changes	$111,000,000
– Decrease in equipment (foreign currency) spending	$5,924,000
– Decrease in other (local currency) spending	$37,295,000
– Decrease in the Praetorian Multiple	$8,486,000
Mean 1990-94 Budget with changes	$59,295,000

IS TANZANIA SPENDING TOO MUCH ON ITS MILITARY?

In terms of the 1995 strategic context, the answer to our question is Yes. The mean annual savings might have amounted to about 51.7 million in the 1990-94 period, an amount equivalent to 2.7% of mean GNP or 5.1% of mean ODA for the 1990-94 period. With the planned Tanzanian force reductions for 1995, which were 2,000 positions deeper than this analysis proposes, the actual dollar saving would have been greater. A caveat, however, is that force reductions are easiest to achieve by reducing recruiting and thereby allowing normal attrition turnover to accomplish a significant portion of the reduction. Such a strategy will result in an increase in the average position cost and the PO&M savings may be less than those projected.

SOCIAL MILITARIZATION ANALYSIS

PRAETORIAN AND SPARTAN INDICES (1990-94 MEANS)

Country	Praetorian Index	Spartan Index	Total Regular Personnel
Rwanda	95.8	0.8	5,120
Zaire	40.1	1.5	27,220
Mozambique	35.8	2.8	42,080
Kenya	29.5	1.1	24,080
Burundi	23.2	1.5	7,060
Tanzania	22.9	2.2	34,600
Malawi	11.3	1.2	9,910
Zambia	6.9	2.7	22,320
Uganda	6.4	3.4	62,000

The national defence focus of the Tanzanian forces was reinforced by the events of the war with Uganda. Tanzania's relatively high Praetorian Index, which is less characteristic of national defence armies, is more likely a feature of the relatively low GNP/capita figure than of economic rent-seeking. In any event Tanzania's Praetorian Index has been declining in recent years. Often force reduction strategies based on reduced recruiting result in reductions being disproportionately heavy among junior ranks, who are paid less, and there is a danger that the Praetorian Index can rise as the force becomes more top-heavy than before.

DEVELOPMENT ISSUES

THE MILITARY AS NATIONAL DEVELOPMENT AGENCY

The Military Balance has noted previously that the Tanzanian two-year conscription period includes "civic duties," which implies the use of the military in what Canadians would term an "assistance to the civil authority" rather than an "aid of the civil power" role. Depending on the nature of these "civic duties," there may be a positive effect on civilian infrastructure development. Since there is no evidence that Tanzania has secured licences to build military equipment locally, this possible development use of the military can be discounted. The military procurement impact on the Tanzanian industrial structure would therefore likely be limited to the effect of works and buildings construction. Available statistics do not allow the extent of this effect to be estimated.

Tanzania has made use of a mixed volunteer professional/conscript system in which the conscripts accounted for 44% of the total personnel strength, or about 20,000. The professional component accounted for four tenths of one percent of the 18-32 male population. The conscript term was two years, and the annual turnover would have been about 10,000, staggered perhaps on a quarterly basis in order to even the impact on the training system. This represented about 4% of the available annual male cohort of approximately 250,000, or about three tenths of one percent of the male population aged 18-32. The military force level in general, and military conscription in particular, would have had a limited effect on the labour market and on unemployment rates. Without an analysis of the specific curriculum of military training programs, it is difficult to assess the amount of transferable skills involved and the amount of human capital formation that takes place. In any event with an annual turnover of three-tenths of one percent of the 18-32 male population it would seem that the human capital formation effect is not large, though perhaps discernible. It is unclear whether the force reductions planned will include both the conscript and the professional components or whether the intent will be to shift to an all-volunteer force—which would limit the actual savings possible.

The Defence Sufficiency Structure analysis recommended a reduction of the Tanzanian defence forces by 22,440 positions. Some concern may be felt about the labour market impact of a reduction. If the current conscript-professional balance is maintained, perhaps 9,200 of that reduction would be conscripts. This could be achieved over a two-year period by reducing the annual intake from 10,000 to 5,000. This might reduce public sector employment by 4,600 for each annual cohort of 250,000 males. In addition, there would be a reduction of approximately 11,600 full-time professional positions.

THE ODA FUNGIBILITY ISSUE

Over the 1990-94 period Tanzania's ODA averaged approximately eleven times the Tanzanian defence budget. A reasonable question is whether the level of ODA has permitted Tanzania to spend more on its military than would otherwise have been the case. With ODA at 139.1% of CGE there is ample donor leverage. However, since Tanzania has already announced force reductions in line with this study's proposals, there appears to be no need for any donor pressure to be applied. Indeed, there may well be an argument for additional donor financial assistance on the model of that provided to Uganda, to assist with the reintegration of redundant military personnel into civilian society.

CASE STUDY 8: KENYA

STRATEGIC THREAT ANALYSIS

A geostrategic Threat Analysis for Kenya should normally consider three areas:
- threats of confrontation with other states with which Kenya shares borders, including Ethiopia, Somalia, Sudan, Kenya, and Uganda,

- the possibility that a civil war or insurrection in a neighbouring country will spill over into Kenyan territory either through combatant forces making use of Kenyan territory, or through the movement of refugees fleeing from that civil war or insurrection, and
- threats to Kenya's internal political stability and armed resistance to the civil authority, possibly aided by the government of one of the neighbouring countries.

THE NEIGHBOURING STATES AS THREATS TO KENYA

Ethiopia appears to have had no great prior history of border disputes with Kenya that might lead to serious concerns about the threat of Ethiopian military action. Indeed, Kenyan concern about Somalian claims against Kenyan territory led to Kenyan verbal support of Ethiopia during the Ogaden war between Somalia and Ethiopia. Nonetheless, the successful revolution in Ethiopia raises the question of the direction of the new Ethiopian government or the prospects of a new civil war as the various factions that make up the new Ethiopian administration continue to compete with each other. There is concern that a Christian-Muslim split might be exploited by traditional meddlers such as Libya or Sudan. Since Ethiopia has a substantial Muslim population that some sources estimate to be almost the same size as that of the Coptic Christians, this conflict cannot be ruled out. However, the Transitional Government has proposed a devolved federal structure that gives each of the nine federal states the right to secede, as a means of accommodating regional ethnic and religious differences. Moreover, the civil war resulted in widespread destruction of the inventories of Soviet equipment held within Ethiopia, and has destroyed so much of the national wealth of Ethiopia that it remains highly questionable that external arms suppliers such as the People's Republic of China would be prepared to sell military equipment to Ethiopia with such a small chance of payment in the immediate future. Thus there is little evidence that Ethiopia would represent a credible strategic threat to Kenya in the short to medium time frame. However, the possibility of renewed civil war in Ethiopia suggests that having to deal with Ethiopian refugees remains a possibility.

Somalia, prior to the civil war that led to the overthrow of the Barre administration and the subsequent descent into chaos, had serious border differences with Kenya. In the 1960s Somalia laid claim to large portions of Kenya's northeastern territories as part of its initiative to consolidate all of the Somali peoples within the Somali state. This was followed by support of the Shifta rising in those territories in the mid-1960s. During the Ogaden war between Somalia and Ethiopia, Kenya gave verbal support to Ethiopia and condemned U.S. support of Somalia. On one occasion in 1978 Kenyan military aircraft forced down an Egyptian plane carrying supplies to Somalia. However, the collapse of the Barre regime and the protracted Somali civil war before and after has, as in Ethiopia, led to the wholesale destruction of military equipment in Somalia. Moreover, the collapse of the government and much of the civilian infrastructure of Somalia leads to the question whether there is any capacity to provide a logistics base for any kind of military operation against Kenya, even if there were any evidence of the existence of a central government authority and the will to do so. Once again the most realistic threat to Kenya appears to be that of having to deal with massive trans-border flows of refugees. Given that Kenya, in the past, has followed policies of ethnic exclusion (should we say "ethnic cleansing"?) of Somalis as part of its security policy we might expect to see some difficulties in responding to further refugee displacement.

Uganda, under dictator Idi Amin, made claims in 1976 to parts of Kenya's western territory. This was followed in 1978 by the Ugandan-Tanzanian war, the ousting of Amin, the restoration of Milton Obote's Uganda People's Congress (UPC), and the subsequent withdrawal of the Tanzanian army. For a period at the conclusion of that war Kenya was the refuge for several hundred Amin officers, though these were eventually returned for trial to the Tanzanian-supervised Ugandan government in 1979. However, Uganda remained in a chaotic state in which tribal rivalries played a major part, particularly among the Nilotic Acholis and the Longos, who formed the majority of the army. Subsequent events in Uganda saw the development of the rebel National Resistance Army (NRA), the overthrow of Obote, a Longo, by Acholis led by Bazilio and Tito Okello, and the eventual acquisition of power by the NRA, led by Yoweri Museveni. Subsequent risings by Bagandan royalists, Nilotic remnants of the Okello-led army, and the Acholi-based Holy Spirit Battalion failed to overthrow the Museveni administration.

The internal policies of the Museveni administration have been directed toward national reconciliation and economic growth. As part of this there have been moves to reduce public sector costs. Since the military accounted for about 25% of central government spending and about 3% of GNP in 1991, reductions in military spending were necessary. A difficulty had been the need to provide employment for NRA members to enhance internal stability during the national reconciliation process. Decisions in 1995 by ODA donors to provide funding for what are, in effect, severance packages for redundant NRA members to facilitate their demobilization is a critical aid in the military reduction process. The Museveni administration's internal policies have been generally successful, but stable international relations with its neighbours are critical to their continued success. Ugandan security policy in general has appeared to emphasize peaceful relations with its neighbours. In April 1990 Uganda concluded a non-aggression treaty with Sudan. In July of the same year Uganda entered into a joint declaration of "peace and stability" with Djibouti, Ethiopia, Kenya, Somalia, and Sudan that included an agreement among the six states not to provide support to opposition groups in the other states. The 1993 Arusha Agreement and its 1994 expansion represented moves to re-establish elements of the East African Community and to enhance economic cooperation between the three principal East African states. Another example is the cooperative venture between Uganda, Tanzania, and South Africa in Alliance Airways, which the partners are trying (1995) to encourage Kenya to join.

However, the successful invasion of neighbouring Rwanda by the RPF, dominated by Tutsi exiles based in Uganda, has been led by Paul Kagame, the former Director of Military Intelligence of the NRA, who is assumed to have the tacit support of elements of the Ugandan NRA and arguably of the government as a whole. Moreover, Uganda has provided access to supplies and support for the SPLA operating in southern Sudan. This willingness to support rebel movements in neighbouring countries to the north and south stands in contrast to the pacific policies to the east. The Kenyan willingness to provide sanctuary to a number of the alleged leaders of the genocidal actions of the previous Rwandan government suggests that the two countries are potentially at cross purposes in the Rwandan crisis, though whether this would lead to a deterioration of Ugandan-Kenyan relations remains to be seen. On balance then, Uganda's declining military capabilities, coupled with cooperative behaviour toward Kenya, argue that it represents a remote strategic threat. Nonetheless, it is quite reasonable to expect a prudent Kenyan strategist, having seen the 1979 invasion of Tanzania by the Ugandan army, and the civil war and chaos that followed in Uganda, and having reasonable grounds to suspect Ugandan army involvement in the Tutsi insurrection in Rwanda, to view Uganda as a possible though remote strategic threat in the long run, though not in the next five years.

The 1977 closing of the border with *Tanzania* following the breakup of the East Africa Community (Kenya, Tanzania, and Uganda) included the cutting off of all mail and telephone links and direct air flights between the two countries. The 1979 visit to Tanzania by Kenyan President Moi included discussions of the border situation, but no headway was made until November 1983, when the two countries agreed to reopen their borders, to allow trade to resume, and to begin discussion about the resolution of the issue of the East Africa Community assets, the bulk of which Kenya had retained. Those discussions also included, as a gesture of goodwill, an agreement that neither would harbour fugitive criminals. Accordingly, in 1983 Tanzania returned to Kenya for trial two of the leaders of the 1982 attempted Kenyan air force coup, who had fled to Tanzania for asylum, and Kenya returned a member of the 1982 attempted coup in Tanzania. Since then relations between the two states have remained peaceable, and with the 1993 and 1994 Arusha accords have moved strongly toward significant economic cooperation. Nor does the initial ideological divide between Kenya and Tanzania, which was a major factor in the breakup of the Community, represent as significant a difference as it once did, with Tanzania's moving away from radical socialist economic policies. The Kenyan strategist should have no concern about recent Tanzanian behaviour and there is no evidence of any Tanzanian intent to threaten Kenyan security. Moreover, the substantial 1995 planned reductions in the Tanzanian forces, which would have amounted to a cut of approximately 50% in personnel strength, represented additional evidence of Tanzania's peaceful intentions. However, while Tanzania is an increasingly unlikely real threat to Kenyan security, it seems prudent to consider a Kenya-Tanzania conflict as a possible though remote contingency to be guarded against.

Sudan has not had a significant history of serious border conflicts with Kenya. However, the border remains ambiguous, in that the administrative and international borders do not coincide. This was of little concern formerly, since the sparsely settled border area had been viewed as of little economic value and remote from the real areas of interest of both countries. However, recent suggestions of oil deposits in the "Elemi triangle" have now heightened border concerns.

The Sudan-Iran linkage has been of increasing concern to all Sudan's neighbours. Military cooperation between the two Islamic states has included the provision of port facilities in Port Sudan to Iran as well as Iranian financial support for the purchase of Chinese-built weaponry by the Sudanese government, which has allowed significant increments to be made to Sudan's military capacity. From a capabilities standpoint this justifies heightened Kenyan concerns. The question of Sudan's intentions may be equally worrisome when one considers the increasing support of violent Islamic fundamentalism by the government of Sudan backed by Iran. This has included training and support of small forces active in southern Egypt and more recently in Eritrea. Other cross-border meddling has involved the support of the Holy Spirit Army/Lord's Resistance Army in northern Uganda, though this can be rationalized as a response to Ugandan support of the SPLA in southern Sudan. Adherents to Islam make up only about 6% of the native Kenyan population and are themselves split along ethno-linguistic lines between the coastal population, which is largely Arabic in origin and influenced by the more radical Islamic Party of Kenya, and those inland, who follow the United Moslems of Africa, which claims membership among African (i.e. non-Arab) Moslems. To this Islamic mix we could add the 400,000 Somali refugees in the northeastern areas. The heightening ethno-linguistic tensions within Kenya between Bantu-speaking and Nilotic-speaking populations, which are becoming increasingly politicized and violent, are a major concern. To add to them the possibility of outside meddling in the Islamic population, or even directly in the Bantu-Nilotic split, is increasingly worrisome. Sudanese cross-border meddling in other states serves as a discomforting precedent.

The Sudanese civil war, which reflects the Nilotic-Semitic ethnic fault line, as well as the Islamic-Christian-Animist religious fault line, would seem to suggest that any direct military initiative of the Sudanese government against Kenya would result in highly fragile logistics lines through territory held by SPLA or SPLA-United forces. An alliance of convenience between the Kenyan Army and guerrilla forces could present a Sudanese force with a difficult situation. Sudanese moves to split the Nuer-based SPLA-United from the Dinka-based SPLA following the fall of the Mengistu government in Ethiopia, a principal logistics support of the SPLA, suggested that SPLA capacities might be in decline. The Sudan/SPLA equation also seemed to be affected by reports of other support for Sudan, including a 1995 report of new French-supplied satellite and perhaps air reconnaissance data on SPLA force locations, suggestions that France intervened to permit Sudanese forces to transit through the Central African Republic to attack SPLA forces from the rear, and a 1996 report that Sudan was using the airport in Bunia as a logistics airhead to supply its forces in south-western Sudan. However, the balance shifted again in late 1996 with a successful SPLA campaign, which almost reached Juba, and reestablished SPLA's hold on parts of southern Sudan. The SPLA campaign appears to draw logistics support from Uganda and possibly Ethiopia again. Kenyan diplomatic efforts, in concert with its partners in the Inter-Governmental Authority on Drought and Development (IGADD), which includes Uganda, Ethiopia, and Eritrea, to contribute to a political settlement of the long running civil war have a strong element of self-interest.

Increasing Sudanese military capabilities, a developing pattern of cross-border meddling, and a potential border dispute should lead a prudent Kenyan general staff to look to its defensive capacity against Sudan.

CIVIL WAR SPILLOVER

Kenya has agreements with each of its neighbours to deny its territory to rebel or opposition forces. Kenya has enough military capability to enforce these agreements if it wishes to do so. However, Kenya has had substantial inflows of refugees from neighbouring civil wars. These are estimated to total by early 1993 some 400,000 Somalis, 80,000 Ethiopians, and 20,000 Sudanese (*Africa South of the Sahara* 1995). Two responses to the refugee problem can involve the Kenyan military: the support of local police forces in ensuring the maintenance of civil authority in controlling refugee movements; and the provision of relief supplies through military logistics capabilities to refugee populations until such time as the civil authority can deal adequately with the problem.

WAR WITH SUDAN

Since Kenya has agreed not to allow the use of its territory by rebel groups, it seems unlikely that Sudan would be drawn into a declaration of war (overt or undeclared) on that basis. This would leave the question of the Elemi triangle as a potential issue if it cannot be resolved diplomatically. The third, and more remote casus belli, might be based on the imperial Islam theme—though this seems less reasonable.

The practical problems that Sudan would have, however, in mounting an invasion of Kenya suggest that such a war is highly improbable. Modern wars are increasingly dominated by the logistics factor—and especially by the quantities of fuel that are consumed by large numbers of armoured fighting vehicles. Consequently, an examination of the logistics capabilities of the Sudanese forces is critical in developing a concept of operations. The nearest railhead to the Kenya border is at Wau—a distance of approximately 1,400 km over roads that are classed as "improved" and "partly improved," with sections of the 600 km road from Juba to the border classed "impassable in bad weather"; and these roads run through territory partially controlled by SPLA, who encircled the towns of Torit and Kapoeta during the late 1995 campaign and who have also periodically cut the rail line from Wau to Babanusa. The river alternative involves a 1,200 km route from Kosti to Juba followed by the same 600 km overland route from Juba to the border; traffic on the White Nile has been attacked in the past by SPLA forces based in the traditional Dinka lands south of Malakal. The three airheads in southern Sudan are located at Wau, Malakal (700 km by river from Juba), and Juba; the capacity of air logistics to supply a field force is limited even in first world states, and that of Sudan is far more limited. Kenya, on the other hand, has a railhead at Kitale (500 km from the border) and a surfaced all-weather road to within a few km of the border. The logistics factor is massively in favour of Kenya. In addition, until and unless the SPLA is decisively defeated, their capacity to disrupt an extraordinarily long and tenuous Sudanese line of communications (LOC) would seem to make the Sudanese logistics problem almost insurmountable.

There appears to be a substantial air advantage to Sudan, with 48 fighters and FGA compared to the 18 of Kenya. However, 18 of the Sudanese aircraft are the short-legged Chinese J-5s and J-6s. Their combat range is not quite the distance between Juba and Kitale and Eldoret, where the main northern Kenyan airfields are located. Were Juba's airfield or fuel supplies to be knocked out, the nearest airfields are at Wau and Malakal, which are beyond the combat radius of both the J-6s and the 11 F-7s/MIG-21s. Given reservations about maintenance levels and sortie rates, the capability of the Sudanese air force to achieve air superiority is highly doubtful, particularly if the Juba base is damaged or knocked out. A sensible Sudanese General Staff should recommend against a war with Kenya on the basis that success would be improbable given the LOC problems. Moreover, any initial success would result in lengthening Sudanese LOCs and weakening its air cover while shortening the Kenyan LOCs. This is not a recipe for success. A concept of operations for a more limited war strategy might involve a border crossing, the seizure of a limited territory, and/or the mauling of one or more Kenyan units. Once concessions had been extracted the raiding force might withdraw. Once again a prudent

Sudanese General Staff planner should advise against the idea. The long and difficult LOC problem makes Sudan equally vulnerable to a followup Kenyan raid which, if it were to knock out the Juba airfield, which is well within the combat radius of Kenyan F-5s operating from Eldoret and Kitale, could place Sudan in a very difficult situation. A Sudanese raid would thus be dependent upon catching all the Kenyan aircraft on the ground; if they were at any of the other five major Kenyan airfields then the raid would fail in its purpose to knock out the Kenyan air force.

In summary the relatively low probability of Sudanese success in a war against Kenya reinforces the low likelihood of such a war Until Sudan has been able to successfully conclude the civil war against the SPLA and to deal successfully with its severe LOC weaknesses.

THE MILITARY BALANCE OF POWER, 1996-97

THE LOCAL STRATEGIC CONTEXT
(RANKED IN ORDER OF ESTIMATED TOTAL COMBAT POTENTIAL)

Country	Air Force				Army			Navy	
	Fighter Sqns	FGA Sqns	COIN Attack Sqns	COIN Transport Sqns	ADEs	IDEs	COIN Bns	Subs	Patrol Craft
Ethiopia	–	5.3	1.1	1.5	3.5	27	NA	–	–
Sudan	0.6	2.4	0.3	1.9	2.8	26	19	–	6
Tanzania	1.5	–	–	0.3	0.2	5	–	–	16
Kenya	–	1.1	3.4	0.8	0.8	2.7+1	2	–	7
Uganda	–	0.3	0.3	0.4	0.2	4	–	–	–
Somalia	–	–	NA	NA	–	–	NA	–	–

Somalia's forces are in almost total disarray. *Ethiopia's* forces are improving but the continuing political fluidity makes capability forecasting still problematical. *Kenya's* F-5s are shown in *The Military Balance* as FGA; since they are equipped with Sidewinder air-to-air missiles they should be classified in the regional context as light fighters and are likely to be superior to Tanzania's fighters. Similarly *The Military Balance* classifies Kenya's Hawk aircraft as COIN aircraft, though the version held by Kenya are better classed as light FGA. Not shown are the 2.4 squadrons of light attack helicopters, including one squadron equipped with TOW anti-tank missiles. They would be a very powerful combat multiplier against opposing armoured vehicles. Kenya's force structure indicates a concern for maintaining a significant COIN capability. Given the fluidity of the situation on its northern and northeastern frontiers this seems a sensible approach.

Tanzania's air defence artillery resources are not shown. The 20 SAM-3 and particularly the 20 SAM-6 missile launchers could be expected to take a heavy toll of ground attack aircraft without anti-missile resources. Nor are the massive Tanzanian field artillery resources shown.

When qualitative differences between aircraft types are taken into account, Sudan's air force is perhaps 40% superior to that of Kenya and could theoretically win an air superiority battle, though it would be very seriously damaged—reduced perhaps by two-thirds. It would, however, still be capable of playing a role in ensuing operations, seriously limiting the ability of Kenya's critical attack helicopters to operate against Sudanese armour. However, the distance factor already cited suggests that a single air superiority battle would be unlikely and that a pattern of local short-term air superiority by either side would be more likely. Given Sudan's strategic dependency on the Juba airfield, a critical question would be the adequacy of air defence warning radars to provide sufficient warning of a Kenyan raid to permit air defence fighters to become airborne to protect the airfield. Kenya, on the other hand, is not as dependent on a single air base, though its air defence artillery appears less capable, particularly in its missile capabilities, than is Sudan's.

When qualitative differences are taken into consideration Sudan has the greatest main battle tank combat capability. Kenya has about 33% of the Sudanese capability and about four times Tanzania's combat power. While Kenyan anti-armour capability is further strengthened by its highly effective anti-tank helicopters, their use would be dependent on the maintenance of local air superiority to protect them from Sudanese fighter aircraft. In theory then, Sudan has the capability to win an armour battle with Kenya. The fly in the ointment, however, is getting the Sudanese MBTs to the front. The maintenance attrition in attempting to drive MBTs 1,400 km is horrendous—the reason why armies use wheeled tank transporters to move MBTs any distance. Moreover, a tank transporter carrying a 35-45 tonne MBT requires good, well maintained roads, a severe and perhaps insurmountable problem for the Sudanese army on the Kenyan front. Kenya, on the other hand, has a much better road system. The long war of attrition, as opposed to the short war of the armoured battle, places a high premium on artillery and infantry resources. Here Sudan holds a four-to-one advantage in artillery and a three and a half-to-one advantage in manpower over Kenya. However, artillery imposes the greatest burden of all on the tonnage capacity of army logistics systems. Here again the inadequacy of the Sudanese transportation network would scupper the advantage in guns, particularly during the rainy season, when the Sudd becomes effectively impassable.

A Sudanese-Kenyan balance of power analysis provides a good example of how theoretical weapons inventory analysis can lead to misleading conclusions if it ignores terrain and space factors. The extremely long LOC of a Sudanese expeditionary force, vulnerable not only to military disruption but also to weather, represents a critical degradation of a theoretical advantage—a factor also apparent in the weak performance of Sudanese government forces in the long-running war against SPLA. Indeed, 1992-94 successes against SPLA were as much attributable to the political success in splitting the SPLA-United faction from SPLA as they were to simple military success. Unless there is clear evidence of a considerable increase in Sudan's military logistics capabilities coupled with massive transportation infrastructure upgrades in southern Sudan, there is little compelling reason for large Kenyan imports of equipment beyond its current holdings. The only purchase that perhaps makes some sense might be in improving the air defence artillery capabilities of the army. However, significant reductions in the Kenyan military capabilities at this time do not seem warranted.

A DEFENCE SUFFICIENCY FORCE STRUCTURE FOR KENYA

The hypothetical Tanzanian current threat is an army corps of one composite division (one armoured brigade, two light infantry brigades, and an artillery brigade), plus one light infantry division (three light infantry brigades plus an artillery brigade). This is supported by an air force of one and a half fighter squadrons. The field artillery component is very powerful and has a significant air defence missile launcher component. Its weakness lies in its lack of mobility and limited expeditionary logistics capability. The existing Kenyan force structure consists of a composite division of one armoured and two light infantry brigades plus two battalions of light artillery supported by an air force of one and a half squadrons of fighter and FGA aircraft, plus two and a half squadrons of attack helicopters. The force is weak in APCs and artillery, relying on its attack helicopters to act in effect as airborne artillery. The Kenyan air force's air-to-air missile inventory gives it a critical advantage in the air battle. This force is sufficiently strong to conduct a successful strategic defensive in a one-front war with Tanzania. The reduction in overall Tanzanian force levels will allow Kenyan force levels to be reduced eventually without impairing Kenyan security.

The hypothetical Ugandan threat is four infantry brigades with limited heavy armour and close support artillery. In a one-front war the existing Kenyan force is more than adequate to deal with the theoretical Ugandan threat. The hypothetical Sudanese threat is made less likely because of terrain and distance factors. However, the overall numerical advantage of the Sudanese air force indicates that some attention should be paid to improving Kenyan air defence artillery capabilities.

The defence requirement of a composite light mechanized division of an armoured brigade, two infantry brigades, an artillery brigade, and a logistics brigade would require approximately 15,000 troops, plus military infrastructure of 5,000, for an army of 20,000, plus air and naval forces of about another 4,000, to a total of about 24,000. This is virtually identical to the existing force of 24,200. It is, in fact, a well designed balanced force and one suspects that Kenyan defence planners intend to gradually add equipment along the lines suggested to increase its mobility and firepower. If Tanzania reduces its force levels Kenya can contemplate reductions of its own—perhaps cutting one infantry brigade. The existing Kenyan defence forces would be capable of handling the COIN requirement.

MILITARY EXPENDITURES: ANALYSIS OF VARIABLES

THE MILITARY EXPENDITURES BALANCE
(BORDERING COUNTRIES IN ORDER OF GNP)

Country	1994			ME/GNP		MI/ME	
	GNP $US millions	ME $US millions	ME/GNP %	1990-94 %	1985-89 %	1990-94 %	1985-89 %
Sudan	NA	NA	NA	12.4	5.1	3.4	17.5
Kenya	6,565	198	2.3	4.0	4.0	12.6	34.7
Uganda	4,414	66	1.5	2.3	5.3	4.9	44.2
Ethiopia	4,947	128	2.6	8.8	29.4	26.4	73.7
Tanzania	2,058	79	3.8	4.8	8.0	13.7	55.2
Somalia	NA	NA	NA	2.5	8.7	66.7	74.0

Appendix 6 concludes that arms imports are not reflected in Military Expenditures for any states. Accordingly, adjusted figures are used. Regional trends in military spending have been dominated by civil war effects in Ethiopia, Somalia, Sudan, and Uganda. Uganda had been reducing military expenditures, Somalia is in a state of chaos in which inventories of weapons are being consumed in inter-clan fighting, and Ethiopia appears to be pursuing an internal conciliation process that may lower military spending and reallocate funds to economic reconstruction. Military expenditures are increasing in Sudan as a consequence of greater efforts to achieve a military resolution to the civil war and the more aggressive foreign policy of supporting fundamentalist forces in neighbouring states. Tanzanian expenditures have declined with the end of the South African-backed civil war in Mozambique and through enhanced cooperation levels with Kenya and Uganda, though the events in Rwanda and Burundi appear to have delayed further decreases.

SENSITIVITY ANALYSIS: THE EXISTING KENYAN SPENDING PATTERN
(MEAN 1990-94)

Spending Category	Budget Share %	$US per Position	Foreign Currency $US millions	Local Currency $US millions	Total $US millions
Equipment	12.6	1,038	25.0	0	25.0
PO&M	87.4	7,176	0	172.8	172.8
Total	100	8,214	25.0	172.8	197.8

CHANGE EFFECTS

- Changing Equipment spending
  by 1% of the Budget $1,978,000   (Foreign Currency)
- Changing Personnel strength by 1,000
  – Change in Equipment spending $1,038,000   (Foreign Currency)
  – Change in PO&M spending $7,176,000   (Local Currency)
  – Total change in Military
    spending $8,214,000
- Changing the Praetorian
  Index by 1 $5,876,000   (Local Currency)

THE DEFENCE SUFFICIENCY BUDGET

The threat analysis supports the existing force structure. Equipment purchases may decline, as there is no great need to massively upgrade Kenyan holdings, though as a percentage of the defence budget they are reasonable at present. Military PO&M spending warrants investigation, however, in order to reduce the Praetorian Index, which at 29.5 was the third highest in East Africa over the 1990-94 period, and 44% higher than the East

African mean of 20.5. A decrease in the Praetorian Index to the East African mean could result in mean annual savings of $52.9 million, an amount equivalent to 0.8% of GNP or 6.0% of ODA for the 1990-94 period.

Mean 1990-94 Budget without changes	$ 197,800,000
Decrease in Praetorian Index	$ 52,900,000
Mean 1989-93 Budget with changes	$ 144,900,00

IS KENYA SPENDING TOO MUCH ON ITS MILITARY?

The answer to our question is Yes and No. In 1990-94 Kenya spent less as a percentage of GNP than all of its neighbours except Uganda. As well it had the lowest military expenditure as a percentage of Central Government Expenditures. However, Kenya's military forces represent an economically privileged elite, with estimated personnel, operations, and maintenance spending levels significantly greater than either the Sub-Saharan or the East African. This seems in part to be directed to the maintenance of military loyalty to the Moi administration—perhaps an uncomfortable precursor to the rise of military Praetorianism in Kenya.

SOCIAL MILITARIZATION ANALYSIS

PRAETORIAN AND SPARTAN INDICES
(1990-94 MEANS)

Country	Praetorian Index	Spartan Index	Total Regular Personnel
Sudan	39.1	3.7	85,560
Kenya	29.5	1.1	24,080
Tanzania	22.9	2.2	34,600
Ethiopia	11.7	2.2	120,000
Uganda	6.4	3.4	62,000
Somalia	NA	2.4	NA

DEVELOPMENT ISSUES

THE MILITARY AS NATIONAL DEVELOPMENT AGENCY

The unusually high ratio of military engineers in the Kenyan Army (close to 20% of total army strength according to *The Military Balance* force structure description, as opposed to the 2-10% of NATO forces and the approximately 5% of most other Sub-Saharan states) suggested that the Kenyan military engineers might be used for national infrastructure development. However, discussions with Canadian and American sources in Nairobi indicated that the Kenyan engineers' substantial construction engineering role is limited to military bases rather than infrastructure construction in the civilian sector. Recent reports (*New African*, July-August, 1996) of the establishment of a small arms ammunition factory at Eldoret in cooperation with the Belgian Corporation Fabrique Nationale de Herstal, a subsidiary of the French GIAT Industries, suggests the possible beginning of an arms export-oriented industrial strategy supported in part by Kenyan military procurement. Other military procurement impacts on the Kenyan industrial structure, however, would likely be limited to the effect of works and buildings construction. Since it appears this role is fulfilled by military engineers, its effect on the local economy will be limited.

Kenya uses a volunteer professional army with high pay scales. Such armies characteristically can only afford a limited force size and consequently have a much smaller effect on unemployment rates in the general labour market, since they constitute such a small portion of it. Kenya's military constitutes approximately 0.8% of the male population between 18 and 32 years of age. Its effect on general unemployment rates in Kenya is therefore insignificant for practical purposes. Such armies, where there is a substantial difference between their compensation scale and that of the general labour market, are also characterized by comparatively low turnover or quit rates. This should be the case in Kenya, and therefore, although the military individual training system represents an investment in human capital formation in technologically advanced skills, the transfer of these to the civilian sector would have a limited, and for all practical purposes insignificant, effect.

THE ODA FUNGIBILITY ISSUE

With ODA at about 443% of military expenditures there is ample opportunity for Kenya to divert its own spending to the military sector. However, with ODA at about 46% of CGE, donor states have considerable leverage to encourage reductions in Kenyan military expenditures if they should choose to do so.

8

THE MIDDLE EAST

THE REGIONAL STRATEGIC CONTEXT

No other region of the world has seen as much inter-state bloodshed since the end of the Second World War as this area. Three major strategic conflicts have remained largely unresolved and have fuelled continuing confrontations.

INTER-STATE ISSUES: THE ARAB-ISRAELI CONFLICT

The first inter-state issue has been the conflict over the establishment of the state of Israel on territory that had been inhabited in part by non-Jewish peoples. The expulsion/withdrawal of a large proportion of the Palestine population from the new state following the first Arab-Israeli war in 1948-49 provided a continuing spur to Arab hostility to the new state, a hostility manifested in a refusal to recognize the international legitimacy of Israel and a dedication to its elimination. The subsequent three Arab-Israeli wars—the Suez conflict of 1956-57 (when Israel allied itself with France and Britain), the Six Days War of 1967, and the Yom Kippur War (or Ramadan War if one's perspective is Arab) of 1973—succeeded only in demonstrating that Israeli military superiority made war an untenable strategic option for the Arab side. This was recognized initially by Egypt in 1979 with the conclusion of the peace treaty that saw territory captured by Israel returned to Egyptian control. That treaty, however, did not resolve the Palestine issue. Continued Israeli occupation of the West Bank, together with suggestions by parties in Israel that the West Bank should be incorporated into a greater Israel, continued to play havoc with Israeli-Arab relations. Israel's continuing occupation of the Syrian Golan Heights, because of its immense military strategic value to Israel's security, formed another contentious issue.

The 1992 election of the Rabin administration in Israel, with its "Land for Peace" foreign policy strategy, led to significant developments that suggested that this long-running conflict might be moving slowly toward resolution. A first step in negotiations led to the "Declaration of Principles on Interim Self-Government Arrangements" and the establishment of the Palestine National Authority in Jericho and the Gaza strip in 1994. The "Declaration of Principles" also promised Israeli-Palestine negotiations on the permanent status of the territories by 1997, though the implementation program is now increasingly behind schedule. In 1994 a separate peace treaty was signed between Jordan and Israel—the second such treaty between Israel and an Arab state. The long-term effects of the 1996 election of the new Likud administration, with its opposition to extensions of Palestine self-rule, the return of the Golan to Syria, and to reductions of Israeli settlements in the West Bank remain to be seen.

PERSIAN GULF SECURITY

The fundamental strategic issue in this theatre concerns the control and security of the oil supplies, which are critical to the economic well-being of the developed world. The Gulf Cooperation Council (GCC) is a loose alliance of militarily weak oil producers led by Saudi Arabia, a group incapable of providing adequately for its members' security. Consequently, the two regional great powers, Iraq and Iran, have vied for strategic dominance in the area.

Under the Shah, Iran sought, with Western acquiescence, to be the Gulf arbiter. After his overthrow in 1979 by the Islamic Revolution, Iraq saw (mistakenly) an opportunity to seize primacy. The 1980-88 Iraq-Iran war was effectively a strategic draw, with the economies of both states badly damaged. The 1990-91 Kuwait War further damaged, though it did not eliminate, Iraq's strategic capacity and its ability to play a dominant role in the theatre. The 1992 Iranian seizure of Abu Musa in the south end of the Gulf, together with additional weapons purchases and continuing support of Muslim fundamentalist groups in the Middle East and North Africa, continues to worry the GCC states who continue, in turn, to look to the West for security guarantees. The critical strategic importance of Gulf oil supplies guarantees that the West, and particularly the United States, will continue to be involved in the theatre.

THE FUTURE OF LEBANON

Lebanon's troubles are driven by both internal and external forces. Internally, Lebanon enjoys the doubtful advantage of quadrapartite religious rivalries between Maronite Christian, Druze, Sunni Islam, and Shia Islam, as well as a variety of smaller interests. The rivalry and bloodshed destroyed any semblance of a coherent central government in Lebanon. Externally, Lebanon had been an object of attention by the Palestine Liberation Organization (PLO) because of its utility as a base for operations against Israel subsequent to the PLO's having been ejected from or else placed under stringent controls by Egypt, Jordan, and Syria. It has been the focus of the attention of the Israelis, who wished to establish a *cordon sanitaire* in Southern Lebanon, in conjunction with Israel's Christian allies, to limit PLO raids into Israel proper. Finally, it has been the object of Syrian ambitions to physically incorporate Lebanon into Greater Syria. The actions of the external players in supporting one internal faction or another has contributed to the impossibility of creating a coherent central government. Conversely, the chaos of the internal situation, which presents an occupying army with a potentially high casualty rate among its occupying forces, together with the danger of a full-scale Israel-Syria confrontation, has limited the ability of the external players to resolve the difficulties.

Recent trends have been for a lower level of violence and greater strategic caution on the part of the external players without much real progress to a peace in Lebanon. Unhappily, the low level of chronic violence seems destined to continue for at least the short to medium term.

THE REGIONAL SOCIO-ECONOMIC BALANCE OF POWER (1990-94 MEANS)

Country	Population (millions)	GNP ($US billions)	ME ($US millions)
Iran	60,400	131,580	5,138
Saudi Arabia	17,100	127,980	27,690
Israel	4,700	68,190	6,532
Egypt	58,700	40,668	1,695
Syria	13,800	59,375	8,890
Iraq	18,800	18,257	12,641
Libya	4,700	29,808	2,415
Sudan	28,000	11,941	1,476
Jordan	3,700	4,968	461

THE REGIONAL MILITARY BALANCE OF POWER, 1996-97

Country	Fighter Squadrons	FGA Squadrons	ABEs	IBEs
Israel	31.6	12.1	14.3	12.7
Egypt	23.2	11.4	12.2	11.7
Syria	20.7	14.6	15.3	9.3
Iraq	11.3	8.1	9.0	19.3
Iran	7.8	10.6	4.8	9.3
Saudi Arabia	7.6	10.2	3.5	5.3
Libya	13.1	10.3	7.4	13.9
Jordan	2.0	4.1	3.8	2.7
Sudan	0.6	2.4	1.1	8.7

Note: Libya does not have the manpower to man the equipment levels it possesses.

INTRA-STATE ISSUES

To these interstate conflicts must be added the additional phenomenon of the continuing rise of Muslim fundamentalism, driven largely by population growth which is outstripping economic growth, the attendant problem of high unemployment rates, wide disparities in income and wealth levels from state to state and within states, and the creation of fertile ground for proponents of radical solutions.

MILITARIZATION LEVELS

Country	Financial: Economy ME/GNP %		Financial: Government ME/CGE %		Spartan Index		Praetorian Index	
	90-94	85-89	90-94	85-89	90-94	85-89	90-94	85-89
Iraq	69.2	49.7	NA	NA	36.1	57.9	20.5	6.2
Saudi Arabia	21.6	19.1	58.0	33.9	9.1	5.8	17.6	20.5
Syria	15.0	22.1	59.3	57.2	32.5	38.7	4.8	5.1
Sudan	12.4	5.1	268.0	106.0	3.7	2.7	39.1	16.1
Israel	10.9	18.0	24.1	30.2	43.7	46.2	2.7	4.3
Jordan	9.3	29.5	25.6	75.8	28.1	29.2	3.0	0.7
Libya	8.1	17.1	16.1	21.9	18.6	21.8	3.8	5.4
Egypt	4.2	10.7	9.7	20.8	14.3	17.1	2.0	5.8
Iran	3.9	8.4	17.0	41.1	12.2	13.6	3.5	4.9
Means	17.18	19.97	59.73	48.36	22.03	25.89	10.78	7.67

MILITARY EXPENDITURE LEVELS AND TRENDS

From about 1983 to 1989, military expenditures in the Arab-Israeli theatre showed a steady and in some cases, such as Egypt, a strikingly steep reduction. The Persian Gulf War does not appear to have affected this process, as it seems that the set of states involved in this long-running conflict have effectively concluded that military conflict cannot provide a political solution and that the example of the Egypt-Israel peace treaty offered a more sensible route to conflict resolution. Unfortunately, the Persian Gulf theatre is quite another situation. With the end of the Iran-Iraq war in 1988 it appeared that military expenditures in this area might also be reduced. However, Iraq's invasion of Kuwait, and threats to the rest of the GCC states, saw expenditures, which had been declining, turn up again in 1989. The post-1991 Gulf War period, with Hussein still in power in Iraq and new worries about the possibilities of Iranian rearmament, saw a short-run increase in military expenditures in the states of this theatre, though this appears to have reversed again in 1993. Among the peripheral states, military expenditures in Libya have parallelled the decline among the Arab-Israeli set, while expenditures in Sudan have increased sharply.

FINANCING MILITARY EXPENDITURES

Because of the immense scale of the military forces involved, the level of military expenditures required to maintain them has meant that with the exception of Saudi Arabia and the GCC states, the remaining states of the region, in addition to reported budgetary expenditures on the military sector, have had to resort to supplier credits on a vast scale, as well as to the conscript premium also on a considerable scale.

THE SOCIAL IMPACT OF MILITARY EXPENDITURES

The heavy reliance on conscription and on quickly deployable reserves has led to an extraordinary level of social militarization in the region. The high level of real military threat in the region has led, however, to Praetorian Index levels that are low in comparison to the other regions of Africa, and in some cases consistent with NATO norms. This suggests that compensation levels for military forces is strongly influenced by the external threat environment. Where the threat level is high, there is a requirement for an efficient deployment of scarce financial resources, particularly when the state is not particularly wealthy. This requirement tends, therefore, to hold down excessive military personnel expenditures and to limit the size of the economically privileged class if, indeed, any exists. This phenomenon stands in striking contrast to that in West Africa, where the weak or effectively non-existent external threat environment has allowed the military of those countries to concentrate upon involvement in the internal political affairs of their countries such that they become a richly rewarded elite of economic rent-takers. Such does not appear to be the case in many of the states of the North East Africa/Middle East region.

The highest Praetorian Index levels are found in Sudan and Saudi Arabia, as are among the lowest Spartan Indices. In Saudi Arabia's case this appears to reflect in part a history of a volunteer military in an extremely wealthy state in which members of the extended Royal Family and their key supporters hold high military offices. With the post-Gulf War buildup in force strength in Saudi Arabia the Praetorian Index has fallen as the Spartan Index has risen. Sudan, however, appears to be more consistent with the Sub-Saharan model than with the Middle East/Persian Gulf model.

THE MILITARY AS DEVELOPMENT FACTOR

This region contains the one state in which the use of the military as a national development agency has been established as a matter of state policy. After the conclusion of the Egyptian-Israeli peace treaty the Egyptian government specifically assigned national economic development roles to its military forces. As a consequence the Egyptian military has become, in effect, a major military parastatal organization with significant operations in infrastructure construction, import substitution policies, particularly in the military equipment fields, economic technology transfer initiatives, military equipment export strategies, and unemployment reduction policies.

In one sense the massive Egyptian military parastatal could be regarded as an alternative model for the defence conversion hypothesis. In this model the structural adjustment option of simply shrinking the military sector and causing heavy short-term economic and labour supply disruptions, which in turn could lead to major social dislocations and political instabilities, is avoided. Instead, the defence sector undergoes a gradual transformation into a series of public sector parastatals that gradually convert themselves from a military to a civilian orientation. The adherents of the traditional defence conversion hypothesis would question the economics of the military parastatal, however. In addition, the scope for economic praetorianism, as retired military officers take positions in the parastatal on the basis of their rank rather than their civilian management skills, should be questioned.

This study was struck by the extent of the Egyptian military parastatal. It was also struck by the absence of significant study of that parastatal in the economic development literature—indeed, the most extensive reports on it have been found in the military and intelligence literatures, where the emphasis has been military rather than economic. This study has barely scratched the surface of what is a fascinating case study of the deliberate use of the military in national development roles. What is required, especially in terms of the ultimate validity of the defence conversion hypothesis, is a far more exhaustive study of the cost effectiveness of the Egyptian military parastatal experiment—and this cost effectiveness assessment must address social cost effectiveness as well as financial cost effectiveness.

CASE STUDY 9: JORDAN

STRATEGIC THREAT ANALYSIS

A geostrategic Threat Analysis for Jordan should normally consider four areas:
- war with Israel either alone or as a member of an Arab coalition,
- war with neighbouring Islamic states, Syria, Iraq, and Saudi Arabia, and
- threats to Jordan's internal political stability and armed resistance to the civil authority stemming from the Palestine expatriate population resident in Jordan.

WAR WITH ISRAEL

One hypothetical scenario might stem from an Israeli decision to invade Jordan in a one-front war. Given Israeli advantages in total force strength, technology, and military performance, Israel would easily win such a war at the operational/strategic level. However, the grand strategic purpose of such a war is difficult to comprehend, especially now that Jordan and Israel have signed a peace treaty—the second between Israel and an Arab state. One consequence would be the acquisition of *all* of the Palestine population and the requirement to administer and police all of their territories. It is difficult to see any Israeli enthusiasm for a doubling of the *intifada* problem, particularly when Israeli policy has been moving toward increased cooperation with the Palestine population. An unprovoked Israeli attack on Jordan would impact heavily on British, French, and American opinion and could result in constraints on critical American financial support and loan guarantees to Israel. It is difficult to view this scenario as a serious contingency. A second scenario, a one-front war launched by Jordan, must be viewed as even more improbable, given the Israeli strength advantage, which would guarantee a quick Jordanian defeat.

The third scenario might be that of a war between Israel and a general Arab coalition. Here the model might be that of the general Arab coalition of 1948, or the more limited coalition of 1967. The grand strategic objective could be the recapture of territory lost in the 1962 war or the 1948 war, or even the elimination of Israel on the 1948 war objectives model. The military strategic plan would involve a three-front (Syria, Jordan, Egypt) war presenting Israel with the most difficult strategic situation, particularly if a general *intifada*-style uprising could be coordinated with the military operations. The outcome of such a conventional war is somewhat more difficult to predict. Paradoxically, however, an impending Arab conventional victory might lead to the most dangerous strategic outcome of all—the use of Israeli nuclear weapons to prevent conventional defeat. However, putting together such a coalition would be exceedingly difficult, since it is not at all obvious what the strategic motivation of each participant might be—particularly in view of the potential costs in either a conventional or a nuclear scenario. It is unclear what Egypt, the most militarily important member of such a coalition, might expect to gain; it is, however, clear what cost Egypt might expect to pay. Jordan's motivation would be equally unclear, particularly since it has concluded a peace treaty with Israel that includes agreements on the always difficult issue of water rights. Syria's objective would be to regain the Golan. Nonetheless, one would conclude that such a coalition is improbable and that this scenario is therefore equally improbable.

However, there is a contingency under which such a scenario becomes more probable. That is the possible succession in Israel of a radical administration so devoted to the Judea/Samaria concept that it might seek to reverse the peace process that the Rabin administration had created and to try to drive all of the remaining Palestine population out of the West Bank, Gaza, and Israel itself. Such a move might so inflame public opinion in the Arab world that the general Arab coalition would come about. Increased public support for the Moslem Brotherhood in Egypt might also contribute to such pressures. However, the effects of the peace initiatives undertaken by the Labour administration are still largely intact, in spite of attempts by extremists on both sides to derail the process, and the Grand Coalition war does not seem likely in the short term (up to five years).

WAR WITH THE NEIGHBOURING ARAB STATES

Saudi Arabia can be excluded as a strategic military threat for several reasons. First, Saudi Arabia has no recent history of initiating war with its neighbours. One must be sceptical of the idea that one of the two remaining Arab monarchies in the Middle East would launch a war against the other. Indeed, the historical relationship between the two monarchies has been positive, and Saudi Arabia has provided financial subsidies to Jordan. While the Jordanian failure to leap aboard the anti-Hussein coalition during the Gulf War led the Saudis to close their joint border and suspend financial support for a period, recent relations between the two have returned to normal. In any event it is difficult to see any benefit to Saudi Arabia in gaining possession of Jordanian territory, since it would result in Saudi Arabia gaining both Israel and Syria as border neighbours, with all the problems that come with managing those relations. Finally, gaining control of Jordan would also mean gaining direct responsibility for the Palestine expatriate population in Jordan, with all the difficulties that that would entail.

Syria's past relations with Jordan have reflected a number of differences, some of which have been serious. During the September 1970 suppression of the Palestine guerrillas in Jordan by the Jordanian army under the direction of King Hussein, a number of Syria-based tank units of the Palestine Liberation Army (PLA) invaded Jordanian territory, where they were ultimately defeated by the Jordanian Army. While these units were not part of the Syrian Army per se, they obviously operated with at least the acquiescence of the Syrian government of the day. That government was overthrown in November of that year, and General Hafiz al-Asad came to power. In the 1973 war with Israel a Jordanian tank corps was sent to the aid of the Syrian Army in the southern part of the Golan sector. On the other hand Syria and Jordan were sharply divided on the Iraq-Iran war: Syria, fearing Iraqi ambitions, supported Iran; Jordan, fearing the threat of Iranian fundamentalism to the oil-rich GCC states, which provide critical financial subsidies to it, supported Iraq. More recently the two states found themselves on opposite sides in the Gulf War: Syria provided troops to the Coalition forces (and gained a freer hand for its operations within Lebanon), but Jordan refused to be part of the Coalition, perhaps fearful of Iraqi retribution when the West eventually lost interest in maintaining the confrontation, and in any event economically dependent to some extent on the profits gained from Iraqi traffic through the Jordanian port of Aqaba. Syrian strategic policy has been primarily directed to the recovery of the Golan and the domination of Lebanon (the "Greater Syria" objective) rather than to a clearly articulated desire to control Jordan. Nonetheless, Jordanian strategists could expect Syria to exert pressure on Jordan to conform or acquiesce to Syrian objectives. Jordanian acquiescence to such pressures, given the Syria-Iraqi differences, could result in counter-pressure from Iraq or in an Israeli reaction, given the importance to Israel of Jordanian territory as a strategic glacis. Syrian possession of the territory south of the Yarmuk River around Irbid, for example, would bypass the Israeli position on the Golan. However, the probability of Syrian aggression against Jordanian territory seems remote, provided that Jordan can maintain control of its territory and preserve a credible military force, which would make an invasion a costly proposition, particularly if a quick *coup de main* could be prevented. While Syria is certainly the more powerful state, it cannot easily deploy all of its military forces against its smaller neighbour, given that it has a substantial force tied down in Lebanon. Also it must be continually concerned about the threat from an Israeli action or, if Saddam Hussein remains in power, from Iraq, when Western no-fly zone enforcement forces finally withdraw, and about relations with Turkey over water rights. Accordingly, the threat from Syria appears marginal at the moment, but one it is one that a prudent Jordanian general staff must be concerned with.

Iraq's relations with Jordan have been less tense in recent years than those with Syria. Jordan, together with the oil-rich states of the GCC, supported Iraq during the Iran-Iraq war. Jordan's port of Aqaba provided an important link with the outside world for Iraq after the war closed its own ports on the Persian Gulf and Syria closed its borders and its oil pipeline to Iraq. Moreover, during the Gulf War Jordan declined to join the coalition against Hussein and was very reluctant to comply with the economic sanctions against Iraq, actions that in the end caused it to lose financial support from the oil states. However, given the unpredictability of Hussein's foreign policies, it would be highly imprudent to rule out the possibility of an Iraqi move against Jordan. Accordingly, a prudent Jordanian general staff would want to maintain sufficient military power to make such an incursion costly and sufficiently time-consuming to allow other states to come to its aid. Paradoxically, however, the state that would be most likely to come to Jordan's aid might well be Israel, in that it would be unwilling to have Iraqi weapons so close to its borders. Such a situation could cause great internal strains within Jordan between the Palestine refugee population and the original Bedouin inhabitants. The defeat of Iraq in the Gulf War has reduced Iraqi military power but has by no means eliminated it. As long as the West is prepared to effectively maintain an air/naval garrison in the Gulf area, Iraqi strategic behaviour will remain relatively quiescent and there will be no overt threat from Iraq against Jordan. With the passage of time, declining Western military capabilities with the end of the Cold War, the desire of Western populations for an increasing "Peace Dividend," and the notoriously short attention span of Western public opinion, there may come a point when the Western garrisons have effectively been removed and the strategic controls on Iraq effectively abandoned. If that point is reached the Middle Eastern strategic context would again become unstable. Consequently, while there appears to be no strategic military threat from Iraq in the short run, Jordan must remain watchful in the long run.

THE INTERNAL SECURITY DIMENSION

The Palestine population in Jordan constitutes about 40-50% of the total population of 4.4 million. In addition, there are approximately one million Palestinians on the West Bank, over which King Hussein relinquished any residual claim of authority in 1988. That restored the Bedouin population to a bare majority position within Jordan. The 1994 creation of the Palestine National Authority in Gaza and Jericho reinforced the Jordan-Palestine disconnection. During the Arab-Israeli conflict following the 1948 war the PLA conducted guerrilla operations against Israel from the territories of adjacent Arab states. This led to Israeli retaliation against Palestine bases in those states and the loss of life and destruction of property therein. Consequently all Arab states took action to control PLA operations to reduce or eliminate Israeli operations against their territories. In Jordan the "Black September" (to use the Palestine term) operation in 1970 resulted in perhaps 10,000 dead and ultimately a tank battle in northern Jordan against PLA units based in Syria. There has thus been a substantial history of Jordan-Palestine conflict and a continuing Jordanian concern over the maintenance of order in the face of Palestine activity. In more recent years this has been exacerbated by the rising influence of more fundamentalist Islamic groups: in 1989, 32 members of the Muslim Brotherhood were elected to the 80-member lower house of parliament; indeed, there were suggestions that had seats been more evenly distributed they might well have secured a majority. For the moment the fundamentalists have adopted a politically moderate posture, but the Jordanian government will be concerned about the prospects for the future. Accordingly there is a legitimate internal security area of concern in both the large Palestine population in Jordan and in the substantial support for the Muslim Brotherhood. The 1996 structural adjustments driven by IMF pressures for budgetary reform will exacerbate these tensions.

SUMMARY

Jordan faces a difficult security situation. It is a small state lying between powerful neighbours, and its territory is strategically important to them. In addition it has a substantial refugee population within its borders amounting to as much as 40-50% of its population. Should internal instability convince its neighbours that it is unable to control its territory there will be a temptation on the part of one or more of them to seize Jordanian territory in order to assure their own security. In turn this could encourage others to take action to counter the first, and the region could drift into another general war that would be in no one's interest. Jordan is an economically weak state and cannot afford to maintain a large military capability and would, no doubt, like to be able to reduce the one it has to a more bearable level. Unfortunately, so long as its neighbours remain armed to the teeth Jordan has little choice but to maintain a military capability that represents a severe economic burden. Jordan is not the cause of the over-militarization of the region, and attempts to pressure it to reduce its military forces without simultaneously reducing that of its neighbours could be strategically counter-productive by creating a power vacuum into which these neighbours might feel compelled to move. The problem is to determine the minimum force level to guarantee Jordanian sovereignty. It is probably quite close to what Jordan already has.

THE MILITARY BALANCE OF POWER, 1996-97

THE LOCAL STRATEGIC CONTEXT
(RANKED IN ORDER OF ESTIMATED TOTAL COMBAT POTENTIAL)

Country	Air Force		Army		Navy	
	Fighter Sqns	Bomber/ FGA Sqns	ADEs	IDEs	Subs	Ships/ Patrol Craft
Israel	24.1+7.5	4+8.1	14.3	4.3+8.3	2	55
Syria	20.7	14.6	15.3	9.3+3.3	–	27
Iraq	11.3	8.1	9.0	20.3	–	8
Saudi Arabia	7.8	10.2	3.5	3+2.3	–	37
Jordan	2.0	4.1	2.8+1	2.7	–	5

Where two figures are shown, the first represents active formations and the second readily mobilizable reserves of aircraft or main battle tanks in storage that could be deployed on mobilization, given adequate warning time. The two Saudi Arabian figures for IDEs show the regular army plus the National Guard, which is directly under royal command.

What is striking about the regional balance of power is the military weakness of Jordan in comparison to its three big neighbours, Israel, Syria, and Iraq (even after its war losses). While the quality of Jordan's troops has long been assessed as among the highest in the Arab world, their quantity is inadequate to the defence of Jordanian territory should one of its neighbours choose to attack. The weak Jordanian economy limits its ability to keep up with advances in equipment technology, particularly in the air force, or to maintain large enough military forces to balance those of its neighbours. Strategies normally adopted by weak states are to seek alliances with powerful neighbours or to adopt conciliatory policies toward them. For Jordan these strategies are of doubtful help, given the intensity of the Arab-Israeli relationship, the potentially predatory nature of both Syria and Iraq, and the strategic centrality of Jordanian territory. Jordan faces the peculiar problems of all buffer states lying between powerful adversaries.

THE COUNTER-INSURGENCY (COIN) DIMENSION

As noted in the conceptual model section, when the main insurgency problem comes in predominantly urban or geographically restricted high population density areas there is a tendency to use normally structured military forces to deal with the requirement. That is the case here.

A DEFENCE SUFFICIENCY STRUCTURE FOR JORDAN

Given the economic base of Jordan, it is impossible to maintain a military force powerful enough to defeat Israel. Jordanian security policy vis-à-vis Israel must be based on diplomacy and the avoidance of hostilities. A force strong enough to respond to non-Israeli external threats must be powerful enough to make an aggressor pay a price sufficient to deter him from aggression. In addition, it must be strong enough to prevent a quick *coup de main* that could overthrow the Jordanian authority before other states could react. A force of an army corps of two armoured and two mechanized divisions plus an air force of perhaps eight squadrons divided between fighters and fighter/ground attack aircraft is about the right size and is, in fact, about the size of the existing Jordanian force. Since Jordan has avoided interference in its internal affairs to this point we can probably conclude that a larger force is not required. Such a force could also back up police forces in the aid to the civil power context.

MILITARY EXPENDITURES: ANALYSIS OF VARIABLES

MILITARY IMPORTS AND MILITARY EXPENDITURES

As noted in Appendix 6, military imports are deemed to be included in reported military expenditures for Egypt, Libya, Iran, and Saudi Arabia, but not for Israel, Syria, and Sudan. Jordan is a special case, in that imports appear to have been included from 1989-93, but not in the previous period.

THE LOCAL STRATEGIC CONTEXT
(BORDERING COUNTRIES IN ORDER OF GNP)

Country	1994			ME/GNP		MI/ME	
	GNP $US millions	ME $US millions	ME/GNP %	1990-94 %	1985-89 %	1990-94 %	1985-89 %
Saudi Arabia	121,400	17,200	14.2	21.6	19.1	27.2	37.3
Israel	76,810	6,588	9.9	10.9	18.0	12.0	15.5
Egypt	42,120	1,742	4.1	4.2	10.7	64.6	54.2
Syria	NA	NA	NA	15.0	22.1	5.8	17.4
Iraq	NA	NA	NA	69.2	49.7	4.9	33.0
Jordan	5,790	434	7.5	9.3	15.7	10.4	46.7

Iraq's GNP was devastated by the Gulf War. If the 1984 GNP figure of $48,250 million were used, Iraq would have the third largest economy in this set. With the exception of Iraq, military spending as a percentage of GNP in the region had been declining from about 1984 until the Iraqi invasion of Kuwait and the ensuing Gulf War. After that war the pattern diverged, with ME/GNP continuing to decline in the "peace treaty" states of Egypt, Israel, and Jordan, but remaining constant or increasing in the two with security concerns vis-à-vis Iraq.

Israel's indigenous arms industry has been estimated by the Office of Technology Assessment of the U.S. Congress (*Global Arms Trade: Commerce in Advanced Military Technology and Weapons*) to account for an additional 25.5% on top of the defence budget. A significant portion of Israeli arms production is exported, some to the United States on a counter-trade basis. *World Military Expenditures and Arms Transfers* shows substantially lower Israeli arms exports than does the Congressional source. Egypt, Iraq, and to a lesser degree, Jordan, have also established indigenous arms production industries, whose size has not been adequately determined in this study. While this does not materially alter the MI/ME figure, it does mean that the MI figure cannot be used as a perfect analogue for equipment spending in those countries.

Like most of the Middle East states, Jordan makes use of conscription. Since conscripts are paid at a substantially lower rate than the professional members of the forces, the conscript premium represents a means of reducing the overall cost of the defence budget. With the conscript portion of Jordan's military forces, at approximately 75% of the total, this premium represents a significant reduction. No attempt has been made, in the absence of comparative pay rates, to estimate its size.

The fundamental problem faced by Jordan is strikingly clear from the macroeconomic statistics. Jordan has a GNP one ninth that of the average of its heavily armed neighbours. It thus has a profound security problem. With a GNP smaller in absolute terms than the military expenditures of most of its neighbours, it simply cannot match their military spending. However, the geostrategic reality has meant that it could not reduce its military spending to a more easily borne level if it wished to retain control of its affairs. The move to a peace treaty with Israel makes a great deal of economic sense to Jordan. Unhappily, its shared borders with the heavily over-armed Syria and Iraq limit the economic benefit of that peace treaty.

SENSITIVITY ANALYSIS: THE EXISTING JORDANIAN SPENDING PATTERN
(MEAN 1990-94)

Spending Category	Budget Share %	$US per Position	Foreign Currency $US millions	Local Currency $US millions	Total $US millions
Equipment	11.6	537	54	0	54
PO&M	88.4	4,078	0	407	407
Total	100	4,614	54	407	461

CHANGE EFFECTS

- Changing Equipment spending
  by 1% of the Defence Budget $4,610,000   (Foreign Currency)

Note: Since Jordan has a limited local armaments industry the actual decrease in Foreign Currency spending may be somewhat less than that estimated.

- Changing Personnel strength by 1,000
  - Change in Equipment spending $537,000   (Foreign Currency)
  - Change in PO&M spending $4,078,000   (Local Currency)
  - Total change in Military
    spending $4,614,000
- Changing the Praetorian
  Index by 1 $134,511,000 (Local Currency)

THE DEFENCE SUFFICIENCY BUDGET

There is little prospect for major reductions of Jordanian military spending in the absence of any general Middle East arms control agreement. It seems unlikely, unfortunately, that such an agreement can be reached while Saddam Hussein remains in power. While the Israeli-Arab confrontation has appeared to be lessening, it is not the only strategic confrontation in the Middle East. Jordanian military spending overall does not appear out of line with its genuine security requirements. Indeed a case can be made that it could well be increased if the Jordanian economy could afford it. Jordan's Praetorian Index is already below the regional mean, and with no evidence that the Jordanian military is exploiting its position to exact an economic rent, there appears little scope for significant gains through cuts in personnel spending. When the age of Jordanian military equipment is examined, particularly that of its combat aircraft, a case can be made that its military equipment expenditures should be increased rather than decreased. Consequently there appears little scope for significant reductions in Jordanian military equipment spending.

IS JORDAN SPENDING TOO MUCH ON ITS MILITARY?

The answer to our question is No. There is no question that Jordan is spending a great deal on the military. From a purely economic perspective the proportion is excessive. From a security perspective, however, Jordan has little choice, being in the classic predicament of an economically weak buffer state between powerful adversaries. One is driven to the conclusion that even at 1994 spending of 7.5% of GNP Jordan is not spending too much.

If the objective is to reduce Jordan's defence burden, then Jordanian foreign/security policy might be directed to the twin objectives of easing the Israel-Arab confrontation (which seems to be the objective of current Jordanian policy) and establishing a regional arms control regime to limit the military forces of Iraq and Syria. Reduction in those forces could permit reductions in Jordanian forces. Such a regime would require a Syrian-Israeli peace treaty as well as a general Arab-Muslim de jure as well as de facto acceptance of the legitimacy of Israel. Such moves would, in turn, depend on the resolution of the Palestine issue and the return of the Golan to Syria. The Iraqi dimension is far more difficult, but equally critical in terms of Syrian security anxieties. Syrian force levels are driven in part by its uneasy relationship with Iraq as well as its concerns with Israel. A resolution of the Golan issue will be unlikely to result in great reductions in Syrian forces without a simultaneous reduction in the Iraqi threat. In turn, Syrian overmilitarization is in part responsible for driving Israeli military levels—which in turn worries other regional states. This is not an easy foreign policy agenda, however desirable it may be. An easier step might be a move toward confidence-building measures of the variety developed through the CDE/CSCE/CCSBMDE process, which culminated in the Stockholm Agreement. Verification procedures for any subsequent arms control regimes could be based on those developed for the Conventional Forces in Europe treaty.

SOCIAL MILITARIZATION ANALYSIS

PRAETORIAN AND SPARTAN INDICES (1990-94 MEANS)

Country	Praetorian Index	Spartan Index	Total Regular Personnel
Iraq	20.5	36.1	602,300
Saudi Arabia	17.6	9.1	152,900
Syria	4.8	32.5	407,200
Jordan	3.0	28.1	99,860
Israel	2.7	43.7	167,800
Egypt	2.0	14.3	432,000

Iraq's high Praetorian Index reflects a substantial demobilization in the post-Gulf War period without a parallel cut in expenditures. Jordan is not excessively militarized in terms of the regional context. Its Spartan Index level is driven by legitimate security concerns and its Praetorian Index level is little above that of Britain, from which it has drawn much of its military sociological traditions.

THE MILITARY AS NATIONAL DEVELOPMENT AGENCY

In 1989, Jordan entered into a licensing agreement to build 100 Hughes/McDonnell Douglas 300/500 helicopters. This represents almost twice the total helicopter holdings of Jordan's air force and twelve times that of this type. It seems unlikely that all are intended for Jordanian use, and the use of military procurement as an element in industrial strategy may be evident. If this were the case, several objectives are possibly being pursued.

First, Jordanian value added would be substituted for the foreign labour component of the aircraft. Second, there may be plans to use the export of Jordanian value added to counterbalance the foreign exchange costs of purchases for Jordanian use. Since assembly will also involve testing, there will be a degree of technology transfer in terms of job skills; if some components are to be manufactured locally, there will be additional technology transferred in the form of skills involved in the manufacture of aircraft parts to exacting technological standards.

The conscription term is two years and the annual intake should be about 38,000, probably staggered on a quarterly or semi-annual basis to even the impact on the training system. This represents about 80% of the annual cohort of about 48,000 males in the 18-22 age group. An intake of this size will cause a discernible reduction in unemployment rates—a social objective in most economies. Whether the conscript training represents human capital formation subsequently transferred to the civilian economy would require a detailed examination of the individual training curriculum.

THE ODA FUNGIBILITY ISSUE

With 1990-94 mean ODA at 121% of reported military expenditures fungibility is clearly possible. With ODA at 31% of CGE, strong donor leverage is available.

CASE STUDY 10: EGYPT

STRATEGIC THREAT ANALYSIS

A geostrategic Threat Analysis for Egypt should normally consider four areas:
- war with Israel either alone or as a member of an Arab coalition,
- war with Iraq or Iran as a result of commitments made to the security of the states of the GCC as a consequence of the Declaration of Damascus of March 6, 1991,
- threats of direct military confrontation with states with which Egypt shares borders, Libya and Sudan, and
- threats to Egypt's internal political stability and armed resistance to the civil authority stemming from the exploitation of economic unrest by the Islamic fundamentalist movement.

THE NEIGHBOURING STATES AS MILITARY THREATS TO EGYPT

Israel remains the primary concern of Egyptian security policy. One scenario for war between Israel and Egypt is based on the contingency of an Israeli invasion of Egypt and a one-front war on the general model of the 1967 war. Given the Israeli advantage in technology and particularly in the performance of its military forces Israel would win such a war at the operational/strategic level. Any grand strategic purpose of such a war, however, is difficult to comprehend. Since the October War of 1972, Israeli-Egyptian strategic relations have been marked by the Israeli policy of relinquishing territory it gained in the Six Days War of 1967—a policy that is described under the rubric of "trading land for peace." This policy successfully led to the peace treaty of 1979, which returned the bulk of the lands occupied to Egypt; the remaining bits were returned to Egypt following international arbitration. The result stabilized the Israeli southern flank, making the threat of a multi-front war with a grand Arab coalition much less likely. The 1994 peace treaty with Jordan and the agreement for the establishment of the Palestine National Authority in Gaza and Jericho by the Labour Party administration built further on the precedent of the 1979 treaty. An Israeli attack on Egypt would destroy one of the greatest successes of Israeli foreign policy, vastly increase the social and economic burdens of policing a hostile population in occupied territories, and run the real danger of bringing critical United States financial support to an end. Consequently this scenario must be viewed as exceedingly unlikely.

A second scenario would postulate a one-front war launched by Egypt—a scenario similar to that of the October war minus the Syrian front. Given Israel's qualitative advantages in both technology and personnel, and the strategic advantage to Israel of fighting a one-front war, Egypt's forces would be defeated at the strategic/operational level. Again there seems to be no strategic purpose in such a war. In addition to the financial and social costs of defeat, it is likely that the Egyptian government would be overthrown. Moreover, the launching of the war would likely lead to the withdrawal of equally crucial U.S. financial aid to Egypt. Finally, there is no grand strategic logic in such an action, since Egyptian diplomacy has achieved the return of all territory lost in the 1967 war. Moreover, the Israel-Jordan peace treaty and the second Arab-Israel peace treaty, as well as the agreement to establish the Palestine National Authority in Gaza and Jericho, has removed or at least considerably lessened the Egyptian isolation within the Arab world that had been caused by the 1979 treaty. This second scenario, then, is not a serious contingency.

A third scenario would see a second Egyptian southern front being opened in coordination with a northern Syrian front with the intention of recapturing the Golan Heights occupied by Israel since the October War. While the strategic advantage to Syria in such a coalition is clear, it is difficult to see any strategic advantage to Egypt in bearing the heavy cost of a war in order to see an Arab neighbour (and sometime rival) regain its territory. Moreover, regardless of the increased difficulty of dealing with a two-front war, it is still highly probable that Israel would once again emerge victorious. Finally, the Labour administration in Israel had indicated a willingness to negotiate a return of the Golan in exchange for a genuine Syria-Israel peace treaty—the "peace for peace" policy—a development that might offer the prospect of a diplomatic rather than a military resolution. This scenario, too, cannot be viewed at this point as a serious one.

The fourth scenario is based on the general Arab coalition of 1948, or the more limited coalition of 1967. The grand strategic objective could be the recapture of territory lost in the 1962 war, or the 1948 war, or even the elimination of Israel on the model of the 1948 war objectives. The military strategic plan would involve a three-front war, with the third front opened by Jordanian forces, perhaps reinforced by Saudi and/or Iraqi forces. This would present Israel with the most difficult strategic situation, particularly if a general *intifada*-style uprising could be coordinated with the military operations. The military outcome of such a war is more difficult to predict. Paradoxically, however, an impending Arab conventional forces victory might well lead to the most dangerous strategic outcome of all—the use of Israeli nuclear weapons to prevent conventional defeat. Moreover, the task of putting together such a coalition would be exceedingly difficult, since it is not at all obvious what the strategic motivation of the participants might be, particularly in view of the potential costs in either a conventional or a nuclear scenario. It is unclear what Egypt, the most militarily important (for without Egypt such a coalition has no chance of victory over Israel) member of such a coalition, might expect to gain; it is, however, clear what cost Egypt might expect to pay. Jordan's strategic calculus must be similar. Syria's objective, of course, would be to regain the Golan. Under normal conditions, such as have prevailed since the 1979 and 1994 treaties, it would seem that such a coalition is improbable and that this scenario is therefore equally improbable.

However, there is a potential contingency under which such a scenario becomes more possible. That is the possible succession in Israel of an extreme administration so devoted to the Judea/Samaria concept that it might seek to drive out all of the remaining Palestine population of the West Bank, of Gaza, and of Israel itself. Such a move might so inflame public opinion in the Arab world that the general Arab coalition would come about. Increases in the level of public support for the Moslem Brotherhood in Egypt might contribute to such pressures in any event. The long term-effect of the 1996 election of the Netanyahu administration in Israel remains to be seen; however, Egypt, Jordan, and the PLO have been restrained in their initial reaction in hopes of influencing the new Likud administration to continue the peace process initiated by its Labour predecessor. This scenario still seems highly unlikely in the short run, and the diplomatic initiatives undertaken thus far may lead to its remaining unlikely in the long run as well. Consequently, prospects for the Grand Coalition war are unlikely in the short (five years) term.

An outbreak of war in the Persian Gulf is a second major concern to Egyptian security policy. The two conceptual threats to Gulf security remain *Iran* and *Iraq*. The response of the Coalition forces to the Iraqi invasion of Kuwait makes an invasion of the GCC states unlikely in the short term. However, there are factors that make the longer term prospects more worrisome. First, with the end of the Cold War there has been a reduction in the forces of the NATO states—particularly the United States, Britain, and France—which provided the bulk of the non-Islamic air and naval forces and all of the non-Islamic land forces during the Gulf War. As this reduction continues, the capability of the NATO states to provide as large a military commitment will lessen and could embolden Iraqi or Iranian leadership—as the 1994 Iraqi military demonstration on the Kuwait border suggested. While the Damascus Declaration of March 1991 committed Syria and Egypt to provide troops to an Arab peacekeeping force to form the framework of a comprehensive "Arab defensive and security system" in return for the provision of financial support by the oil-rich (and security-poor) Gulf states to the Syrian and Egyptian economies, it appears that by 1992 Saudi Arabia had effectively lost confidence in the credibility of the Egyptian/Syrian force and preferred that Saudi security be guaranteed by the United States. The quick American response to Hussein's 1994 military demonstration in southern Iraq and the orchestration of Security Council Resolution 949 appear to have further strengthened the Saudi belief that only the United States can be trusted as a security guarantor. As long as the United States maintains its military capabilities the prospects for aggression by either Iran or Iraq remain relatively modest. However, the capacity of the United States to remain the world's protector is not infinite—particularly as its allies continue to run down their own capabilities.

Iran's strategic intentions in the Gulf region remain murky. While the Iran-Iraq war, together with the Iranian Islamic revolution, had a devastating impact on Iranian military capabilities, there are indications that Iran is continuing to rebuild its equipment stocks. Moreover, the revelation of Chinese technical assistance to the Iranian nuclear program and the prospect of the purchase of one or more Russian power reactors leads to legitimate concerns as to whether Iran is pursuing a nuclear weapons program in addition to its power and research reactor programs. The purchase of Soviet Kilo class conventionally-powered attack submarines, together with the seizure of Abu Musa island, creates a potential pressure point on the security of oil tanker traffic through the entrance to the Persian Gulf. Another concern is the possibility of the emergence of Iranian-backed internal subversion forces in one or more of the GCC states, particularly where local grievances have not been adequately addressed by the traditional leaderships in those states. Here the continuing issue of Islamic fundamentalist movements, which are perceived to be heavily supported by Iran, are an increasing complication.

Iraq too remains worrisome. While massive numbers of equipments were captured, destroyed, and damaged in the Gulf War, it still retained substantial stocks. Moreover, Iraq's extensive indigenous technical capacity and a process of cannibalization of parts and repairs has allowed a considerable amount of rebuilding to take place. Hussein's leadership structure remains in place and the Republican Guard was less damaged in the war than many analysts at the time believed.

The chances of an overt war with *Libya* seem very remote, simply on the basis of the power differential between the two states. While Libya has spent its oil revenues lavishly on the purchase of Soviet equipment, to the point that it now has probably the world's largest stockpile of obsolete Soviet hardware, it has never had the population base to man that equipment. Nor has the battlefield performance of various Libyan expeditionary forces ever proved impressive. A Libyan-Egyptian war would thus be quickly resolved in Egypt's favour and Libya knows this. However, Libya possesses considerable strategic nuisance capability in that it can force Egypt to deploy forces on its western border in order to maintain order in that area. Moreover, Libyan support of the Moslem Brotherhood and other similar factions within Egypt can increase the Egyptian internal security problem. In addition, the recent Libyan proposals for a political union of Libya and Sudan provide another element of considerable nuisance value toward Egypt, particularly in that they may suggest some de facto cooperation between Libya and Iran. However, the Libyan pattern of direct behaviour vis-à-vis Egypt to this point has been one of drawing back at the point that it appears that Egyptian patience is becoming exhausted.

The Sudanese situation is more complicated. At the heart of Egypt-Sudan strategic relations are two key issues. The first focuses on the ever-present concern over the distribution of the Nile's water resources, which are strategically critical to Egypt. Under the 1959 Nile Waters Agreement Egypt gets approximately 75% of the Nile's water, and the 1995 threat by Sudan to abrogate this treaty has contributed to the ongoing Egypt-Sudan crisis. The second issue is the extent of Sudanese support for the violent fundamentalist movements, initially in southern Egypt but now more apparent in northern Egypt too, and the suspicion that Sudan may have been behind the attempted assassination of President Mubarak in Addis Abbaba.

The two issues have become more interlinked as a result of the growing relationship between Sudan and Iran. One element of this relationship has been the granting of port facilities at Port Sudan on the Red Sea coast to Iran. When combined with the Iranian purchase from Russia of Kilo-class conventional submarines, this has led to Egyptian worries about the potential threat posed by these submarines to Suez canal traffic—a key source of Egyptian foreign exchange—particularly if they were based in Port Sudan. While this threat is at the moment more a political than a military one, the still murky intent of the Iranian rearmament program continues to concern Egypt, and it has approached the U.S. government about the acquisition of ASW frigates/destroyers to counter this concern. Another concern has been the continuing buildup of Sudan's military capabilities. There have been suggestions that their expansion has been based in part on the provision of Iranian financial assistance. Iranian financial support has been held to be behind the violent fundamentalist training camps established in Sudan, which have been implicated in cross-border meddling in Eritrea as well as in Egypt. The Sudanese buildup is probably directed to the successful conclusion of the Sudanese civil war, rather than to threatening Egypt.

THE INTERNAL SECURITY DIMENSION

The history of the last fifteen to twenty years provides ample support for the thesis that Egypt has a genuine internal security problem that must be dealt with. A quick survey might begin with the armed assault in 1974 by the "Islamic Liberation Organization" on the Technical Military Academy. From 1974 onward, senior officers of the Egyptian army were increasingly concerned with the efforts to infiltrate the junior officer and other ranks structure of the army on the part of the Society of Muslim Brethren and its more extremist allies "al Takfir wa'l-Higra" and "Shabab Muhammad." The kidnapping and murder of a cabinet minister by the extremist Muslim group "al Takfir wa'l-Higra" in 1977 was followed by massive riots when the government proposed to remove food subsidies. The period 1977-81 was marked by armed clashes between Muslim extremists and members of the Coptic Christian Community (over 6% of the population of Egypt) and the bombing of Coptic properties. The year 1981 was marked by the assassination of President Sadat by a group of soldiers (al-Jihad), led by a junior officer.

The 1981-85 period was more quiet, likely as a consequence of the security forces crackdown in reaction to the assassination. In 1984 the Society of Muslim Brethren joined forces with the nationalist Wafd party, and the coalition gained 14.5% of the vote in elections that were seen as relatively honest. In 1985, however, with the impact of a recession, came renewed troubles, when militants hijacked an Egyptian aircraft. 1986 saw the hijacking of the Achille Lauro, massive riots by the conscript-based Central Security Forces when it was rumoured that the government was contemplating an extension of the conscription period, and a massive demonstration at the funeral of Omar Tilmansi, the Supreme Guide of the Society of Muslim Brethren. In 1987 there were a series of incidents triggered by the "Egyptian Revolution," a neo-Nasserite youth group with suspected Libyan and Abu Nidal linkages; meanwhile the Society of Muslim Brethren shifted its electoral support leftward to the Socialist Labour Party. There was a series of incidents linked to Iranian support in 1988. In 1992 the Muslim fundamentalist-Coptic clashes recurred. In mid- and late 1992 a number of attacks were made by Muslim fundamentalists against tourists, particularly in the South; these attacks had the further economic effect of reducing tourist traffic to Egypt in 1993 by 37% from its 1992 peak. 1994 saw an assassination attempt against

President Mubarak after his re-election. A further assassination attempt was made in 1995 in Addis Abbaba, and increased terrorist activity took place in Minya province in upper Egypt.

The potential level of support for Islamic fundamentalism can perhaps be gauged by seeing the change in the level of support for the Wafd and Socialist Labour parties between the 1984 and 1987 elections. The shift of the Muslim Brethren between the two parties saw a shift of about 6.5% of the popular vote with them. This might amount to about 3.25 million of the then estimated Egyptian population of 50 million.

There is thus a legitimate requirement for substantial Egyptian internal security forces.

IMPLIED FORCE REQUIREMENT

Though the prospect of war with Israel seems thus to be remote, there will still be pressure to maintain a level of military capability that in size and equipment is linked in some traditional balance of power fashion to the capabilities of Israeli forces. Conceptually it may be possible to reduce such a level of holdings on the basis of a regional arms control treaty. Realistically, however, the multipolar relationships in the region would require so many states to become parties to such an agreement that the chances of its ever coming into being seem exceedingly remote.

While an actual war in the GCC area seems unlikely, there is a requirement for the maintenance of a credible conventional military deterrent capability like that contemplated by the Damascus Declaration, even though that declaration appears to have become effectively moribund. Such a capability implies the ability of Egypt to maintain an expeditionary force capability that, in conjunction with the GCC states' own forces, together with U.S. expeditionary capabilities, could serve to deter either Iraq or Iran. Such a Egyptian deterrent capability would be predominantly land-based, since even with the rundown in NATO states forces, there would likely still be adequate Western naval and air capabilities to back up the GCC states.

The requirements against both Libya and Sudan appear to be border guard forces capable of being backed up by heavier military forces if required.

THE MILITARY BALANCE OF POWER, 1996-97

THE LOCAL STRATEGIC CONTEXT
(RANKED IN ORDER OF ESTIMATED TOTAL COMBAT POTENTIAL)

Country	Air Force		Army		Navy	
	Fighter Sqns	Bomber/ FGA Sqns	ADEs	IDEs	Subs	Ships
Israel	24.1+7.5	4.0+8.1	14.3	4.3+8.3	2	3
Egypt	23.2	11.4	12.2	11.7	8	7
Iraq	11.3	8.1	9.0	20.3	–	1
Iran	7.8	10.6	4.8	9.3	2	7
Libya	13.1	10.3	7.7	13.9	4	6
Saudi Arabia	7.8	10.2	3.5	3+2.3	–	8
Rest of GCC	2.6	8.8	2.3	3.0	–	6
Sudan	0.6	2.4	1.0	8.7	–	–

Iran's figures are complicated by the existence of two armies, the regular army and the Revolutionary Guard Corps. The 24 "divisions" and additional independent "brigades" of the latter appear to be at most about one quarter the strength of normal divisions and weakly equipped. Only the regular army formations are shown in this analysis, but the Revolutionary Guards are included in the paramilitary calculation in the Spartan Index section. *The Military Balance* notes that approximately half the Iranian air force aircraft of U.S. origin are of doubtful serviceability. Two additional submarines are on order.

Libya's organizational figures are highly suspect. *The Military Balance* estimates that about 55% of Libyan main battle tanks are in storage as well as "many" aircraft. A quick scan of equipment holdings, claimed organizations, and personnel totals leads to the conclusion that Libya cannot man its organizations with the personnel totals listed. Libya has probably adopted the Soviet concept of Category II (partially manned) and Category III (equipment warehouse) brigades/squadrons with at least half the Libyan formations falling into Category III. Libyan reserve personnel, if the figures are trustworthy, would appear to be sufficient to man about half of the Category III formations at best. Accordingly, in a best case scenario Libya could claim one quarter to one half of its listed formations as available on mobilization.

Saudi Arabia's two figures for IDEs show the regular army plus the National Guard, which is directly under royal command.

In the Suez/Sinai theatre, a war between Israel and Egypt would require Israel, as a matter of strategic prudence, to maintain covering forces able to contain both Syria and Jordan while it concentrated its attack on Egypt. Given the combat multiplier that the active defence has in operations, together with the operational and tactical superiority of the Israeli Defence Forces, a covering force sufficient to contain the maximum Syrian/Jordanian forces of 19 armoured divisions and 10 infantry divisions might be set at 6-7 Israeli armoured and 3-4 infantry divisions. This might leave 6-7 armoured and 8-9 infantry divisions available to invade Egypt. An Egyptian force of about 10 armoured divisions and 7 infantry divisions might be considered to be sufficient to deny such an Israeli force a quick strategic victory and to shift the basis of the war to a protracted campaign. Since Israeli strategic thought since the 1948 war has favoured the avoidance of a long campaign and has emphasized the successful pre-emptive strike leading to quick victory, such an Egyptian strategic concept might be expected to increase Israeli strategic caution and to deter a war.

In the Nile theatre Egypt's bordering neighbours, Sudan and Libya, are comparatively militarily weak and represent no more than a limited threat. A force of two corps, each consisting of two armoured divisions and a mechanized infantry division, would be perfectly adequate to balance Libya, and one additional corps on the same model could handle Sudan. The total required would be six armoured divisions and three infantry divisions. It seems highly unlikely that in the case of the hypothetical Israel-Egypt war either state would ally itself with Israel against its fellow Muslim state. Consequently, Egypt should not have to expect to prepare for a two- or three-front war.

The Persian Gulf theatre balance of power is striking in that the smaller Arab states (Saudi Arabia and the rest of the GCC states) are militarily weak in comparison to the big three Arab states of Egypt, Syria, and Iraq (even after its war losses).

Since Syrian strategic ambitions appear to be directed to the gradual incorporation of Lebanon into "Greater Syria" and the recovery of the Golan from Israel, it is likely that Syrian interest in the GCC area would be directed to the preservation of whatever subsidies the GCC states might be persuaded to pay in order to ensure that Syrian forces help tie down Iraqi forces on its northern frontier; thus Syria is not considered to represent a strategic threat to the GCC states any more than Egypt is. During the Gulf War Syria contributed an armoured division and a commando brigade to the Coalition garrison in Saudi Arabia.

Iran, though Muslim, is not an Arab state. During the regime of the pro-Western Shah, Iran was seen by the West as a dominant and stabilizing force in the Persian Gulf, though traditional Arab-Persian rivalry meant that the Gulf Arab states did not necessarily share that perspective. The revolution, with its strident anti-Western rhetoric, its Islamic Shi'i fundamentalism, and the U.S. hostage-taking incident, led to great security concerns among the Gulf Arab states. However, the long Iran-Iraq war resulted in a serious degradation of Iranian military combat power. Following the resolution of that war, there does not yet appear, contrary to Western fears and expectations, to have been a profound attempt on the part of the Iranian government to build up a military power capability similar to that developed under the Shah. The consequence is that Iran does not really possess a serious power projection capability at this time. Consequently, at the moment Iran does not represent a real threat to the Gulf states, since any land invasion would have to pass through Iraq, and the prospects of such cooperation seem remote. Moreover, Iran does not have the amphibious capability to launch a seaborne invasion across the Persian Gulf, and in any event the Saudi air force has sufficient strength to crush such a move. Continuing procurement of Chinese anti-ship missiles suggests that a potential Iranian naval interdiction capability may be being developed to threaten oil tanker traffic, however. An Egyptian expeditionary force designed to check Iraq could also serve as a check on Iran.

Saddam Hussein's Iraq must still be considered by the GCC states to be a real security threat. The key issue for the GCC would be the minimum force that would serve to deter Iraqi aggression in the future, particularly in a world in which the NATO states have run down their military forces at the end of the Cold War and might thereby lack the wherewithal to mount another "Desert Shield/Desert Storm" operation. As was the case with the hypothetical Israeli invasion of Egypt, there would be a requirement for Iraq to maintain covering forces to contain any potential moves by neighbouring states. Here their behaviour during the Gulf War might be seen as indicative of their behaviour in any future Iraq-GCC confrontation. Both Jordan and Iran remained out of the war and declined to join the Coalition. Syria joined the Coalition but limited its active participation to the provision of a single armoured division to the Coalition forces in Saudi Arabia/Kuwait. For Iraq to contain the maximum Syrian/Iranian forces of about 21 armoured and 18 infantry divisions might require weaker than normal covering forces of about 4 armoured and 10 infantry divisions, leaving 4 armoured and 10 infantry divisions for the invasion force. The Saudi/GCC forces could deploy a maximum of about 6 armoured and 8 infantry division equivalents, though their capacity for command and control of such a force (in effect an army of four corps) appears speculative at this point, given that the Saudis prior to the Gulf War had no formations larger than brigades. Moreover, the non-Saudi forces—in theory the equivalent of 2.3 armoured divisions and 3 infantry divisions—have not been trained as divisional structures, and their effectiveness as higher formations, even if deployed together, remains open to question. The Egyptian contribution to the Coalition forces during the Gulf War was a corps of one armoured and one mechanized division plus a Ranger (light forces) brigade, which fought together effectively as a corps. The deployment of larger forces, however, in the absence of Western logistics structures seems problematical.

The combination of the Nile theatre and Gulf theatre requirements would thus come to about three corps equivalents, or about 6 armoured and 3 infantry divisions. That of the Suez/Sinai theatre would come to about 10 armoured and 10 infantry divisions.

THE COUNTER-INSURGENCY (COIN) DIMENSION

As noted in the conceptual model section, where the dominant insurgency problem comes in a predominantly urban or geographically restricted high population density areas there is a tendency to use normally structured military forces to deal with the requirement. In Egypt's case this requirement is dealt with on two levels: the Central Security Forces provide the initial response, and where they prove inadequate units of the regular army are employed.

A DEFENCE SUFFICIENCY FORCE STRUCTURE FOR EGYPT

The pattern of Israeli-Egyptian strategic behaviour argues that war is unlikely to be initiated by either side under the current circumstances, and that with the Jordan-Israel peace treaty, the Israel-PLO accords, and establishment of the Palestine National Authority in Gaza and Jericho, the prospects of such a war are increasingly remote. Nonetheless, a conservative and prudent Egyptian General Staff will argue that such a war is a contingency that must be planned for and that a minimum military force structure adequate to deter potential Israeli aggression must be maintained. Given the volatility of popular opinion and the enthusiasm for confrontation among the Muslim fundamentalists it would be difficult for the Egyptian government to be seen to be adopting a weakened defence policy without inflaming popular concerns. In any event, given the role that the Egyptian military has played in Egyptian politics and government from the time of the Free Officer movement to the present, and its importance in preserving the government from the threat of violent action by the Muslim Brethren and their allies, as well as in acting as an agency of last resort to control the Central Security Forces, it will be difficult for the government to deny what is on the face of it a reasonable position on the part of the General Staff. Such a force might reasonably be argued to require 10 armored and 7 infantry divisions for the Suez/Sinai theatre.

Since it is highly unlikely that Egypt would be involved in a two-front war, confronting Muslim forces on the one hand and Israeli forces on the other, the two threat clusters can be considered separately rather than together:

- The Libya Covering Force   2 armoured and 4 infantry divisions
- The Sudanese Covering Force   1 armoured and 2 infantry divisions
- The GCC Expeditionary Force   1 armoured and 2 infantry divisions
- Summary   4 armoured and 8 infantry divisions

The Minimum Defence Sufficiency Structure will be the larger of the above two requirements—10 armoured and 7 infantry divisions plus supporting air force and air defence troops. This is close enough to the existing Egyptian defence structure of 12.2 armoured division equivalents and 11.7 infantry division equivalents to suggest that the existing structure is reasonable within the current local geostrategic context, particularly if qualitative differences were factored into the analysis.

This study recognizes the existence of a legitimate internal security threat. In the absence of an analysis of the police capabilities of the various levels of government in Egypt, we are unable to determine whether the existing Central Security Forces are excessive. As will be noted later, however, an additional purpose of the Central Security Forces appears to be to reduce unemployment—a legitimate social though not necessarily constabulary purpose. In summary, then, it does not appear that the existing force structure is excessive.

MILITARY EXPENDITURE: ANALYSIS OF VARIABLES

THE LOCAL STRATEGIC CONTEXT
(BORDERING COUNTRIES IN ORDER OF GNP)

Country	1994			ME/GNP		MI/ME	
	GNP $US millions	ME $US millions	ME/GNP %	1990-94 %	1985-89 %	1990-94 %	1985-89 %
Iran	125,000	9,052	2.4	3.9	8.4	23.5	29.5
Saudi Arabia	121,400	17,200	14.2	21.6	19.1	27.2	37.3
Israel	76,810	6,588	9.9	10.9	18.0	12.0	15.5
Egypt	42,120	1,742	4.1	4.2	10.7	64.6	54.2
Libya	32,900	1,399	4.3	8.1	17.1	18.3	34.3
Iraq	NA	NA	NA	69.2	49.7	4.9	33.0
Sudan	NA	NA	NA	12.4	5.1	3.4	17.5

As noted in Appendix 6, military equipment imports are deemed to be included in reported military expenditures for Egypt, Iran, Iraq, and Libya, though not for Israel and Sudan. Reported expenditures have been adjusted in the following tables. The Gulf War had a devastating effect on Iraq's GNP. In 1984 it amounted to $48,250 millions and would have placed Iraq in fourth position in this table.

Except for Iraq and Sudan, the trend in military expenditures, until the invasion of Kuwait, had been sharply downward, reflecting a de facto easing of the Arab-Israeli confrontation. Since the Persian Gulf war there has been an upward turn in Saudi military expenditures—particularly in the import of high-performance Western equipment directed to Persian Gulf security concerns. The reports of Iranian purchases of equipment from China and Russia, as well as increased support for Muslim fundamentalist groups in the area, may cause a reversal of military spending declines in other Arab states. This may heighten Israeli security concerns, though the Arab increases would be directed toward other Arab and Iranian threats.

After the Gulf War the United Sttaes agreed to cancel Egyptian debts incurred to purchase U.S. equipments. This resulted in a significant decrease in the defence burden, as well as in foreign exchange reserves obligations. However, since Egypt possesses an indigenous defence industrial base, we cannot assume that equipment spending is limited to arms imports. The existence of the massive Egyptian military parastatal, to be described later, which engages in the sale of commodities and goods directly to the market sectors, suggests that there are very significant flows of funds into the military sector that are not included in reported military expenditures. Moreover, the military imports share of reported military expenditures at 50.7% seems about twice as high as one might expect, particularly for a state with an indigenous arms industry. Consequently, the Egyptian military expenditures figures used in this section must be viewed as highly suspect and are probably quite significantly higher.

Like most of the Middle East states Egypt makes use of conscription. Since conscripts are paid at a substantially lower rate than the professional members of the forces, the conscript premium represents a means of reducing the overall cost of the defence budget. With the conscript portion of Egypt's military forces at approximately 62% of the total in 1994-95 this represents a significant reduction. No attempt has been made, in the absence of comparative pay rates, to estimate the size of this premium.

SENSITIVITY ANALYSIS: THE EXISTING EGYPTIAN SPENDING PATTERN
(MEAN 1990-94)

Spending Category	Budget Share %	$US per Position	Foreign Currency $US millions	Local Currency $US millions	Total $US millions
Equipment	64.6	2,535	1,095	0	1,095
PO&M	35.4	1,388	0	600	600
Total	100	3,923	1,095	600	1,695

CHANGE EFFECTS

- Changing Equipment spending
  by 1% of the Budget $ 16,950,000   (Foreign Currency)

Note: Since Egypt has a substantial local armaments industry, the actual decrease in Foreign Currency spending will be less than that estimated.

- Changing Personnel strength by 1,000
  – Change in Equipment spending $2,535,000   (Foreign Currency)
  – Change in PO&M spending $1,388,000   (Local Currency)
  – Total change in Military
    spending $3,923,000
- Changing the Praetorian
  Index by 1 $299,376,000   (Local Currency)

Egypt's Praetorian Index is already below the regional mean. The actual size of the suspected off-budget revenues will affect this index, but the magnitude is uncertain.

THE DEFENCE SUFFICIENCY BUDGET

Given that the existing Egyptian force structure can be reasonably justified, the Egyptian defence budget does not appear to be unreasonable, particularly when judged by regional patterns of military spending per soldier. However, there are serious reservations as to whether reported Egyptian military spending accurately reflects actual spending—and this study concludes that it does not, since there are too many apparent sources of off-budget revenues that do not appear to be reported. On the other hand, the Egyptian military was assigned a specific national development role, whose scope is substantial but which reflects non-military objectives. From this perspective the reported defence budget might be properly adjusted downward to the extent that military resources are used for non-military development purposes. Until such time as these two potentially very large variables can be more fully understood, it will remain very difficult to make a judgment as to what the defence sufficiency budget should be.

IS EGYPT SPENDING TOO MUCH ON ITS MILITARY?

This study has mixed views as to whether Egypt is spending excessively on its military in the regional geostrategic context—a position based in part on concerns about the true extent of such military spending, given the extent of the military parastatal and the difficulty in trying to disaggregate its mix of security and development priorities. While Egypt's military combat potential is substantially larger than what would be required to deal with military threats from Libya and/or Sudan, those threats have no real impact on Egyptian military spending levels.

What appears to drive Egyptian military spending is a combination of three objectives: maintaining a credible deterrent capability vis-à-vis Israel—motivated not only by pressure from the Egyptian military, but also by popular hostility toward Israel, as well as a nationalistic desire to restore and maintain the Egyptian leadership role in the Arab Community; maintaining "Oil States" financial subsidies to Egypt for which the quid pro quo is the maintenance of a credible military expeditionary capability that can provide some degree of security reinforcement or guarantee against the residual Iran-Iraq threat to those states; and preserving the government against the threat of internal revolution led by nationalistic/fundamentalist forces, which threat is exacerbated by economic/population pressures.

If the objective is to be the reduction of the Egyptian defence burden, then Egyptian foreign policy and security objectives might be directed to the establishment of a regional arms control regime, with the objective of limiting the military forces of Israel and Iraq. Reduction in those force levels would then permit reductions in Egyptian force levels. Verification procedures for such an arms control regime could be based on those developed for the Conventional Forces in Europe treaty. To achieve Israeli agreement to such a regime would require also the accession of Syria to the regime as well as general Arab-Muslim de jure as well as de facto acceptance of the legitimacy of the State of Israel. Such accessions would, in turn, appear to require additional progress on the Palestine issue and a resolution of the issue of the return of the Golan to Syria. To achieve Iraqi agreement to such a regime would require the removal of Saddam Hussein from power and his replacement by a conciliatory administration. This is not an easy foreign policy agenda, however desirable it would be.

SOCIAL MILITARIZATION ANALYSIS

PRAETORIAN AND SPARTAN INDICES (1990-94 MEANS)

Country	Praetorian Index	Spartan Index	Total Regular Personnel
Sudan	39.1	3.7	85,560
Iraq	20.5	36.1	602,300
Saudi Arabia	17.6	9.1	152,900
Iran	3.5	12.2	514,000
Libya	3.8	18.6	79,000
Israel	2.7	43.7	167,800
Egypt	2.0	14.3	432,000

Two items stand out more clearly in Appendix 7: the very powerful reserve forces of Israel, and the very large paramilitary component of the Egyptian security structure. The Israeli reserves are kept in a high state of readiness through an annual commitment of two weeks refresher training and two weeks operational duty. The consequence, as demonstrated in each of the Arab-Israeli wars, has been a capability to mobilize exceedingly quickly—more rapidly than any other country in the world—and to be able thereby to effectively sextuple the army's active manpower. In effect, because of their quick mobilization time they can be viewed almost as having a standing army capability six times the size of their apparent one. The very large Egyptian paramilitary capability is located primarily (96%) in two components, the 60,000 strong National Guard and the 300,000 Central Security Forces. The conscript-based (three-year period) and poorly paid Central Security Forces' principal urban duties consist of guarding public buildings, embassies, public offices, banks, roads, and bridges. Their 1986 riot, triggered by rumours that the conscript period was to be extended to four years, was suppressed by the army with a cost of sixty dead and three hundred wounded. Their reliability may therefore be of some concern to the government.

States whose Praetorian indices lie significantly above the regional norms are ones in which the military represents an economically privileged elite. Where those forces are conscript-based, the professionals among them are likely to be even more economically privileged. Such economic privilege may be achieved either through elevated pay scales or through inflated rank structures. These conditions appear to exist in Sudan as well as Saudi Arabia. From a policy perspective this analysis suggests that one way to achieve more economical defence spending would be to do a comparative examination of the individual pay systems and/or rank structures of various countries, as a step toward a reduction in the privileged class status of military elites.

Egypt's Spartan Index is in the middle of the local context. The paramilitary component is, however, by far the largest in the area. If the paramilitary component were removed, then Egypt would have the lowest Spartan index in the area, with the exception of Sudan. To suggest cuts in the Central Security Forces, which constitute 81% of the paramilitary component, would require an examination of Egyptian police forces to determine the extent to which the Central Security Forces execute a normal police function rather than a paramilitary function. The threat from Muslim fundamentalism, which is to a considerable extent a consequence of Egyptian poverty, appears to be a principal driving force behind the maintenance of such large paramilitary forces both as a means of maintaining security and as a means of reducing potential unrest by sopping up a significant portion of the labour surplus. Moreover, Iranian meddling both in Egypt and in Sudan in support of Muslim fundamentalism continues to be an issue that might be expected to lead to strong resistance to cuts in the size of the security forces.

DEVELOPMENT ISSUES

THE MILITARY AS NATIONAL DEVELOPMENT AGENCY

Following the Camp David accords in 1978 the Egyptian military was assigned a national development role. It appears that the organization to implement this objective overlaps functions within the Ministry of Military Production. Three main organizations are involved:

- the National Service Project Organization (NASPO),
- the National Organization for Military Production (NOMP), and
- the Arab Organization for Industrialization (AOI).

This set of organizations appears to encompass an unusual military parastatal, which has been provided with a number of highly beneficial advantages over its private sector counterparts. They are not required to pay taxes, or to obtain import licenses or business permits. Nor are they accountable for normal profit and loss considerations. They are able in some cases to draw on conscript labour, which provides a considerable labour cost advantage, since the conscript wage rate (£E12-16 per month in 1993) is about one third that of the private sector. The provision of housing, uniforms, and rations to the conscripts might amount to an additional £E15-20 per month at 1993 market rates, but this should be discounted to the parastatal cost of production of those goods, which would reduce it significantly. We suspect that the effective parastatal personnel costs are about half those of the private sector. These organizations are provided with tariff protection for goods they produce (sources in the Canadian Embassy in Cairo estimated the tariff on imported television sets to be 200%), and in some cases (according to an IMF source) they are able to exclude the import of certain goods entirely. They are able to import components that are in limited supply or not available to the private sector.

NASPO was established in 1978 to control the organized production of civilian goods. Total FY1985 production was estimated, in the U.S. Department of Defence (DOD) Area Handbook *Egypt: A Country Study*, to be £E1,183 million. It is composed of four major divisions:

- *Military Agriculture* (£E488 million in FY1985) This accounted for 18% of the total Egyptian national food production in that year. In FY 1986, 5,000 troops and 500 officers were assigned to this component.

It is estimated that 90% of production is used by the military and Ministry of the Interior troops (including the conscript-based Central Security Forces) and the remaining 10% is sold into the civilian market.

- *Military Civilian Manufacturing* (£E347 million in FY1985) Products include clothing, doors, window frames, stationery, pharmaceuticals, microscopes.
- *Construction* (£E174 million in FY1985) The 1982-86 Five Year Plan assigned to this component the responsibility for the installation of approximately 40% of the telephone links in Egypt. In addition it was responsible for construction of power lines, sewers, bridges, overpasses, and land reclamation projects.
- *Other Goods and Services* (£E144 in FY1985) The military-controlled oil fields, with estimated offshore sales of up to $100 million U.S., may be included here.

In 1986 the creation of new "development regiments" was announced. These were to be assigned approximately 30,000 conscripts, who would receive special training following the normal period of basic training.

NODP production in the 1980s was estimated at about $240 million U.S. annually from 16 factories with 50,000 workers divided into six main production groups, plus a training centre and technical institute. A sub-contractor tier accounted for some $60 million U.S. in components production. An additional feature of NODP appears to be the following of the traditional Soviet model of split military and civilian production, where civilian goods production fills in the time not devoted to military production. Apparently the higher quality control necessary for military production gives the military-produced civilian goods a better reputation in the marketplace than competing civilian production. Some sources in Cairo in during the 1993 interviews estimated the then current division as 60% military and 40% civilian; had that been the case in the 1980s the civilian production might have been as much as $160 million U.S., for a total NODP production of $400 million U.S. annually.

The following groups and centres of production have been identified in the U.S. DOD *Area Handbook* and their military specialization indicated; it is conjectured that the main company title where named represents their civilian goods specialization rather than an attempt to conceal their military nature:

- Arms Production Group
  - The Abu Zaabal Company for Engineering Industries (artillery and tanks)
  - The Al Maadi Company for Engineering Industries (infantry weapons)
  - The Hulwan Company for Machine Tools (mortars and rocket launchers)
- Ammunition Production Group
  - The Hulwan Company for Engineering Industries (ammunition components)
  - The Heliopolis Company for Chemical Industries (ammunition and bombs)
  - Other factories at Shubra, Aboukir, and El Mansura
- Chemical and Explosives Group
  - Factories at Abu Zaadal and Kata
- Electronics Group
  - The Banha Company for Electronic Industries (communications equipment)
- Metallic Production Group
  - Factories at Helwan
- Field Services Equipment
  - Factory at Helwan

AOI was established in 1975 to be a joint venture with Qatar, Saudi Arabia, and the UAE in which the Gulf states would contribute capital ($260 million each), Egypt would contribute factories at Helwan (aircraft and engines), Sakr (missiles), and Keder (armoured vehicles), which would provide labour, technology, and skilled management. Technology would be acquired from Western—mostly British and French—sources. The Camp David accords resulted in Egyptian isolation and the organization became a purely Egyptian one in 1979. The AOI acts as a holding company with nine factories. It employs 20,000 workers and in the 1980s produced $100 million U.S. annually. Again, there appears to be some degree of civilian goods production—including proposals for school desks and tables for a Canadian International Development Agency (CIDA) project, and wind turbines for a Danish International Development Agency (DANIDA) project—though the extent of such production is unknown.

Known joint ventures identified in the *Yearbook of World Armaments and Disarmaments* published by the Stockholm International Peace Research Institute (SIPRI), and the DOD *Egypt: A Country Study*, include the following:

- Arab-British Dynamics Co. (1977 – BAe 30%): 7,412 Swingfire anti-tank missiles
- Arab-American Vehicle Co. (1978 – AMC Corp. 49%): CJ-6 Jeeps
- Arab-British Helicopter Co. (1978 – Westland 30%): Lynx, Mi-8 helicopters
- Arab-British Engine Co. (1978 – Rolls Royce 30%): Gem, Mirage, and Alphajet engines
- Arab-French Aircraft Co. (1978 – Dassault Breguet 36%): Alphajets
- Arab-French Engine Co. (1978 – SNECMA 15%): aircraft engines
- Arab Electronics Co. (1978 – Thomson-CSF 30%): military electronics
- Arab International Optronics (private sector JV ? %): military optronics

In addition, Egyptian subsidiaries of AOI handle licensed production arrangements such as the assembly of Turcano trainers (Brazil) and Chenyang fighters (China). U.S. licensing agreements included agreements to build 996 AIM-9P air-to-air missiles, and 25 AN/TPS-63 surveillance radars. A major licensing agreement has been that for the production of 540 Abrahms M-1 main battle tanks (with an estimated value of $2 billion U.S.), for which the United States would supply engines, transmissions, armour, and fire control systems, with the remaining parts produced in Egypt. The agreement appears to involve some degree of technology transfer, which Egypt planned to use in the upgrade of U.S. M-60 tanks transferred to Egypt as part of the "cascading" process following the reduction of U.S. equipment holdings as a consequence of the Conventional Forces in Europe arms control agreements. In addition there has been some evidence of a move toward an indigenous design capability with the reverse engineering of the Soviet BM-21 multiple rocket launcher as the Saqr-18 and the development of the Fahd wheeled armoured personnel carrier. There had also been a joint project with Argentina and Iraq to develop the Condor missile, though this has since been abandoned.

Export sales have been emphasized, with sales to Iraq (Saqr-18 and ammunition to as much as $1 billion U.S. in 1982-83), Kuwait (the Fahd APC), Somalia (rebuilt T-54 MBTs), and Sudan (Swingfire missiles). Other sales have gone to Algeria, Gabon, Nigeria, Saudi Arabia, Senegal, Zaire, Zambia, and Zimbabwe. Export sales of the Abrahms main battle tank to Saudi Arabia are an objective—though it appears that the Saudis would prefer U.S.-built M1A1s.

Consequently, the use of military procurement as an element in industrial strategy seems clearly evident. First, Egyptian value added has replaced the foreign labour component of the equipment. Second, part of the production has been exported in order to use the export of Egyptian value added to counterbalance the foreign exchange impact of purchases for Egyptian use. Since assembly will also involve testing, there will be a degree of technology transfer in the form of of job skills; if some components are manufactured locally, there will be additional technology transferred in the form of the skills involved in the manufacture of aircraft and other parts to exacting technological standards.

The Egyptian conscription system supplies the armed forces, the Central Security Forces, prison guards, and "military economic service units." The conscription age is 20, and the annual pool from which conscripts are drawn is about 525,000. The size of the annual draft is somewhat unclear. That for the armed forces is about 85,000; some sources suggest that the military takes the top third of those selected, with the bottom two-thirds employed elsewhere; this might imply a total draft of about 250,000. The 300,000-strong (some sources have suggested the actual figure is closer to 500,000) Central Security Forces might account for an additional 85,000 to 100,000, with the remainder assigned to the NASPO or the "development regiments" (which accounted for 30,000 conscripts in 1986). The two intakes would represent about 35% of the annual cohort of males in the 18-22 age group. A conscript intake of this size will, at its least, cause a discernible reduction in unemployment rates—a social objective in most economies. The issue of whether and how much of the military training received by conscripts represents human capital formation that is subsequently transferred to the civilian economy would require a detailed examination of the curriculum of the individual training programs undergone by the conscripts. Some military trades have clear civilian analogues while others do not; the question as to whether general military training contributes to human capital formation in terms of general life skills is a subject of some debate in the specialist literature, and the issue remains to be conclusively resolved. An official of the Egyptian Ministry of Foreign Affairs in Cairo assured this author that it did indeed do so.

The Egyptian military has a substantial role in infrastructure development. As noted above, the 1982-86 Five Year Plan assigned to NASPO the responsibility for the installation of approximately 40% of the telephone links in Egypt, as well as for the construction of power lines, sewers, bridges and overpasses, and for land reclamation projects. The "development regiments" cited above probably supply a major portion of the unskilled labour for such projects. In addition, it was indicated to this study that certain technical military elements, such as engineering and communications branches personnel, were used in telephone line construction and road and bridge building.

In summary it seems clear that Egypt has created as a deliberate matter of defence, industrial, and national development policy a very substantial military-agricultural/industrial parastatal that has both military and civilian agricultural and industrial production elements as well as national infrastructure development elements. As such the Egyptian military parastatal would seem particularly useful as the basis of a series of case studies concerning the use of military forces in non-military national development roles.

THE ODA FUNGIBILITY ISSUE

With mean 1990-94 ODA at 212% of military expenditures there is ample opportunity for fungibility. In theory, with ODA at 20.5% of CGE, there is significant donor leverage. However, the importance of Egypt to U.S. Middle East regional security policies effectively eliminates any prospect of the use of ODA leverage to reduce Egyptian military expenditures.

9

DETERMINING THE EXTENT OF MILITARY OVERSPENDING

This study was initiated in part in response to a remark by IMF Managing Director Michel Camdessus that implied that an appropriate level of military expenditures could be set arbitrarily—in his speech he suggested a maximum of 4.5% of GNP.

Of the ten countries studied in the case studies, eight had military expenditures in 1994 under the Camdessus line: one (Morocco) at it, and one (Jordan) beyond it. The study concluded that, when judged on the basis of the local international strategic threat environment faced by each country, expenditures of both states whose spending equaled or exceeded the norm could be justified on the basis of the local strategic context. However, the military expenditures of only one of the states (Egypt) whose spending lay below the Camdessus line could be fully justified in terms of the local international strategic context. Accordingly, this study rejects the validity of the 4.5% Camdessus line or, more importantly—since the Camdessus 4.5% of GNP Line was deliberately selected as a "straw man"—of any arbitrarily selected percentage of GNP as a universal measure of an appropriate level of military expenditures.

This then leaves the international donor community with the question of what alternative analytical yardsticks might be used in the quest for reductions in excessive military spending in developing countries—reductions that might lead to a re-allocation of moneys to the achievement of alternative economic or social policy priorities. This study prefers a strategic threat assessment approach based upon a traditional capabilities/intentions model to determine whether the force structure of an individual country is reasonable in terms of its surrounding international context. Seven of the ten countries examined were held to be spending more on their military than necessary in terms of the force structure required for their strategic threat context. However, the underlying reasons for that excessive expenditure varied considerably, and these variations illustrate the difficulties that the donor analytic community must be prepared to face in bringing pressure upon developing countries to reduce their expenditures, particularly since the military establishments of those countries can be expected to resist cuts in their funding.

Of the seven with military expenditures judged to be excessive, one (Zimbabwe) was felt to have made a strategic policy misjudgment in attempting to create a defence capability that was economically unsustainable and should be abandoned in favour of alternative foreign and security policy initiatives. In any event, subsequent political developments in the principal threat state, the Republic of South Africa, have reduced the external threat level to a point that the existing Zimbabwe defence establishment represents an unneeded level of military capability. An alternative explanation is that the Mugabe administration has sought to provide lifetime career employment to the military members of the black independence forces.

Four countries (Burkina Faso, Mali, Cameroon, and Kenya) showed strong evidence of excessive levels of military Praetorianism—the tendency of military forces to take advantage of their position to exact an economic rent. In the two West African states, military Praetorianism had evolved into the classical form, with the military establishments taking over the reins of government by means of coups. In Cameroon, on the other hand, a less intrusive form of military Praetorianism seems evident, with the military seeking preserve an authoritarian government rather than replace it. Kenya's military forces have followed a professional national defence model rather than a Praetorian one to this point; however, the Moi administration has followed a pattern of high levels of military spending, in part as a means of ensuring the loyalty of the military—a development that is often a precursor to Praetorianism, and the recent upward spike in Kenya's Praetorian Index must be viewed as worrisome.

Zambia's military overspending appears to stem from overmanning in its force structure—an example, perhaps, of the military inefficiency hypothesis.

Tanzania's military has followed the professional national defence model, and its overspending has represented a conservative and thus slow reaction to the reduced threat level in the surrounding strategic environment rather than any move toward Praetorianism. Given the deteriorating situation in the entire Great Lakes area, such a conservative reaction is defensible, and the late 1996 decision to suspend further reductions can be viewed as reasonable under the circumstances.

The exceedingly complex sets of negotiations between Israel and its

Arab neighbours had seemed to offer increasing hopes for a set of simultaneous reductions in military force structures expenditures. Indeed, Jordan seems to have drawn the conclusion that it will be safe to begin the process of force reductions, since the prospect of war with Israel seems increasingly remote. The difficulty in achieving generalized area-wide force reductions, however, lies in the fact that not all regional threats can be analyzed solely in terms of the Arab-Israeli axis: events in the Persian Gulf theatre influence force structures in bordering states in the Mediterranean theatre, which, in turn, affect other states in that theatre. Attempts to exert leverage to achieve force reductions in the Mediterranean theatre without taking the Persian Gulf theatre into account can be expected to have mixed results at best.

Nor should analysts be too quick to ignore non-military objectives in the maintenance of what might appear to be overly large military force structures. The national development objectives assigned to the Egyptian military forces after the Egypt-Israel peace treaty have been used to justify a larger military establishment (which for the purposes of this paper is taken to include the Central Security Forces) in Egypt than might otherwise be the case. The process of creating a purely civilian bureaucracy to administer such national development programs while simultaneously reducing the military bureaucracy that is currently administering them would be complex and costly—particularly if the principle of conscription were to be followed in order to maximize the social impact on unemployment rates that the current system provides.

FINANCIAL MILITARIZATION MEASURES

The tools most frequently used to gauge the policy priorities of ruling elites by measuring financial militarization have been the economic (ME/GNP), and the governmental (ME/CGE). A central problem of these financial measures is uncertainty as to whether all military expenditures have been included in official defence budgets, or whether they are limited primarily to personnel, operations, and maintenance expenditures. This study concluded that in many cases military equipment purchased from foreign suppliers has constituted an "off budget" expense that should properly be included in the military expenditure calculus. What was unexpected, however, were the indications that military establishments might have "off budget" revenue sources as well—such "revenues" might include, for example, the imputed financial value of the foodstuffs

THE MILITARIZATION MATRIX

Region/Country	Threat Level and Trend	Defence Sufficiency?	Overspending?	Economic Militarization (ME/GNP) Compared to Regional Norm	Fiscal Militarization (ME/CGE) Compared to Regional Norm	Spartan Militarization Compared to Regional Norm	Praetorian Militarization Compared to Regional Norm
SAHARAN AFRICA/MIDDLE EAST							
Egypt	Moderate, Unstable	Appropriate	No	Much Lower	Much Lower	Much Lower	Much Lower
Jordan	High, Unstable	Difficult	No	Lower	Lower	Higher	Much Lower
Morocco	Moderate, Unstable	Appropriate	No	Higher	Higher	Higher	Higher
SUB-SAHARAN AFRICA							
West Africa							
Burkina Faso	Low, Stable	Appropriate	Yes	Much Higher	Much Higher	Lower	Much Higher
Mali	Low, Stable	Appropriate	Yes	Higher	Much Higher	Lower	Much Higher
Central Africa							
Cameroon	Unstable	Appropriate	Yes	Much Lower	Much Lower	Much Lower	Higher
Southern Africa							
Zambia	Low, Stable	Appropriate	Yes	Lower	Lower	Lower	Much Lower
Zimbabwe	Low, Declining	Excessive	Yes	Higher	Higher	Higher	Lower
East Africa							
Kenya	Moderate, Declining	Appropriate	Yes	Much Lower	Much Lower	Much Lower	Lower
Tanzania	Low, Unstable	Arguable	Yes, but Reducing	Lower	Lower	Higher	Lower

produced by the Egyptian "military-agricultural complex" for consumption by its forces, or some portion of the revenues generated by the sale of civilian goods produced by military factories. Another example of "off budget" revenues might be found in the frequently expressed suspicion that the Nigerian forces enjoy a portion of the oil production revenues of that country and that the true Nigerian ME/GNP figure might well be considerably higher than that reported. What would be particularly useful, therefore, would be the general adoption of completely transparent defence budgets by aid-receiving countries in accordance with the United Nations Centre for Disarmament Defence Expenditures Disaggregation Model cited in Appendix 2. Whether the international donor community has enough leverage to foster the creation of an international corps of military forensic accountants and military forensic economists to audit such accounts is, of course, an interesting question—but the exercise might prove highly useful for all concerned.

SOCIAL MILITARIZATION MEASURES

The Spartan Index is a relatively familiar idea, though the inclusion of paramilitary forces is less common. However, it is perhaps worthwhile to spend some time considering the antecedents of Spartanism—and why some states have very large Spartan scores whereas others seem able to get along with much less. The most obvious antecedent is the existence of an apprehension of a war threat—whether it be of international war with another sovereign state or of civil war within the state. A second condition seems to be associated with some post-civil war states in which the victorious rebel forces have been engaged in a long guerrilla war. With their forces dependent upon large numbers of young people whose guerrilla career has prevented them from gaining any significant amount of education or civil employment-related training, there is a natural tendency to maintain larger than necessary forces as a means of providing them with employment and the wherewithal to support their families. A third factor is found in certain countries who were strongly influenced by Marxist-Leninist governmental models that include large conscript-based standing armies. And finally there is a limited number of states that appear to maintain larger than required forces as a means of reducing unemployment levels.

The most interesting social militarization measure to emerge from this study, however, was the Praetorian Index, which represents, in effect, a hybrid social/economic measure that was originally introduced to permit cross-country comparisons, since it is essentially independent of exchange rate effects, the bane of all cross-country comparisons involving developing countries. The extent to which it might be independent of purchasing power parity effects has not been examined, though one is intuitively led to the thought that it would be. The very wide range of country-to-country Praetorian Index values led to the conclusion that the Index did capture to a considerable degree the presence of Praetorianism, and led further to an identification of opportunities for reductions in military expenditures that were not evident through a simple force structure analysis. A simple two-by-two matrix of the Spartan and Praetorian Index scores produced other insights. The first came in a comparison of Sub-Saharan and Middle East/Saharan means, which shows clearly the effect of a history of inter-state wars in the one area, and of civil war in the other.

Region	Mean Spartan Index	Mean Praetorian Index
Middle East/ Saharan	19.1	6.9
Sub-Saharan	3.2	20.9

A closer examination of each region separately was made on a three-by-three matrix with boundaries set at the mean Index score plus or minus 0.43 standard deviations—a procedure that divides the statistical distribution into three approximately equal parts along each axis.

Middle East/ Saharan Region	Low Praetorian (PI<4.4)	Middle Praetorian (4.4<PI>9.3)	High Praetorian (PI>9.3)
High Spartan (SI>24.4)	Israel, Jordan	Syria	Iraq
Middle Spartan (13.9<SI>24.4)	Libya, Egypt		
Low Spartan (SI<13.9)	Iran, Algeria	Morocco Mauritania, Tunisia	Saudi Arabia

Note: Within cells ranked by SI.

Sub-Saharan Region	Low Praetorian (PI<13.7)	Middle Praetorian (13.7<PI>28.1)	High Praetorian (PI>28.1)
High Spartan (SI>4.3)	Congo (11.4) Botswana (10.8) Chad (7.4) Zimbabwe (8.5) Gabon (7.2) Guinea-Bissau (3.7)	South Africa (14.7)	
Middle Spartan (2.0<SI>4.3)	Ethiopia (11.7) Guinea (8.8) Zambia (6.9) Uganda (6.4)	Tanzania (22.9) CAR (19.8)	Sudan (39.1) Mozambique (35.8)
Low Spartan (SI<2.0)	Malawi (11.3) Togo (10.7) Nigeria (8.8)	Sierra Leone (24.0) Niger (23.5) Burundi (23.2) Cameroon (23.1) Benin (20.5) Mali (19.4) Senegal (17.3) Ghana (14.8)	Rwanda (95.8) Zaire (40.1) The Gambia (31.5) Burkina Faso (30.2) Kenya (29.5) Côte d'Ivoire (29.0)

Note: Within cells ranked by PI, the lack of 1990-94 military expenditures data for Angola, Equatorial Guinea, Liberia, and Somalia prevent the calculation of Praetorian Indices.

Iraq's high Praetorian Index is influenced by two special factors: the high operations and maintenance costs of its wars with Iran and later with the United States-led coalition following its invasion of Kuwait, and by the greater percentage decline in its regular military strength than in its military expenditures after the Kuwait War. The Republican Guard, though, certainly fits the early Roman model. Saudi Arabia's high Praetorian Index is more likely to be the result of the need to keep its military forces loyal.

THE PRAETORIAN CYCLE

In both matrices there is a pattern of two dominant axes—a Praetorian axis and a Spartan axis, with a relatively small number of outliers that do not fit comfortably into either. One interpretation of this phenomenon is that we are seeing the division of the set into national-defence oriented armies (the Spartan axis) and internal control-oriented armies (the Praetorian axis), with outliers perhaps in transition from one form into another, or perhaps with mixed purposes. A second interpretation might distinguish between the Saharan/Middle East group, whose principal perceived threats are primarily interstate, and the Sub-Saharan group, whose principal perceived threats are now primarily intrastate.

A closer look at the year-to-year variations in the two indices in individual Sub-Saharan countries suggests the existence of what might be termed a "Praetorian cycle," which begins with a middle or high PI characteristic of an Authoritarian state, in which the military protects the civilian ruling elite, or a Praetorian state, in which the military itself rules. If the excesses of the elite become so great that a resistance movement emerges, the initial response of the threatened elite is to increase spending on its existing relatively small regular and paramilitary forces both to ensure their loyalty and to cover the increased O&M costs of a repressive campaign against the resistance forces—a pattern that explains the fact that the Praetorian Index spikes upward as a precursor of civil war. When the civil war breaks out, the response of the threatened elite is to add to the numbers of its regular and paramilitary forces, with the result that the SI rises and the PI falls. The post-civil war pattern depends on whether the state evolves toward a more democratic form, in which case both SI and PI decline, as in Uganda; back toward the Authoritarian or Praetorian form, with a constant or slightly declining SI but a continuing high PI, as in Togo; into terminal collapse, as in Liberia; or into a frozen state in which the revolutionary army is maintained as a means of providing employment for the revolutionary fighters, who lack employable skills suited to a civilian economy, whereupon the SI remains relatively constant while the PI declines, as in Zimbabwe.

To this we might add as a variant a "Marxist-Leninist Praetorian" cycle, which is a better fit for those Sub-Saharan states influenced by Soviet/Chinese military models during the Cold War, which possess large conscript-based military forces. No less authoritarian than their ordinary Praetorian counterparts, they characteristically have much lower PIs simply on the basis of having much larger military forces. Their cycle might thus follow a similar pattern to that of the regular Praetorian cycle—Ethiopia, for example, is more easily analyzed as a Marxist-Leninist Praetorian cycle post-civil war state that appears to be making the transition to the more democratic form in which both PI and SI are falling.

TESTING THE PRAETORIAN CYCLE HYPOTHESIS

Rwanda had been a upper middle Praetorian state with a PI of 21.7 in 1989. Its PI began to shoot up in 1990, reaching 59.5, and peaked at 119.3 in 1993, just before the catastrophe—the highest PI level of any state examined in this study. This phenomenon led to the initial hypothesis that a sudden sharp increase in the PI (the trebling in 1990) might be a leading indicator of a state about to collapse into civil war. The civil war collapse took place so quickly that the expected SI increase was not evident. In 1995, during the period of the successor RPF administration, the SI has made its expected upward move from 0.7 to 5.0—an indication that the Rwandan civil war may be far from over.

Other states have shown similar patterns. Liberia's PI almost doubled, rising from 8.8 in 1985 to 15.6 in 1987, with a subsequent SI increase from 3.1 in 1988 to 3.8 in 1989; the government was overthrown in 1990 and the country dissolved into a multi-factional civil war and chaos. Uganda's PI almost tripled, from 15.0 in 1984 to 43.0 in 1985, just prior to the rebel NRA victory in 1986. The Gambia's PI rose from 8.9 in 1990 to 34.0 in 1992, and reached 47.4 in 1994, when the government was overthrown by a coup. Sierra Leone's PI more than doubled between 1990 (14.4) and 1992 (29.5), when General Momoh's government was overthrown by a coup, fell to 16.6 in 1993 as the new government of Captain Strasser enjoyed a brief honeymoon, and spiked again to 37.0 as Sierra Leone seemed to be beginning to plunge down the Liberia track; the Spartan expansion had taken place in 1991 with almost a doubling of military forces. Sudan's PI demonstrated the upward spike pattern between 1990 (15.0) and 1992 (58.0), which was paralled by a rise in the SI from 2.8 to 4.6 by 1995. Central African Republic's PI had a significant rise between 1993 (20.8) and 1994 (36.9) that predated the attempted coup in 1996, which was put down through the intervention of French forces stationed in that country. Togo's PI rose from 4.7 in 1986 to 12.6 in 1987, and again from 13.6 in 1989 to 20.0 in 1990 and 24.3 in 1994. In both instances the general unrest in Togo was successfully contained by the Eyadema administration, in 1986 with the military assistance of France, and the 1995 PI dropped back to 16.6.

Two PI rises that do not follow the described pattern, were those in Ghana between 1990 (5.3) and 1991 (13.0) and in Burkina Faso between 1993 (25.1) and 1994 (41.1). In both cases, however, the increase in PI was brought about by a reduction in force strength that took place more quickly than reductions in military spending. Ghana's SI dropped from 0.8 in 1990 to 0.5 in 1991 and 0.4 in 1992, when the PI rose further to 23.5 before declining to 19.4 in 1994. The rise in Burkina Faso's PI stemmed from a transfer of 1,400 positions from the army to the paramilitary Gendarmerie; had those positions remained within the army, the Burkinabe PI would not have changed significantly. Consequently, these two instances do not invalidate the Praetorian cycle hypothesis.

If the Praetorian cycle hypothesis is substantially correct, then it should be possible by means of this measure to forecast instability—to identify those states that are "at risk." The following states would be on that list. Burundi's PI increased from 24.4 in 1990 to 30.2 in 1993 and then dropped to 17.8 in 1994 as a result of a military expansion, as its SI doubled from 1.2 to 2.4; the 1996 coup is consistent with the Praetorian cycle, and civil war looks increasingly likely. Zaire's PI increased steadily from 7.2 in 1982 to a high of 56.1 in 1993, though it dropped back to 31.2 in 1994; nonetheless Zaire must now be considered at great risk; the late 1996 events in the Great Lakes area of Zaire appear to validate the hypothesis. While the Eyadema administration succeeded in containing the two previous waves of civil unrest, Togo must still be considered to be at risk. The annulment of the June 1993 Nigerian election results by General Babangida, which was followed by the November 1993 coup led by General Sani Abacha against the Transition Council headed by Earnest Shonekan, is a classical Praetorian coup. It was paralleled by a 42% rise in Nigeria's PI from 7.0 in 1992 to 10.0 in 1994. Depending on how much of Nigeria's oil revenues remain as an "off budget" component of military expenditures, the real changes in Nigeria's PI may be substantially greater. Kenya has had genuine external security concerns that enforced a national defence orientation and the development of a respected professional army. However, the Kenyan Army has consistently enjoyed a high PI, suggesting an interest on the part of the Moi administration in ensuring its loyalty. A 40% PI spike from 1981 to 1983 was followed by a force expansion in 1987, with the SI rising from 0.7 to 1.1. A further 55% PI increase from 25.1 in 1987 to 39.2 in 1993 has been parallelled by a 275% expansion of paramilitary forces. Increases of this magnitude could be cause for concern that Kenya's forces are beginning to move away from the National Defence model toward a Praetorian model.

Cameroon's PI dropped from 30.9 in 1993 to 17.2 in 1994 because of a military expansion, as the SI rose from 0.9 to 1.8, which might suggest a progression along the Praetorian cycle. However, the border conflict with Nigeria provides a legitimate inter-state security concern and possible justification for the force expansion. Cameroon's PI had remained relatively constant over the previous ten years and showed no characteristic upward spike.

The post-civil war stage of the Praetorian cycle has seen different evolutions with Uganda and Ethiopia making significant progress, while the situation in Mozambique remains less clear but hopeful. In Ethiopia the new government has reduced its military forces, with the SI dropping from 9.6 in 1989 to 2.2 in 1995, while the PI remains relatively low at 11.7. Uganda's PI dropped from 25.5 in 1987 to 5.0 in 1988, reflecting the inclusion of the NRA rebel forces in the official military forces and a doubling of the SI from 2.3 to 4.4. From 1988 to 1994 there was a gradual drop in the SI to 2.6, as a slow partial demobilization took place. Military expenditures were also reduced such that the PI rose only marginally from 5.0 to 5.7 by 1994. The 1994-95 decision of the international donor community to provide funds to support the further demobilization of the Ugandan civil war army and the return of its soldiers to employment in the civilian sector must be viewed as a highly sensible policy that would have allowed the process to go further. Unfortunately, the increasing hostility between Sudan and Uganda has led to an increase in planned Ugandan defence spending.

Mozambique differs from Ethiopia and Uganda in that the civil war ended with the exhaustion of both sides rather than with a clear victory by the revolutionary forces. This has left a fairly high residual Spartan militarization, as large numbers conscripted into government security forces are only partially demobilized, as a consequence of continuing security anxieties on the part of the government. With some reduction in military strengths but without corresponding cuts in military expenditures, and with the disastrous effect of the war on the economy and thus on GNP per capita, the level of Praetorianism remains comparatively high. A danger lies in the possible evolution to (or a return to) Praetorianism as the government turns to the military as a means of keeping itself in power. Further complications arise from the wartime imports of military equipment and the resulting large foreign debts, the servicing of which can consume capital needed for economic investment in a reconstruction economy. Mozambique's military is to be downsized fairly rapidly, and the SI and PI can be expected to change significantly, but the ultimate end of the process is still unclear.

THE DEFENCE CONVERSION PARADIGM: THE MILITARY AND NATIONAL DEVELOPMENT

The conventional military or defence conversion paradigm presumes a successful shift of the military-industrial base from the production of military goods to the production of civilian goods. Simultaneously the military establishment is downsized through the demobilization of military personnel to civilian status. A problem in practice, however, stems from the reality that product development, marketing, and financial management skills appropriate for dealing with a single public sector customer are not necessarily the same as those required for the successful development of products for the competitive environment of the private sector. The indifferent private sector track record of major U.S. high-technology defence contractors in the post-Cold War period provides an illustrative example of this. Similarly, the retraining of individuals made surplus by the military force structure downsizing for employment in civilian life is often problematical, particularly where their training has been in military skill specialities for which there are few civilian analogues—a problem that seems likely to be larger in low-technology developing country military forces than in high-technology developed country forces, where a larger percentage of the total force structure is involved in maintenance and logistic functions.

One of the difficulties with post-war demobilization programs in Africa is that individual members of rebel forces who have been engaged in lengthy guerrilla operations almost invariably have little education and few skills appropriate to employment in a civilian economy in any of the agricultural, commercial, industrial, or service sectors. Coletta et al., in *The Transition from War to Peace in Sub-Saharan Africa* (1996), note in three separate case studies of "demobilization and reintegration programs (DRPs)" that in Ethiopia "almost two-thirds of ex-combatants have not gone beyond primary school," in Namibia "guerrilla ex-combatants have low educational and skills levels," and in Uganda "their educational and skills levels are low." Moreover, in all three countries half or more of ex-combatants were married and had children to support; they had joined the army or guerrilla forces in their late teens or early twenties, and remained in the army or guerrilla forces for periods in some cases of over ten years. DRPs characteristically provided cash payments, transitional social safety nets for periods of about two years, some training and assistance, and access to land. Whether such programs are adequate in the long term remains to be seen: Coletta et al. report that in Zimbabwe only about 10% of ex-combatants were formally employed or self-employed in the private sector by 1988, some ten years after the Lancaster House agreement of 1979, which ended the conflict. The long-term economic and social distress of many of the ex-combatants, stemming from their lack of human capital as a consequence of their war service, thus leads to the question whether there might be alternative strategies to that of the DRPs.

The discovery of the very extensive Egyptian military parastatal that has emerged out of the assignment of national development roles to the Egyptian military sector was one of the unanticipated outcomes of this study—especially since it appears to have gone essentially unnoticed both in the military and economic development literature. The Egyptian military parastatal represents a most fascinating active case study, which is deserving of much broader and more intensive research than was within the scope of this study. It provides, in effect, an interesting paradigm shift from the standard military conversion literature.

The Egyptian defence conversion paradigm appears to be one in which the military itself has been converted through the adoption of additional or substitute non-military national development roles and objectives, though the military organization itself remains intact and retains as well much of its traditional purely military roles and objectives. Within this paradigm, the military structure's experience in individual training is applied in part to the development of military skills with civilian analogues, as well as non-military skills, such that in theory the individual upon completion of the period of enlistment is returned to the civilian sector with an improved skill set, which allows a potentially more successful transition from military to civilian employment. In addition, the employment of conscript forces in public infrastructure construction and other development tasks, as well as in the defence industries, permits the wage component of their costs to be reduced by the substitution of conscript labour for more expensive private contractor work forces or regular government employees. In addition, the subtraction of the conscript labour force from the civilian labour pool has the effect of lowering unemployment levels among young single adult males—the most socially volatile of all age cohorts.

The Egyptian model is, interestingly, dependent upon the existence of a conscript-based military force, since the much more expensive volunteer force offers its military employees, in effect, a lifetime employment contract, which results in a much smaller annual replacement turnover.

Whether it is a cost-effective model in terms of its development outcomes (including those relating to social stability) is, of course, another question entirely, one that could usefully be made the primary research question of a deeper, comprehensive study of the Egyptian model as an initial stage in the evaluation of its potential applicability in other developing countries as an policy alternative to the conventional defence conversion models.

Applied to the Sub-Saharan context, the Egyptian defence conversion might see the military forces assigned national development roles, following either the Egyptian model or else that of the Canadian Defence Structure Review of 1975 (Appendix 1), in which there are two overarching objectives—to achieve national development goals, and to upgrade the human capital of the military force members to the point that they would have a better prospect of reintegrating into civilian society than a more transitory program might provide.

APPENDIX 1

NATIONAL DEVELOPMENT TASKS: CANADIAN DEFENCE
STRUCTURE REVIEW OF 1975

The 1975 Canadian Defence Structure Review provides a useful starting point for the analysis of the concept of the Military in National Development Roles. It included as one of the roles of the Canadian Department of National Defence that of "National Development." Sixteen specific Department of National Defence (DND) Tasks were set out as the means of achieving that role:

"1. To provide surveillance in conjunction with other government departments of waters over which Canada exercises jurisdiction, to detect the discharge of pollutants from ships, fishing violations, and unauthorized exploration or exploitation of the resources of the sea bed.
2. To provide bilingual and bicultural programs within the Canadian Armed Forces.
3. To provide sea, land, and air transportation of freight and passengers to other government departments, and outside agencies.
4. To provide administrative and logistics services in support of scientific, operational, and R&D projects for other governments and departments.
5. To participate in and provide administrative and logistics support for national and international events, displays and exhibitions.
6. To provide the use of DND personnel, buildings, equipment and facilities to other government agencies and to the private sector.
7. To provide construction services and support to other government departments in emergency situations and in remote areas.
8. To support the Department of Indian Affairs and Northern Development in the development of Inuit and Indian peoples.
9. To coordinate, control and conduct search and rescue operations for aircraft in distress within the Canadian assigned area of responsibility.
10. To coordinate and, in collaboration with the Canadian Coast Guard, control and conduct Search and Rescue operations for ships in distress within the Canadian assigned area of responsibility.
11. To provide sea, land and air forces to aid civil authorities in instances of civil disaster and emergency situations, including emergency ordanance disposal and accidents involving nuclear materials.

12. To conduct mercy flights and other miscellaneous humanitarian tasks.
13. To conduct ground searches.
14. To participate in the Canadian response to international disasters and distress.
15. The provision of training and logistic support to youth development through Summer Youth Employment Programs and other activities.
16. To support Community activities such as St. John's Ambulance, Red Cross and recreational programs."

APPENDIX 2

UNITED NATIONS CENTRE FOR DISARMAMENT: DEFENCE EXPENDITURES DISAGGREGATION MODEL

The UN Centre for Disarmament uses the following system of categorizing or disaggregating defence expenditures. It is essentially the same as that used in NATO budget disaggregation.

(1) Operating Costs

    (a) *Personnel*
        i. Conscripts
        ii. Other Military
        iii. Civilian

    (b) *Operations and Maintenance*
        i. Current-use Materials
        ii. Maintenance and Repairs
        iii. Purchased Services
        iv. Rent
        v. Other

(2) Procurement and Construction

    (a) *Procurement*
        i. Aircraft and Engines
        ii. Missiles, including Conventional Warheads
        iii. Nuclear Warheads and Bombs
        iv. Ships and Boats
        v. Armoured Vehicles
        vi. Artillery
        vii. Other Ordnance and Ground Force Arms
        viii. Ammunition
        ix. Electronics and Communications
        x. Non-armoured Vehicles
        xi. Others

(b) Construction
- i. Air Bases
- ii. Missile Sites
- iii. Naval Bases
- iv. Electronics (radar sites, for example)
- v. Personnel (barracks, for example)
- vi. Medical (hospitals, for example)
- vii. Training
- viii. Warehouses, Depots
- ix. Command and Administration
- x. Fortifications
- xi. Shelters
- xii. Lands
- xiii. Others

(3) Research and Development

(a) Basic and Applied
(b) Development, Testing, and Evaluation

APPENDIX 3

AFRICAN DEBTORS TO THE FORMER SOVIET UNION
(as of December 1991)

Country	FSU Military Debt $US millions	FSU Military Debt as % of Total FSU	FSU Military Debt as % of Total Debt	FSU Military Debt as % of GNP
Ethiopia	3,676.7	85.5	18.5	60.6
Algeria	3,672.9	91.6	14.1	8.1
Angola	3,174.3	100	45.3	42.0
Libya	2,408.2	100	44.8	8.3
Egypt	2,329.7	99.1	7.3	5.9
Mozambique	1,011.2	72.7	19.8	95.4
Tanzania	477.8	89.5	9.7	16.7
Zambia	407.1	99.2	5.6	13.0
Somalia	253.8	58.6	11.9	42.2
Congo	247.6	71.2	5.7	12.6
Mali	174.5	39.4	7.6	8.2
Guinea	135.6	36.8	6.2	5.6
Uganda	50.1	88.8	2.8	1.4
Benin	45.3	75.2	4.3	2.6
Nigeria	44.7	100	0.1	1.6
Burundi	18	100	2.1	2.1
Burkina Faso	5.7	100	0.8	neg.
Chad	3.7	96.5	1.0	neg.
Central African Republic	1.9	100	0.2	neg.
Ghana	1.5	13.7	neg.	neg.
Sudan	1.2	61.5	neg.	neg.

Notes:

1. Source: Vneshecon Bank (Soviet External Trade Bank); published by *Moscow News*; cited in "Russia to Swap African Debts for Food," *New African*, July, 1992, p. 33. London: IC Publications.
2. 1991 Exchange rate used for calculations: R1.0 = $US 0.7222. Source: *The Military Balance 1991-92*.
3. Total debt includes long-term, medium-term, short-term public and private sector debts. Source: *The Military Balance 1991-92*. Military Debt includes interest yet to be paid as of 1991.
4. GNP figures are for the year closest to 1991. Source: *The Military Balance 1991-92*.

APPENDIX 4

NATO DISTRIBUTION OF DEFENCE EXPENDITURES BY CATEGORY (AVERAGE 1985-89)

Country	Equipment	Personnel	Operations and Maintenance	Infrastructure
Belgium	12.0	62.9	20.7	3.8
Denmark	14.5	56.1	25.9	2.8
Germany	14.9	48.6	30.5	5.8
Netherlands	20.1	52.6	22.0	3.8
Norway	23.1	43.1	25.3	11.0
NATO North Mean	16.9	52.6	24.9	5.4
Greece	18.2	60.4	18.6	4.0
Italy	19.7	57.5	20.0	2.5
Portugal	7.8	66.4	20.9	6.0
Spain	15.0	53.2	23.0	3.7
Turkey	18.8	35.4	39.7	4.9
NATO South Mean	15.9	54.6	24.4	4.2
Canada	19.7	46.2	31.5	1.7
United Kingdom	24.9	38.8	32.3	4.0
United States	25.5	36.9	35.7	1.8
NATO West Mean	23.3	40.6	33.2	2.5
NATO Mean	18.9	50.6	26.6	4.3

Notes:

1. Source: NATO *Facts and Figures* 1989.
2. Luxembourg data is excluded.
3. Infrastructure is that designated as nato infrastructure. Infrastructure for national purposes is not included. This may be a reason that the infrastructure figures for the two North American states are lower than for the European states.

APPENDIX 5

DISTRIBUTION OF CANADIAN MILITARY PERSONNEL BY MILITARY OCCUPATION CODE (MOC) 1994

MOCs with No Clear Civilian Analogue	
Naval Deck Officer	1,338
Infantry Officer	1,086
Artillery Officer	588
Armour Officer	544
Air Weapons Controller	329
Intelligence Officer	164
Infantry	4,704
Armour Crewman	1,597
Field Artillery	1,282
Field Engineer	731
Boatswain	730
Weapons Systems Tech	686
Intelligence Systems Tech	629
Naval Weapons Tech	601
Naval Combat Information Op	516
Naval Electonic Sensor Op	450
Naval Signalman	414
Hull Tech	407
Air Defence Tech	405
Naval Acoustic Op	401
Naval Radioman	400
Air Defence Artillery	400
Land Weapons Tech	391
Naval Tactical Systems Tech	387
Naval Comms Tech	273
Intelligence Op	255
Avionics Tech	239
Naval Acoustic Tech	234
Naval Electronic Systems Tech	184
Ammunition Tech	180
Land Firecontrol Tech	174
Search and Rescue Tech	129
Land Optronic Tech	81
Land Firecontrol System Tech	77
Total	**21,006**

MOCs with Civilian Analogues	
Pilot	2,509
Logistics Officer	1,801
Comms Electronics Engineer	1,242
Air Engineer	1,131
Air Navigator	1,058
Marine Engineer	922
Military Engineer	739
Electrical and Mech Engineer	536
Medical Doctor	429
Nurse	369
Personnel Administration	360
Air Traffic Controller	335
Security	212
Dentist	200
Health Care Administrator	151
Training Development	133
Personnel Selection	119
Public Affairs	90
Chaplain (P)	90
Pharmacist	87
Legal Officer	77
Physical Training	69
Social Worker	53
Chaplain (RC)	53
Medical Associate	40
Physiotherapist	35
Dental Assistant	21
Music	15
Pastoral Assistant	15
Postal	14
Flight Engineer Officer	8
Supply Technician	3,888
Administratice Clerk	3,251
Transport Operator	2,609
Vehicle Tech	2,439
Airframe Tech	1,687
Military Policeman	1,627

Cook	1,508	Structures Tech	179
Medical Assistant	1,354	Refinishing Tech	164
Aero Engine Tech	1,350	Ocean Operator	163
Comms/Radar Systems Tech	1,241	Terminal Equipment Tech	162
Finance Clerk	1,150	Refrigeration Mech	159
Instrument Electronics Tech	1,007	Postal Clerk	132
Radio Tech	1,038	Electrician	125
Communications Research	1,015	Electrical Generating Systems	125
Teletype Operator	842	Plumber/Gasfitter	102
Traffic Tech	770	Preventative Medicine Tech	90
Firefighter	689	Medical Laboratory Tech	88
Marine Engineering Tech	653	Surveyor	82
Steward	644	Water, Sanitation Tech	81
Marine Engineering Mech	565	Machinist	77
Radar Tech	498	Mechanical Systems Tech	76
Safety Tech	443	Clearance Diver Tech	74
Marine Engineering	415	X-Ray Tech	71
Artificer	412	Dental Laboratory Tech	69
Musician	381	Dental Hygienist	65
Flight Engineer	368	Draughtsman	63
Photographic Tech	358	Stationary Engineer	62
Marine Electrical Tech	354	Clearance Diver	51
PT Instructor	342	Map Reproduction Tech	41
Air Traffic Controller	340	Electro-Mechanical Tech	39
Aviation Tech	334	Aeromedical Tech	36
Lineman	329	Operating Room Assistant	29
Teletype and Cypher Tech	310	Dental Equipment Tech	20
Meteorologic Tech	289		
Metals Tech	278	Total	51,671
Communications Tech	269		
Material Tech	263		
Air Electrical Services Tech	217		
Construction Maint Tech	210		
Engineer Equipment Tech	199		
Marine Electrician	195		
Dental Assistant	195		
Construction Engr Proc Tech	184		

Abbreviations:

Comms - Communications
Engr - Engineering
Mech - Mechanic
Op - Operator
Proc - Process
Tech - Technician

APPENDIX 6

PARTIAL CORRELATION ANALYSIS:
MILITARY IMPORTS/MILITARY EXPENDITURES

Country	MI/ME on GNP			MI/ME on CGE			MI/ME on ME−1			MI in ME?	Comment
	R	pR	DPs	R	pR	DPs	R	pR	DPs		
Algeria	0.58	0.58	11	0.89	0.92	7	0.31	0.53	10	Y	WMEAT - Y
Angola	NA	NA	–	NA	NA	–	NA	NA	NA	N	MI>ME 2 DPs
Benin	0.35	0.27	8	0.95	0.08	5	NA	NA	NA	N	MI=0 6/11 DPs
Botswana	0.07	0.38	11	0.00	0.33	11	−0.34	0.19	10	Y?	Inspection
Burkina Faso	0.40	−0.13	11	0.30	−0.08	6	0.53	0.05	10	N	
Burundi	−0.12	−0.16	11	0.00	−0.16	11	−0.12	0.08	10	N	
Cameroon	0.25	0.33	11	−0.01	0.29	9	0.51	0.64	10	N?	Inspection
Central African Republic	NA	NA	–	NA	NA	NA	NA	NA	NA	N	No MI
Chad	0.32	−0.11	10	0.26	−0.14	9	0.40	−0.05	5	N	MI>ME 6 DPs
Congo	−0.21	−0.51	8	−0.78	−0.11	4	−0.99	−0.99	4	N	
Côte d'Ivoire	−0.65	−0.21	11	NA	NA	NA	−0.21	−0.11	10	N	
Egypt	0.41	0.84	11	0.84	0.84	11	0.77	0.79	11	Y	WMEAT - Y
Equatorial Guinea	NA	NA	–	NA	NA	NA	NA	NA	NA	NA	No ME rep 89/93
Ethiopia	0.30	0.32	10	0.39	0.32	10	0.28	0.24	7	N	MI>ME 6/8 DPs
Gabon	−0.29	−0.27	10	−0.26	−0.24	9	−0.47	−0.65	6	N	
Ghana	−0.38	−0.50	11	−0.27	−0.50	10	−0.60	−0.45	9	N	
Guinea	−0.16	−0.32	6	−0.85	−0.85	4	NA	NA	NA	N	
Guinea-Bissau	−0.44	−0.37	8	0.09	0.19	6	NA	NA	NA	N	MI>ME 5/78 DPs

Country	MI/ME on GNP			MI/ME on CGE			MI/ME on ME−1			MI in ME?	Comment
	R	pR	DPs	R	pR	DPs	R	pR	DPs		
Iran	0.78	0.89	11	0.83	0.89	11	0.86	0.94	10	Y	
Iraq	0.63	0.90	8	NA	NA	NA	0.89	0.90	7	Y	
Israel	0.09	0.15	11	0.09	0.15	10	0.06	0.26	10	N	Arms Producer
Jordan	0.95	0.95	9	0.95	0.95	9	0.61	0.47	4	Y*	N 80/7, Y 89/94
Kenya	0.48	0.46	11	0.45	0.46	11	0.52	0.46	10	N	Inspection
Liberia	NA	NA	NA	NA	NA	NA	NA	NA	NA	NA	
Libya	0.99	0.98	7	NA	NA	NA	NA	NA	NA	Y	
Malawi	0.57	0.49	11	0.79	0.78	9	0.62	0.49	10	N	Inspection
Mali	0.29	0.56	9	0.68	0.53	7	−0.18	−0.18	5	N	
Mauritania	0.01	0.03	9	NA	NA	NA	0.02	0.03	5	N	MI=0 7/11 DPs
Morocco	−0.04	0.16	9	0.06	0.08	8	0.20	0.18	8	N	
Mozambique	−0.45	−0.84	8	0.21	−0.82	4	−0.90	−0.81	4	N	
Namibia	−0.90	−0.81	5	−0.90	−0.81	4	−0.90	−0.81	4	N	
Niger	−0.39	−0.28	9	−0.30	0.08	6	NA	NA	NA	N	MI=0 7/11 DPs
Nigeria	0.70	0.75	10	0.53	0.75	9	−0.56	−0.49	4	N	MI>ME 5/11DPs
Rwanda	−0.44	−0.51	8	−0.67	−0.51	8	−0.39	0.04	7	N	
Saudi Arabia	0.50	0.53	11	0.72	0.86	9	0.44	0.51	10	Y	Gulf War Effect
Senegal	−0.02	−0.02	11	0.01	−0.21	7	−0.04	−0.02	10	N	
Sierra Leone	−0.16	−0.11	9	−0.49	−0.10	8	−0.35	−0.33	4	N	MI=0 9/11 DPs
Somalia	−0.20	0.40	4	NA	NA	NA	NA	NA	NA	N	MI>ME 4/4 DPs
South Africa	0.39	0.35	11	0.38	0.35	11	0.47	0.38	10	Y	Arms Producer
Sudan	0.02	−0.44	9	NA	NA	−	0.23	0.41	8	N	
Swaziland	NA	NA	NA	NA	NA	−	NA	NA	NA	N	No MI
Syria	0.29	0.36	7	0.27	0.34	6	0.35	0.31	6	N	
Tanzania	−0.29	−0.78	9	−0.53	−0.78	9	NA	NA	NA	N	MI>ME 4/9 DPs
The Gambia	0.95	−0.49	5	0.99	0.41	3	NA	NA	NA	N	MI=0 3/5; >ME 2/4

Country	MI/ME on GNP			MI/ME on CGE			MI/ME on ME−1			MI in ME?	Comment
	R	pR	DPs	R	pR	DPs	R	pR	DPs		
Togo	0.21	0.08	10	0.49	0.09	7	0.38	0.78	5	N	MI=0 6/10 DPs
Tunisia	0.42	−0.09	11	0.02	−0.01	10	−0.03	−0.01	10	N	
Uganda	0.41	0.38	11	0.53	0.38	11	0.38	0.35	10	N	
Zaire	−0.25	0.00	7	−0.37	0.00	7	NA	NA	NA	N	
Zambia	0.28	0.25	7	0.19	0.25	7	NA	NA	NA	N	
Zimbabwe	0.39	0.49	11	0.29	0.36	11	0.72	0.72	10	N*	

Notes:

Partial correlation analysis allows for a situation wherein the effect of the factor of interest may be masked by the effect of another factor. The effect of the masking factor is held constant by the use of a partial correlation that allows the effect of the factor of interest to be seen independently.

If the partial correlation coefficient (pR) is larger than the simple correlation coefficient (R), then the relationship is stronger than the simple correlation coefficient suggests. The partial correlation in this case can correct for a false negative—or it may simply show that the positive relationship is stronger than the simple correlation suggests.

If the partial correlation (pR) is smaller than the simple correlation (R), then the relationship is weaker than the simple correlation suggests. The smaller partial correlation corrects for a false positive.

No attempt has been made to calculate or use the normal tests of statistical significance. The data series used are too short and too many data points are missing in many cases for such tests to be reliably used. Accordingly, different analysts may make different judgments for specific countries than is the case in this study.

No attempt was made to use multiple regression analysis, because the short data series and missing datapoints would render the results of a multiple regression analysis of doubtful validity.

In certain cases it appears that a country has changed from excluding MI from reported ME to including MI in ME. This appears to be the case for Jordan as noted. It may also be the case with respect to Nigeria.

APPENDIX 7

SOCIAL AND SOCIOECONOMIC MILITARIZATION: PRAETORIAN AND SPARTAN INDICES 1990-94 MEANS

Country	ME/ Soldier	MEE/ Soldier	PO&M/ Soldier	GNP/ Capita	Praetorian Index	Regular (000)	Reserve (000)	Paramilitary (000)	Spartan Index
Algeria	7,443	1,003	6,440	1,539	4.2	4.8	0.5	1.6	6.9
Angola	NA	NA	NA	NA	NA	10.4	—	1.7	12.1
Benin	5,914	271	5,643	276	20.5	0.9	—	0.5	1.4
Botswana	32,682	3,444	29,238	2,708	10.8	4.6	—	0.8	5.4
Burkina Faso	6,675	1,034	5,640	187	30.2	0.8	0.4	0.2	1.5
Burundi	4,788	907	3,881	167	23.2	1.2	—	0.3	1.5
Cameroon	11,638	349	11,288	489	23.1	0.7	—	0.4	1.1
Central African Republic	6,232	0	6,232	315	19.8	1.2	—	0.9	2.1
Chad	2,270	1,031	1,238	167	7.4	4.7	—	0.9	5.6
Congo	6,785	561	6,224	576	11.8	4.6	—	2.6	7.2
Côte d'Ivoire	12,310	0	12,310	425	29.0	0.5	0.1	0.6	1.2
Egypt	3,923	2,535	1,388	693	2.0	7.9	0.8	6.4	14.3
East Guinea	NA	NA	NA	312	NA	3.3	—	5.1	8.4
Ethiopia	1,067	0	1,067	91	11.7	2.2	—	—	2.2
Gabon	26,741	844	25,897	3,616	7.2	4.3	—	4.4	8.7
Ghana	4,625	150	4,475	303	14.8	0.5	—	0.3	0.8
Guinea	4,835	557	4,278	484	8.8	1.6	—	1.6	3.1
Guinea-Bissau	1,103	305	798	215	3.7	6.9	—	1.9	1.6
Iran	9,996	2,350	7,646	2,178	3.5	8.5	0.5	3.2	12.2
Iraq	20,988	1,035	19,953	972	20.5	32.1	2.9	1.1	36.1
Israel	44,241	5,313	38,927	14,509	2.7	35.7	7.9	0.1	43.7
Jordan	4,614	537	4,078	1,347	3.0	27.1	0.8	0.2	28.1
Kenya	8,214	1,038	7,176	244	29.5	0.9	—	0.2	1.1
Liberia	4,577	282	4,295	NA	NA	3.8	—	—	3.8
Libya	24,566	442	24,524	6,397	3.8	117.0	0.7	0.9	18.6

211

Country	ME/Soldier	MEE/Soldier	PO&M/Soldier	GNP/Capita	Praetorian Index	Regular (000)	Reserve (000)	Paramilitary (000)	Spartan Index
Malawi	1,958	404	1,554	138	11.3	1.0	—	0.2	1.2
Mali	4,584	599	3,985	206	19.4	0.8	—	0.9	1.8
Mauritania	2,639	0	2,639	436	6.1	6.6	—	2.6	9.2
Morocco	7,626	629	6,996	1,035	6.8	7.2	0.4	4.8	12.4
Mozambique	3,351	1,022	2,329	65	35.8	2.8	—	—	2.8
Namibia	8,245	0	8,245	1,858	4.4	5.0	—	—	5.9
Niger	4,416	0	4,146	176	23.5	0.5	—	0.6	1.1
Nigeria	4,584	839	3,746	423	8.8	0.9	—	0.1	1.0
Rwanda	25,312	3,516	21,797	228	95.8	0.6	—	0.2	0.8
Saudi Arabia	181,099	49,345	13,754	7,484	17.6	8.9	0.1	0.1	9.1
Senegal	8,495	690	7,805	451	17.3	1.3	—	0.2	1.5
Sierra Leone	3,892	360	3,532	162	24.0	1.3	—	—	1.3
Somalia	NA	NA	NA	NA	NA	NA	—	2.4	2.4
South Africa	51,363	10,273	41,090	2,801	14.7	1.8	1.0	2.5	5.2
Sudan	17,248	589	16,659	426	39.1	3.1	—	0.6	3.7
Swaziland	5,724	0	5,724	1,080	4.9	3.3	—	3.4	6.7
Syria	21,833	1,263	20,570	4,296	4.8	29.5	2.4	0.6	32.5
Tanzania	1,926	264	1,662	73	22.9	1.8	0.3	—	2.2
The Gambia	14,881	2,381	12,500	397	31.5	0.9	—	0.7	1.6
Togo	5,108	180	4,928	246	10.7	1.4	—	0.2	1.6
Tunisia	13,099	952	12,147	1,676	7.2	4.2	—	2.3	6.5
Uganda	1,458	71	1,387	218	6.4	3.4	—	—	3.4
Zaire	7,952	874	7,078	177	40.1	0.7	—	0.8	1.5
Zambia	2,841	287	2,554	368	6.9	2.6	—	0.2	2.7
Zimbabwe	4,880	932	3,948	466	8.5	4.7	—	2.3	7.0

APPENDIX 8

FINANCIAL MILITARIZATION
ME/GNP AND ME/CGE

Country	ME/GNP %			ME/CGE %		
	1994	1990-94	1985-89	1994	1990-94	1985-89
Algeria	3.3	2.3	2.9	7.5	6.8 (2)	7.7
Angola	NA	NA	36.8	NA	NA	NA
Benin	2.3	1.9	2.3	NA	15.4	20.4
Botswana	6.0	5.6	4.4	14.1	11.7	9.2
Burkina Faso	2.6	3.0 (3)	3.8	NA	17.6	26.5
Burundi	4.2	3.5 (3)	4.6	22.3	18.3 (3)	29.5
Cameroon	1.9	1.7	1.8	NA	8.2 (4)	8.7 (4)
Central African Republic	3.2	2.4 (3)	1.1 (1)	NA	NA (2)	4.3 (1)
Chad	7.1	6.4 (4)	13.8	NA	20.7 (4)	43.4 (4)
Congo	4.1	5.3 (3)	6.5 (3)	NA	13.0 (4)	15.0 (1)
Côte d'Ivoire	1.1	1.5 (4)	1.9	NA	NA	NA
Egypt	4.1	4.2	10.7	8.9	9.7 (2)	20.8
East Guinea	1.8	NA	NA	NA	NA	NA
Ethiopia	2.6	8.8 (3)	29.4 (4)	9.1	37.4 (3)	113.0 (4)
Gabon	3.2	3.2 (2)	4.9	NA	9.8 (2)	11.9 (4)
Ghana	0.8	0.8 (4)	1.3	NA	4.7 (4)	9.0
Guinea	1.5	1.6 (3)	3.4 (2)	NA	7.1 (1)	21.8 (1)
Guinea-Bissau	3.3	3.6 (2)	15.8 (4)	NA	8.2 (2)	29.4 (4)
Iran	2.4	3.9	8.4	7.4	17.0	41.1
Iraq	NA	69.2 (3)	49.7	NA	NA	NA
Israel	9.9	10.9	18.0	22.1	24.1 (4)	30.2
Jordan	7.5	9.3 (4)	29.5 (4)	21.9	25.6 (4)	75.8 (4)
Kenya	2.3	3.1	4.0	7.2	10.4	14.0
Liberia	NA	NA	4.0 (4)	NA	NA	14.0 (4)
Libya	4.3	8.1 (4)	17.1 (2)	NA	16.1 (1)	21.9 (1)
Malawi	1.0	1.5	2.7	NA	5.5 (3)	8.2
Mali	1.8	1.9 (3)	4.7	NA	14.6 (2)	15.8
Mauritania	3.7	4.0	6.7 (3)	NA	NA	24.2 (1)
Morocco	4.5	5.3	6.9 (3)	15.3	17.5 (4)	22.5 (3)
Mozambique	8.7	13.8	39.4 (3)	NA	49.9	157.0 (3)
Namibia	1.9	2.2 (4)	NA	NA	5.7 (4)	NA
Niger	0.9	1.1 (4)	1.7 (4)	NA	5.6 (3)	8.5 (3)

Country	ME/GNP %			ME/CGE %		
	1994	1990-94	1985-89	1994	1990-94	1985-89
Nigeria	0.8	0.9 (4)	1.9	5.0	4.2 (3)	9.1
Rwanda	NA	7.2	2.2 (3)	NA	28.9	12.7 (3)
Saudi Arabia	14.2	21.6	19.1	NA	58.0 (4)	33.9
Senegal	1.8	2.4	2.7	NA	8.3 (2)	14.2
Sierra Leone	4.9	3.0 (4)	1.1 (4)	20.2	14.4 (3)	6.5 (4)
Somalia	NA	2.5 (1)	8.7 (2)	NA	NA	84.4 (2)
South Africa	2.4	3.2	4.1	7.4	10.0	12.6
Sudan	NA	12.4 (4)	5.1	NA	268.0 (2)	106.0
Swaziland	1.7	1.6 (3)	1.1	4.1	5.1 (3)	4.0 (4)
Syria	NA	15.0 (2)	22.1 (4)	NA	59.3 (2)	57.2 (4)
Tanzania	3.8	4.8(4)	8.0 (4)	8.3	12.9 (3)	33.6
The Gambia	3.8	3.5 (3)	4.1 (1)	NA	17.4 (1)	32.5
Togo	2.7	3.0	3.2 (4)	NA	11.6 (3)	10.5 (4)
Tunisia	3.6	3.0	3.2	NA	9.3 (4)	10.9
Uganda	1.5	2.3	5.3	7.6	12.4	54.2
Zaire	2.1	3.0	2.7 (4)	44.2	18.5	18.4 (4)
Zambia	1.4	2.0 (2)	3.6 (2)	5.4	6.9 (1)	9.0(2)
Zimbabwe	3.7	4.6	6.4	NA	12.6	15.2

APPENDIX 9

MILITARY CAPABILITIES (1996-97)

Country	Fighter Squadrons	FGA Squadrons	ABEs	IBEs	Subs	Major Surface	Patrol Craft
Algeria	8.1	3.1	9.6	18.0	2	6	21
Angola	0.6	1.1	4	4	–	–	5
Benin	–	–	–	1.3	–	–	1
Botswana	–	–	0.5	1.7	–	–	–
Burkina Faso	–	–	–	2.9	–	–	–
Burundi	–	–	–	1.7	–	–	–
Cameroon	0.3	0.3	–	5.3	–	–	2
Central African Republic	–	–	–	2.0	–	–	–
Chad	–	–	0.6	NA	–	–	–
Congo	–	1.4	0.4	1.3	–	–	6
Côte d'Ivoire	–	0.3	–	1.4	–	–	4
Egypt	23.2	11.4	36.6	35.1	8	7	43
East Guinea	–	–	–	0.3	–	–	4
Ethiopia	–	5.3	3.5	27	–	–	–
Gabon	–	0.6	–	1.3	–	–	3
Ghana	–	–	–	2.3	–	–	4
Guinea	–	0.5	0.4	2.3	–	–	9
Guinea-Bissau	–	0.2	0.1	1.7	–	–	8
Iran	7.8	10.6	14.4	27.9	2	7	36
Iraq	11.3	8.1	27.0	58.0	–	1	7
Israel	31.6	12.1	43.0	38.0	2	3	52
Jordan	2.0	4.1	11.5	8.0	–	–	5
Kenya	–	1.1	0.8	2.7	–	–	6
Liberia	–	–	–	–	–	–	–
Libya	13.1	10.3	23.1	41.7	4	6	32
Malawi	–	–	–	1.3	–	–	–
Mali	0.7	0.3	0.2	2	–	–	–
Mauritania	–	–	0.1	2.1	–	–	7
Morocco	0.9	4.1	5.3	29.7	–	3	27
Mozambique	–	2.7	0.8	2.0	–	–	10
Namibia	–	–	–	1.7	–	–	3
Niger	–	–	–	1.0	–	–	–

Country	Fighter Squadrons	FGA Squadrons	ABEs	IBEs	Subs	Major Surface	Patrol Craft
Nigeria	–	3.6	2.0	7.7	–	2	50
Rwanda	–	–	–	NA	–	–	–
Saudi Arabia	7.8	10.2	10.5	5.3	–	8	29
Senegal	–	–	–	3.0	–	–	10
Sierra Leone	–	–	–	2.3	–	–	5
Somalia	–	–	–	–	–	–	–
South Africa	0.7	14.6	2.5	6	3	–	12
Sudan	0.6	2.4	2.8	26	–	–	6
Swaziland	–	–	–	–	–	–	–
Syria	20.7	14.6	45.9	28	–	2	27
Tanzania	1.5	–	0.2	5	–	–	16
The Gambia	–	–	–	0.7	–	–	4
Togo	–	0.3	–	2.2	–	–	2
Tunisia	–	0.9	1.0	5	–	–	23
Uganda	–	0.3	0.2	4	–	–	–
Zaire	–	0.5	0.6	10	–	–	7
Zambia	0.8	0.8	0.3	2	–	–	–
Zimbabwe	0.9	1.4	0.4	7.3	–	–	–

SOURCES

GENERAL

Financial analysis for less developed countries presents a problem, in that the usual sources do not consistently agree with each other, even though they make use of many of the same source documents. In part this arises from discrepancies in the national government's reported figures and in part from various estimates made by the external reporting agency. In some cases, subsequent issues of a source document will correct errors discovered in earlier editions. Since this study undertakes extensive cross-country comparisons, a major concern has been the consistency of figures, and we have therefore preferred to concentrate on a limited number of databases in order to reduce inter-source variations as much as possible. Principal use has been made, therefore, of *The Military Balance* for military organizations and weapons inventories, of *World Military Expenditures and Arms Transfers* for most economic figures, and *The World Development Report* and *Human Development Report* for figures relating to official development aid. Other investigators have preferred the *Yearbook of World Armaments and Disarmaments*; for a useful and extensive technical analysis of the various sources see Ball (1988).

This study has also noted the very large variations in national economic data as a consequence of variations in exchange rates, which have led to some significant changes in economic rankings over various editions of *World Military Expenditures and Arms Transfers*. Some analysts have proposed the use of Purchasing Power Parity rates in an attempt to avoid this phenomenon, but this study has not attempted any comparative analysis using that approach. Fortunately, the Praetorian Index is independent of exchange rate effects.

MILITARY ORGANIZATIONS AND EQUIPMENT HOLDINGS AND STRATEGIC OVERVIEW

The Military Balance (1980-1981 to 1996-1997). London: The International Institute for Strategic Studies.
Strategic Survey (various years). London: The International Institute for Strategic Studies.

ECONOMIC DATA AND ARMS TRADE DATA

Global Arms Trade: Commerce in Advanced Military Technology and Weapons (1991). Washington: United States Congress Office of Technology Assessment.
Human Development Report (1992 to 1996). Washington: The World Bank.
World Development Report (1992 to 1996). Washington: The World Bank.
Sivard, R.L. (1991). *World Military and Social Expenditures, 1991.* Washington: World Priorities.
World Military Expenditures and Arms Transfers (various years). Washington: United States Arms Control and Disarmament Agency.
Yearbook of World Armaments and Disarmaments (various years). Stockholm: Stockholm International Peace Research Institute.

TECHNICAL MILITARY WEAPONS SYSTEMS DATA, MODELLING, AND ANALYSIS

Chant, C. (1989). *Aircraft Armaments Recognition.* London: Ian Allan.
———. (1990). *Land Forces of the World.* New York: Crescent.
Epstein, J.M. (1990). *Conventional Force Reductions: A Dynamic Assessment.* New York: Brookings.
Foss, C.F. (1994). *Jane's Armour and Artillery, 1994-95.* Coulsdon: Jane's Information Group.
Hoeber, F.P. ed. (1981). *Military Applications of Modelling.* New York: Gordon and Breach.
Huber, R.K. ed. (1990). *Military Stability.* Baden-Baden: Nomos Verlagsgesellschaft.
———. (1984). *Systems Analysis and Modelling in Defence.* New York: Plenum.
Jackson, P.A. ed. (1995) *Jane's All the World's Aircraft 1995-96.* Coulsdon: Jane's Information Group.
Sharp, R. ed. *Jane's Fighting Ships, 1995-96.* Coulsdon: Jane's Information Group.

INSIGHTS CONCERNING THE MILITARIZATION ISSUE

Ball, N. (1988). *Security and Economy in the Third World.* Princeton: Princeton University Press.

———. (1992). *Pressing for Peace: Can Aid Induce Reform?* Washington: Overseas Development Council.
Bueno de Mesquita, B. (1981) *The War Trap.* New Haven: Yale University Press.
Colletta, N.J., M. Kostner, and I. Wiederhofer (1996). *The Transition from War to Peace in Sub-Saharan Africa.* Washington: The World Bank.
———. (1996). *Case Studies in War-to-Peace Transition: The Demobilization and Reintegration of Ex-Combatants in Ethiopia, Namibia, and Uganda.* Washington: The World Bank.
Deger, S. (1986). *Military Expenditures in Third World Countries.* London: Rutledge & Kegan Paul.
Fontanel, J. (1990) "The Economic Effects of Military Expenditure in Third World Countries," in *The Journal of Peace Research,* vol. 27, no. 4.
Hewitt, D. (1991). *Military Expenditure: Econometric Testing of Economic and Political Influences.* Washington: International Monetary Fund Working Paper WP/91/53.
———. (1991). *Military Expenditures: International Comparison of Trends.* Washington: International Monetary Fund Working Paper WP/91/54.
———. (1991) "What Determines Military Expenditures," in *Finance and Development,* vol. 28, no. 4.
———. (1991) "Military Expenditures in the Developing World," in *Finance and Development,* vol. 28, no. 3.
Lamb, G. and V. Kallab (1992). *Military Expenditure and Economic Development: A Symposium on Research Issues.* Washington: The World Bank.
Miller, R. (1992). *Aid as Peacemaker: Canadian Development Assistance and Third World Conflict.* Ottawa: Carleton University Press.

AFRICAN HISTORICAL DATA

Adam, H., and K. Moodley (1992). *Democratizing Southern Africa: Challenges for Canadian Policy.* Ottawa: Canadian Institute for International Peace and Security.
Bender, G.J., J.S. Coleman, and R.I. Sklar (1985). *African Crisis Areas and U.S. Foreign Policy.* Berkeley: University of California Press.
Conteh-Morgan, E. (1993). "Conflict and Militarization in Africa: Past Trends and New Scenarios" in *Conflict Quarterly.* Winter. Fredericton: Centre for Conflict Studies, University of New Brunswick.

Hanson, J., and S. MacNish (1995). *The Republic of South Africa: Prospects and Problems.* Toronto: The Canadian Institute of Strategic Studies.
July, Robert W. (1980). *A History of the African People* (3/e). New York: Charles Scribner's.
Manning, P. (1988). *Francophone Sub-Saharan Africa, 1880-1985.* Cambridge: Cambridge University Press.
Metz, H.C. (1991) *Egypt: A Country Study.* Washington: Library of Congress.
Various editors (1988, 1992). UNESCO General History of Africa. 7 volumes. Paris: UNESCO.
Various editors (various years). *New African Yearbook.* London: IC Publications.
World Bank (1994). *Adjustment in Africa: Reforms, Results, and the Road Ahead.* Oxford: Oxford University Press.

AFRICAN CONTEMPORARY DATA

Africa Events (various issues). London: Dar-es-Salaam Ltd.
Africa South of the Sahara (various editions and years) London: Europa.
Africa Report (various issues). New York: The African-American Institute.
African Business (various issues). London: IC Publications.
New African (various issues). London: IC Publications.
Southern Africa Report (various issues). Toronto: Toronto Committee for Links between Southern Africa and Canada.
The Economist (various issues). London: The Economist.
The Middle East (various issues). London: IC Publications.
West Africa (various issues). London: West Africa Pub.